POLITICAL WATERS

POLITICAL WATERS

The Long, Dirty,

Contentious,

Incredibly Expensive

but

Eventually Triumphant

History of

Boston Harbor—

A Unique

Environmental

Success Story

———

ERIC JAY DOLIN

University of Massachusetts Press

AMHERST AND BOSTON

LC 2003025336
ISBN 1-55849-445-6

Designed by Dennis Anderson
Set in Janson Text
Printed and bound by The Maple-Vail Book Manufacturing Group

Library of Congress Cataloging-in-Publication Data

Dolin, Eric Jay.
    Political waters : the long, dirty, contentious, incredibly expensive
but eventually triumphant history of Boston Harbor—a unique
environmental success story / Eric Jay Dolin.
        p. cm.
Includes bibliographical references and index.
    ISBN 1-55849-445-6 (cloth : alk. paper)
    1. Water—Pollution—Massachusetts—Boston Harbor—History. 2. Sewage
disposal in the ocean—Massachusetts—Boston Harbor—History. 3. Water
quality management—Massachusetts—Boston Harbor—History. I. Title.
TD225.B7D65 2004
363.739'4'0974461—dc22   2003025336

British Library Cataloguing in Publication data are available.

Illustrations courtesy Massachusetts Water Resources Authority
unless otherwise credited.

To Jennifer,
simply the best

Contents

Illustrations follow pages 50 and 194.

Acknowledgments

When I was a doctoral student at MIT in the early 1990s, I wrote my dissertation on the role of the courts in remedial adjudication involving environmental institutions, using the cleanup of Boston Harbor as my case study. That formative experience inspired me to want to learn more about how the harbor got polluted and cleaned up, and it gave me a trajectory for piecing together the entire story, which is presented in this book. The professors who most influenced me and whom I would like to thank for their early support include Lawrence Susskind (MIT), Bernard Frieden (MIT), Lawrence Bacow (formerly with MIT, now president of Tufts), and Alan Altshuler (Harvard's John F. Kennedy School of Government).

I also owe a great debt to Mary Lydon and Elizabeth Steele at the Massachusetts Water Resources Authority (MWRA). Mary is the authority's librarian, and Liz, who was at one time Mary's assistant, is now with the legal department. Both of them were always ready, willing, and able to answer my questions and requests for information. Many other people at the MWRA have graciously helped me. They include Barbara Allen, Rita Berkeley, Michael Connor, Pat Costigan, Dick Fox, David Gilmartin, Rebecca Kenney, Nancy Kurtz, Paul Levy, Tom Lindberg, Doug MacDonald, Richard Mills, Kristen Patneaude, Virginia Renick, Andrea Rex, Tim Watkins, and Jonathan Yeo.

Others who shared their perspectives with me and to whom I am grateful include Steve Angelo, Noel Barrata, Ron DeCeasare, Michael Deland, Harlan Doliner, Jeffry Fowley, Dick Fox, Paul Garrity, Charles V. Gibbs, Charles M. Haar, Eric Hall, Donald R. F. Harleman, William Kane, Barry Kaplan, Peter Koff, Madeleine Kolb, Steven Lipman, John Lishman, A. D. Mazzone, Joe G. Moore Jr., Kenneth Moraff, Neil O'Brien, Brian Pitt, Virginia Renick, Peter Shelley, Michael Sloman, John Snedeker, Jekabs Vittands, and Douglas Wilkins.

This book exists because Clark Dougan, senior editor at the University of Massachusetts Press, read my proposal and said this looks interesting. To him and the rest of the staff at the press, thank you for believing in this project. Carol Betsch, the press's managing editor, did a great job of shepherding the book through the process and was given a very able assist by copy editor Karen Bosc. Another person at the University of Massachusetts who deserves thanks is Richard Delaney, the executive director of the Urban Harbor's Institute at the university's Boston campus. His work on pulling together the Boston Harbor Symposium in 2001 was particularly important for it gave me access to the thoughts and perspectives of key players in the cleanup of Boston Harbor.

To gather many of the older documents concerning sewage and Boston Harbor I relied on the assistance of John J. McColgan and Kristen Swett of the Archives and Records Center of the City of Boston's Archives and Records Management Division. Both through the mail and during my visit to the archives, they helped me track down copies of numerous materials, quite a few of which are unique to the archive's collections.

While I was at MIT, the Sea Grant College Program helped me become intimately acquainted with many of the source materials on sewage and Boston Harbor by sponsoring and then publishing my book *Dirty Water/Clean Water: An Annotated Chronology of Events Surrounding the Degradation and Cleanup of Boston Harbor* (1990). For that I thank Madeleine Hall-Arber, Norm Doeling, Karen Hartley, and Carolyn Levi.

Books can only be as good as the information on which they are built. Thus, my gratitude goes to all of the authors cited in the notes. Their work and their insights enabled me to tell this story.

My wife, Jennifer, and my children, Lily and Harry, made the physical and mental act of writing this book possible. They were supportive throughout and didn't grumble when I went to the computer to write early in the morning, at night, or on the weekends. Jennifer also read the manuscript and offered excellent suggestions for improving it. Although her immediate inclination upon reviewing hundreds of pages on sewage was to tell me the manuscript was full of crap, she suppressed that urge and instead told me it was very interesting crap. Her honesty and sense of humor are much appreciated.

Lastly, I want to acknowledge all of the people who have been and continue to be part of the most recent chapter in the ongoing history of sewage management in the Boston area. It is because of them that this story has a clean ending.

Acronyms

BHP	Boston Harbor Project
BOD	biochemical oxygen demand
CLF	Conservation Law Foundation
CPM	critical path method
CSO	combined sewer overflow
EMMA	Boston Harbor–Eastern Massachusetts Metropolitan Area Wastewater Management and Engineering Study
EPA	Environmental Protection Agency
MDC	Metropolitan District Commission
mgd	million gallons per day
MWRA	Massachusetts Water Resources Authority
NIMBY	"not in my backyard"
POTW	publicly owned treatment works
TBM	tunnel boring machine

POLITICAL WATERS

Introduction

Dirty Water, Clean Water

Boston Harbor is America's harbor. It served as a colonial gateway to the world, witnessed the Boston Tea Party, and helped Boston transform itself from an outpost of a few hardy settlers into a bustling metropolis and self-proclaimed hub of the universe. For hundreds of years, Boston Harbor was also a cesspool. Long before Bostonians dumped tea into the harbor to protest English taxes, they dumped sewage there. As the Boston area grew and prospered, its sewage problems worsened, as did the harbor's health, to the point that in the 1980s the harbor was widely considered the most polluted in the country and often ridiculed as the "harbor of shame." Then, in one of the most impressive environmental comebacks in American history, the harbor was dramatically cleaned up. And all it took was two lawsuits, two courts, dozens of lawyers, the creation of a powerful sewage authority, thousands of workers, millions of labor hours, and billions of dollars.

Although sewage courses through the veins of Boston's history, few of the books written about the city do more than briefly mention it. That is understandable. After all, sewage, which broadly consists of human and other organic and nonorganic wastes, is not the most pleasant topic. Yet, the way in which the Boston area has managed and mismanaged its sewage is a fascinating story. Soon after the colonists arrived, they started building sewers, and Bostonians and their neighbors have been building sewers ever since. Throughout Boston's history, the topic of sewage and what to do with it has floated in and out of the public's consciousness. At times the sewage question has been largely ignored or has been just one of many issues vying for attention. At other times sewage has risen high on the public's agenda. In that way the history of sewage in Boston presents a portrait of punctuated equilibrium in which periods of relative calm have been disturbed by eruptions of fear, disgust, outrage, anger, and ultimately action.

1

From the founding of Boston in 1630 through the mid-1800s, the sewage question, while ever present, rarely became a major issue. The main exception was in the late 1700s and early 1800s, when fears that disease was being transmitted by gaseous emanations from decomposing waste caused local heath organizations and politicians to enact measures aimed at improving the collection and disposal of sewage. The next major sewage crisis occurred in the 1870s. Hundreds of years of private initiative and less than fifty years of municipal oversight had given Boston a haphazard, somewhat ad hoc system of sewers, many of which did a miserable job of performing the task for which they were designed—transporting waste away from homes and businesses down to the harbor's edge. In the parts of the city that had sewers, the sanitary conditions were often atrocious, and where sewers had yet to reach, conditions were even worse. Overflowing sewer pipes and puddles of sewage in homes and streets were common. And when the sewage did reach the harbor's edge it collected in the shallow waters, where it decayed, giving off a horrible stench. The greatest concern was, as it had been during the previous crisis, that such conditions would lead to outbreaks of disease, a notion that had gained credence with the recent sanitary awakening, which had more firmly established the connection between poor sanitation and ill health. The local medical community, sanitary engineers, and the general public demanded change, and they got it in 1884, when Boston finished building a labyrinthine network of sewers designed to collect the region's sewage and carry it, virtually untreated, to discharge points at the bottom of Boston Harbor. Over the next twenty years, two similar networks of sewers were built north and south of the city.

The consensus at the time was that by collecting the area's sewage and consigning it to the depths of the harbor, the city would resolve the problems that had led to the construction of the three sewage systems. On the issue of disposal, in particular, sanitarians and engineers believed that the harbor's great volume, combined with daily tides, would quickly disperse and render innocuous the daily deluge of waste generated by local inhabitants. The new sewage systems did greatly improve the removal of sewage from the cities and towns but confidence in the harbor's powers of dilution proved unfounded and led to the next sewage crisis. This one resulted in the construction of two sewage plants designed to provide a low level of treatment to the sewage before it was discharged to the harbor. But these plants failed to solve the problem, and as the local population swelled, the already miserable state of the harbor grew worse. It got so bad, in fact, that the greatest sewage crisis in the history of the Boston area was precipitated, the resolution of which resulted in the cleanup I described at the beginning.

Sewage management is rarely as compelling as higher-profile environmental issues such as global climate change, the loss of species, or the destruction of tropical rainforests—but, as the history of the Boston area shows, it can be. Boston's struggle to deal with its sewage is an epic story of failure and success replete with colorful characters, political, bureaucratic, and legal twists and turns, and engineering feats, as well as the involvement of massive amounts of money. And, in the end, it all hinged on the very basic, often overlooked, yet monumentally important act of getting rid responsibly of the waste people produce every day.

1

"A Very Stinking Puddle"

On March 22, 1630, a small flotilla left England's shores and began the long journey across the Atlantic Ocean to America. The passengers were English Protestants called Puritans intent on escaping religious persecution and establishing a new home on the shores of what they referred to as the "Northern Parte of Virginia," which would later become New England. The Puritans first sighted land near Cape Ann and then made their way down the coast, with some of them anchoring near Salem and a larger contingent heading farther south to Charlestown. By the fall of 1630, however, the lack of drinking water in Charlestown led many of the Puritan leaders and their followers to cross the Charles River and to settle on the Shawmut Peninsula, where there was a freshwater spring. The new arrivals christened the peninsula Boston, after a town in Lincolnshire, England, from which many of them hailed. Two years later, in 1632, Boston became the capital of the Massachusetts Bay Colony.[1]

Boston was only about two miles long and a mile wide at its broadest point. It was connected to the mainland by a narrow peninsula, called Boston Neck, which was completely covered during bad weather when the seas engulfed it, rendering Boston a temporary island.[2] Rising above the lowlands were three prominent hills, originally referred to as Trimountain, which included Cotton Hill, Mount Vernon Hill, and Sentry Hill (later called Beacon Hill). Boston's hills provided an interesting geographic coincidence. During the Puritans' voyage across the Atlantic, John Winthrop, who would become the first governor of the colony, presented to his fellow travelers on the lead ship, *Arbella*, a speech entitled "A Modell of Christian Charity." He told them that their mission was to create a "civill and ecclesiasticall" form of government that placed the public good ahead of private interests, and thereby became a beacon of hope and an example to others. "For we must consider," he concluded, "that we shall be as a City upon a Hill."[3] Boston qualified not only as a figurative "City upon a Hill" but as a literal one as well.

The most impressive and important feature of Boston was its harbor. Upon seeing it in the early 1630s, William Wood, an English chronicler of the New World, penned the following description.

> The chiefe and usuall Harbour . . . which is close aboard the plantations, in which most of our ships com to anchor, being the nearest their mart, and usuall place of landing of passengers; it is a safe and pleasant Harbour within, having but one common and safe entrance, and than not very broad, there scarce being room for 3 ships to come in board and board at a time, but being once within, there is room for the Anchorage of 500 ships.
>
> This Harbour is made by a great company of islands, whose high cliffes shoulder out the boisterous seas, yet easily deceive any unskillfull Pilote; preferring many faire openings and broad sounds, which afford too shallow waters for any Ships, though navigable for Boates and small pinnaces.[4]

Bostonians faced many challenges. One of the most basic was what to do with their waste. The answer depended on the type of waste in question. To deal with human excrement, many of the colonists built privy vaults or leaching cesspools. The former were basically holes in the ground, lined with wood or stone, or sometimes unlined, topped by a wooden plank or seat with an opening. Privy vaults were located near houses or in cellars. When outside, the vault was typically enclosed in a wooden structure designed both for privacy and for containment of noxious fumes. The vaults were covered with dirt or ashes after each use and then replaced when full or periodically emptied by men called scavengers who carted the waste away, either to the outskirts of town or to the edge of the harbor. In later years, when ordinances restricted the work of these scavengers to the nighttime, the waste they carried off was politely referred to as "nightsoil."[5] The main difference between privy vaults and cesspools was that in the latter the wastes were not confined in a vault, but rather were free to leach outward from the source of deposit through a bed of crushed stone.[6] Of course, for those who had neither access to nor interest in using either of these rudimentary receptacles for bodily evacuation, the oldest form of getting rid of one's waste was still available—direct application to the ground. The new Bostonians also generated large quantities of organic waste in their kitchens, from discarded vegetables, meat, and liquids. This waste, along with other forms of garbage, as well as manure from horses and livestock, and the excess water from lands and cellars, commonly ended up in the streets and alleys of the growing town, or found its way to local waterways, including the harbor.

Waste disposal became a problem early in Boston's history. A scant four years after settling the area, in September 1634, the selectmen of Boston passed on ordinance restricting the manner in which waste was discarded, stating that "no person shall leave any fish or garbage neere the said Bridge or common landing place between the 2 Creeks whereby any anoyance may come to the people that pass that way, upon paine to forfeit for every such offence five shillings."[7] In 1647, the General Court of the new Colony weighed in on this practice, making it "unlawful for any person to cast any dung, draught, or dirt, or any thing to fill up the Cove [the area where Haymarket Square is today], or to annoy the Neighbours, upon the penalty of forty shillings, the one half to the Country, the other half to the Wharfinger."[8] Five years later, the Boston selectmen, concerned that existing laws were either ineffective or too limited or both, ordered that "noe person inhabiting within this Town shall throw forth or lay any intralls of beast or fowles or garbidg or Carion or dead dogs or Catts or any other dead beast or stiinkering thing, in any hie way or dich or Common within this neck of land of Boston, but ar injoynend to bury all such things that soe they may prevent all anoyanc unto any."[9] That same year, the hitherto largely private practice of constructing privies came under the purview of local authorities who passed an ordinance "prohibiting on pain of a twenty shilling penalty the placement of a privy within twenty feet of a highway or neighboring house, unless properly constructed with a vault six feet deep."[10]

Early Sewers

Sometime during the 1600s, Bostonians built their first sewers. The exact date is not known, but it was certainly well before 1700. The process of constructing a sewer was ad hoc and based on individual initiative. When a homeowner determined that a sewer was necessary, he either began building it himself or persuaded his neighbors to shoulder part of the burden, both physical and financial. Obtaining permission for such activities was a formality that was often overlooked. If, at a later date, other neighbors wanted to use the sewer, they would be asked to pay for this right, and when repairs of the communal sewer were needed, all of those who benefited from it were asked to pitch in to cover the costs. These sewers were either above ground gutters or underground conduits intended to carry off rainwater from yards and roofs, kitchen wastes, and the discharge of pumps used to drain cellars. Human excrement was expressly excluded. Given Boston's hilly topography, most sewers found their outlets on the shores of the harbor and the tributaries leading to the harbor. After all, the goal was to get the waste and excess water away from the houses as quickly and easily as possible, and the sloping streets and large expanse of water surrounding the town provided an easy means to that end.

It was not long before this virtually unregulated form of sewer construction became a public nuisance. Not only were streets ripped up with little thought given to the consequences of these actions on fellow inhabitants and the general commerce, but disputes also arose over who would pay the bills for laying and repairing drains and how such bills would be apportioned. This was especially problematic when people who had had no hand in building the sewers sought to connect their house drains to them.

To address these problems, in September 1701 the Boston selectmen ordered "that no person shall henceforth dig up the Ground in any of the Streets, Lanes or High-ways in the Town, for the laying or repairing any Drain, without the leave or approbation of two or more of the Selectmen."[11] For example, in 1704 the selectmen permitted Francis Thrasher to construct a sewer that was "not only a Generall good and Benefit by freeing the Street from the Usual annoyance with Water and mire by the Often Stoppage and breaking of Small wooden Truncks or drains . . . but a more peculiar benefit to ye Neighborhood as a Common Shore [sewer] for draining of their Cellars and conveying away their waste water."[12] The selectmen also ordered all those entering the new drain to pay part of the costs of construction.

In 1709 the General Court formalized the process of laying, maintaining, and paying for sewers and extended it beyond the borders of Boston with "An Act for Regulating of Drains and Common Shores [sewers]." According to the act's preamble, the law was aimed at the "preventing of inconveniences and damages by frequent breaking up the highwayes, streets and lanes of towns, for the laying and repairing of drains, or common shores, and of differences arising among partners in such drains, or common shores, about their proportion of the charge for making or repairing the same."[13] Again, those who wished to lay a sewer had to get permission of the selectmen, and lacking such, would be subject to a fine of twenty shillings that would, in turn, be given to the "poor" of the town. All of the sewers had to be "substantially done with brick or stone, in such manner as the selectmen of the town shall direct." The method of paying for the sewers was similar to earlier informal and formal processes.

> It shall and may be lawful to and for any one or more of the inhabitants of any town, at his or her own cost and charge, to make and lay a common shore, or main drain, for the benefit of themselves and others that shall think fit to join therein. And every person that shall afterwards enter his or her particular drain into such common shore, or main drain, or by any more remote means receive benefit thereby, for the draining of their cellars or lands, shall be obliged to pay unto the owner or owners of such common shore, or main drain, a proportionable part of the charge of making or repairing the same, or so much thereof as shall be below the place where any particular drain joins or enters thereinto, at the judgement of the selectmen of the town, or a major part of them: *saving* a right of appeal the court of general sessions of the peace, to the party aggrieved at any such determination.[14]

For many years thereafter, the selectmen faithfully discharged their duty. Between 1708 and 1738 alone, the town of Boston issued more than 650 sewer construction permits.[15] On October 5, 1738, for example, the selectmen granted liberty to "Mr. George Monk to Dig up the Ground in Orange Street in Order to lay a Drain from his Cellar in Bennets Pasture so Called in to the Common Shore in said Street, Upon Condition that he forthwith make good the Ground, and keep the same in Repair from time to time to the Satisfaction of the Select Men."[16] The selectmen also were called on many times to settle disputes over the apportionment of costs relating to sewers. One such case occurred on December 10, 1717, when the three "trustees for the Proprietors of the common Shore or main drayn running through Prince Street" came before the selectmen with a request. These proprietors had built and paid for a 790-foot sewer of stone. Since the time of construction, other people living along the sewer had "joyned their particular draines thereto & receive[d] benefit by having their cellars drained thro the same." The trustees presented the selectmen with an accounting of what they believed the people who had recently "joyned" owed to the proprietors who had originally borne the entire cost of the sewer. The selectmen agreed with the trustees' accounting and ordered twenty-four individuals and one "brick school house" to pay the trustees varying amounts, with each amount defined as some fraction of the original cost of that portion of the sewer that lay below the point of connection. A Mr. James How, for example, was ordered to pay for one thirty-sixth of 430 feet of the sewer, at a cost of a little less than eighteen shillings.[17]

Throughout the remainder of the eighteenth century, and until the incorporation of the city of Boston in 1822, the rules governing sewers remained largely the same, with a few key revisions. In 1754, the General Court took up the issue of repair more fully. Until then, those who connected to sewers were required to defray the costs of repairing only that portion of the sewer that lay below the point of connection. This arrangement failed to fully recognize the common-property nature of the sewers and that keeping them in good repair was in the interest of all who benefited from the sewer no matter where they sat along the sewer's course. The new law, therefore, required that all persons, both above and below the area in need of repair, pay their fair share of the repair costs as judged by the selectmen.[18] In 1763 another provision was added to the law, requiring people interested in opening and repairing sewers to notify all affected persons so that the latter had the opportunity to voice their objections to the selectmen who, in turn, had the power to either uphold or reject the objections.[19] In 1767 the Boston selectmen, alarmed by the "great Damage done to the Streets" by the shoddy workmanship of those laying the sewers, reserved the right to appoint the builder before granting a permit.[20] Then, in 1796, the provincial law was modified again, requiring those wanting to initiate repairs to advertise their intent at least seven days before taking action so that the potentially aggrieved might make their concerns known to the selectmen.[21] Although many sewers built during this period and afterward were "substantially done with brick or stone," some were made from hollowed-out timber.

In building sewers, Bostonians were following an ancient practice. Archeological digs have uncovered sewers going back thousands of years. There were few similarities, however, between the sewers of Boston and those of the great societies of the past. The Minoan civilization (3000–1000 B.C.) and the Indus civilization (circa 25000 B.C.) had extensive sewer systems, made of stone and brick, that were designed to carry off household and human waste, as well as stormwater runoff from the land and roofs.[22] These systems were well constructed, as is evidenced by the comments of a twentieth-century observer of a Minoan ruin on the island of Crete: "One day, after a heavy downpour of rain, I was interested to find that all the drains acted perfectly, and I saw water flow from sewers through which a man could walk upright. I doubt there is any other instance of a drainage system acting after 4,000 years."[23] The Romans also had an extensive sewerage system that included the famous Cloaca Maxima, or main drain, which is still in working condition today, a monument to Roman engineering talent.[24]

Although Boston's sewers were rudimentary in comparison with these and other advanced ancient sewers, they were quite similar to those in contemporary England or the cities of Europe, where the norm was for sewers to be simple culverts or underground conduits, sometimes lined with stone, brick, or wood. As many sanitary historians have noted, sewer construction between ancient times and the early 1800s had not evolved, but rather devolved. Not until the mid-1800s would sewerage systems approach and then exceed the scale and complexity of those that had been built many thousands of years before.[25]

During the 1700s, Boston achieved mixed success in dealing with its waste and runoff waters. A visitor to Boston in 1740 observed, "There are sixty streets, forty-one lanes, and eighteen alleys, besides squares, courts, etc. The streets are well paved, and lying upon a descent. The Town is, for the generality, as dry and clean as any I remember to have seen."[26] In 1759 another visitor noted, "The buildings in Boston are in general good; the streets are open and spacious, and well paved; and the whole has much the air of some our best country towns in England."[27] Yet, despite these observations, some serious problems remained, and if these visitors had come at different times or, perhaps, seen a wider cross section of the town, their opinions likely would not have been as positive. Sewers were often clogged and household waste either backed up into the houses from which it was sent or accumulated on the streets. In 1747, for example, Water Street became a source of concern for residents who complained that the street contained "for the greatest part of the Year a Slough of Dirt and Filth so that the way is almost impassable whereby the Inhabitants of the Town as well as Passengers are greatly impeded, and those that dwell near greatly Injured."[28] Defective sewers also caused runoff from the lands to accumulate in puddles after heavy rains. Privy vaults and cesspools often overflowed and saturated the lands with human waste, and, in the process, created a horrible smell. Many people carelessly dumped the contents of their privy vaults, along with other waste, on abandoned lands. During the 1750s, a defunct tannery was used in this manner, creating a situation that was "not only very inconvenient to the Inhabitants that dwell near, but extremely offensive especially in the Summer Season, when they have no comfort or satisfaction in their own Houses, occasioned by the disagreeable stench arising from this Nuisance."[29]

The work of scavengers and street sweepers was sometimes of questionable quality. The "nightsoil" dredged out of the privy vaults often slopped over the sides of uncovered carts as it was transported away from residential areas, leaving behind a pungent trail of waste. A newspaper reporter in 1800 gave voice to the feelings of many Bostonians when he asked "how long the citizens of Middle and Fish-streets and on towards Hancock's Wharf, are to be stiffled by the intolerable stench arising from the *filth* spilled from carts devoted to the *dirty goddess*? Almost every morning their olfactory nerves are saluted with the unwholesome effluvia, and their healths endangered by the carelessness or perhaps design of those nocturnal *goldfinders*. The Board of Health have frequently ordered them to discharge their *'oozing'* cargo in suitable places, without effect."[30] Much of the waste that was carted away or transported through sewers or over the streets made its way to the harbor, a fact that was painfully obvious to observers who spent time near the town's shoreline. One of them, Dr. Alexander Hamilton, visiting Boston in 1744, saw the town dock at low tide and called it "a very stinking puddle."[31]

Fear of Disease Spurs Change

Olfactory distress, aesthetics, and the need to make streets passable were not the only concerns driving the move to improve the sewerage of Boston and the disposition of human wastes. For many years, Bostonians had been subject to epidemics of disease, including scarlet fever, typhoid, and other maladies undefined. Medical science was still in a rudimentary state, and doctors did not know the exact causes of these diseases. Some argued that they were contagious, while many more believed that the primary vectors were "miasmas" or gaseous emanations from putrefying organic matter and waste. The weight of the miasmic theory was partly responsible for earlier efforts to build sewers in the city and to ensure that privy vaults were properly constructed and kept a safe distance from houses. According to John B. Blake, the notion that "gaseous effluvia" could cause disease was an old idea. "The *Regimen Sanitatis Salernitanum*, written in the twelfth century, offered this advice.

> Though all ill savours do not breed infection,
> Yet sure infection commeth most by smelling.
> Who smelleth still perfumed, his complexion
> Is not perfum'd by Poet Martials telling,
> Yet for your lodging roomes give this direction,

In houses where you mind to make your dwelling,
That neere the same there be no evil sents
Of puddle-waters, or of excrements,
Let aire be cleere and light, and free from faults,
That come of secret passages and vaults."[32]

In Boston, the need to keep putrefying organic waste away from people took on added urgency when the first epidemic of yellow fever swept through the town. It began during the summer of 1798, with the first victims being a family living near a wharf not far from the town dock. Medical experts claimed that the cause could be traced to the exhalations from rotting fish and other putrescible matter. To remedy the situation, the suspect waters were heavily limed. Dr. Isaac Rand, the president of the Massachusetts Medical Society, later described the general market area where similar gaseous vectors could have arisen.

> The [town] dock is the receptacle of a large sewer, in which the cloacinae of the county jail and the neighboring houses discharge their contents; and is surrounded by warehouses, which contained a great number of raw hides from the West Indies, and the Cape de Verd Islands; and a large quantity of beef not sufficiently salted. . . . Besides, being in the vicinity of Faneuil Hall market, all the putrid meat and decayed vegetables were thrown into it; all the filth of Court-street, Cornhill, Hanover-street, Wing's-lane, Union-street, and Dock-square, flows into it.[33]

One of Rand's colleagues, Dr. Samuel Brown, noted that such circumstances helped "to destroy the salubrity of the surrounding atmosphere, by loading it with animal effluvia, perceivable by the smell, many times, at the distance of a hundred yards or more." When people living in the path of winds blowing off Mill Pond, which abutted the Charles River, came down with yellow fever, Brown fixed blame again. "The inhabitants contiguous to the pond, and others, throw dead dogs, cats, putrid meat, fish, and rotten vegetables into it; and drown many small animals there: the filth of the streets flow into it in every direction, and it is the receiver of the vaults surrounding the pond."[34] The yellow fever abated by October 1798, after a severe northeaster and the season's first frost, but not before it had taken 145 lives.

Fearing another epidemic and believing that steps could be taken to avoid such an event, the people of Boston, acting through a committee of notables, requested that the General Court authorize the creation of a local board of health. The court complied and in March 1799 the Boston Board of Health was established; Paul Revere became its first president.[35] The six-member board quickly issued a series of regulations aimed at improving the sanitation of the town and offering a better defense against future outbreaks of disease. Fishmongers were required to place fish waste in sealed containers, the sale of rotting meat was prohibited, and human corpses had to be buried at least six feet underground. The use of privy vaults and sewers also came under scrutiny. To stop the vaults from freely flowing onto the lands, owners were required to keep the contents of their vaults at least eighteen inches from the surface or risk being labeled a nuisance subject to remedial action. During the warmest half of the year, from May 1 through November 1, when heat helped turn the contents of vaults into a fetid stew, one had to obtain a permit from the board before even opening a vault, lest the neighborhood become unwittingly enveloped in potentially pestilential fumes. Then, to make the disposal of vault contents a less messy affair, the board provided three covered scavenger carts and, according to Blake, "they obtained permission from the respective owners to use the West Boston Bridge, the Charles River Bridge, and Russell's and Tileston's wharves to dump the contents into deep water."[36]

The board viewed the proper use of sewers as essential to promoting health. Therefore, it ordered that "no waste water shall be suffered to run upon the surface of streets from any house, building, or yard abutting on a street in which there is a common sewer, but the same shall be led therein by the owners of the buildings."[37] The board further recommended that the connections between house drains and sewers be fitted with valves "to prevent the foul air and stench from issuing therefrom, which is known to be of a very noxious quality, and dangerous to health."[38] One reason that sewers produced great quantities of "foul air and stench" is that they were often clogged with waste, a situation that effectively transformed the sewers from mechanisms for transporting liquids and solids into "elongated cesspools." The board wanted many of the worst sewers cleaned and when it discovered that it lacked the authority to force private owners to take up that task, it sometimes stepped in. In one instance, the board paid scavengers $117.66 to cart away 113 loads of rotting materials that had been dredged from the Market Square sewer. At the end of the board's first year in operation, it presented a list of accomplishments, including the emptying and cleaning of 137 privy vaults and 27 "offensive drains."[39]

The board's efforts certainly improved the sanitation of the town, as did the continued construction of sewers. But Boston's evolving system of dealing with household and human waste, as well as runoff from the lands, was still far from perfect. The work of scavengers continued to be ridiculed. The state of hauling off the waste from privy vaults became so bad that in 1811, the Board of Health enlisted the services of Jeremiah Bridge, who boasted the use of a particularly effective cleaning system, and in effect gave him the monopoly on this business. According to Blake, "many disliked paying Bridge's prices. . . . Others wanted a share of the business and farmers resented being cut off from this source of manure. As a result, many citizens failed to have their vaults emptied on time or had it done by unlicensed collectors without permission. Despite frequent threats and regular prosecutions, this phase of the sanitary program remained a persistent source of trouble."[40]

The sewers, too, remained a source of trouble. Josiah Quincy, the second mayor of the city of Boston, reflected on the sorry state of sewer construction in his *Municipal History of the Town and City of Boston*, which he penned in 1852. His comments cover the period from the early 1700s through the incorporation of the city of Boston in 1822. "No system could be more inconvenient to the public, or embarrassing to private persons," Quincy said. "The streets were opened with little care, the drains built according to the opinion of private interest and economy; and constant and interminable vexations [and] occasions of dispute occurred between the owners of the drain and those who entered it, as to the degree of benefit and proportion of contributions."[41]

A particularly vivid and disturbing picture of how bad things could get was offered by Jonathan Kilham, a member of the Boston Board of Health who was called on to investigate the state of the common sewer in Bang's Alley. The board had built the sewer in 1809 and for many years since had been unable to either collect the full assessment from the abutters or get them to properly maintain the sewer. Kilham recounted his visit to Bang's Alley in 1818.

> Complaint having been made at this Office that the whole of Bang's Court is in such a State of filth of every species as endangers the Health of the Citizens generally—viz Their Privies Are Overflowing the common Sewer stopd & every waste water Conveyance Stagnant—Old Rotten Cheese exposd to the sun & air and every species of filth that can be namd in Heaps Having viewd the premises I declare the whole Court to be a Nuisance of the most dangerous nature And direct the Secretary to notify . . . [the property owners of Bang's Alley] to empty their Vaults—Open their Common Sewer, Clear their Waste Water drains—And remove from the surface every species of filth their Collected within Six Days.[42]

Not surprisingly, given the widespread problems the board was having enforcing its regulations, the property owners in Bang's Alley ignored the official entreaties to improve the sanitation of their property. Although scenes such as Bang's Alley were not uncommon, all of Boston's sewers were not in disrepair. Many Bostonians endeavored to maintain their sewers in good working order, if for no other reason than it made life more pleasant. Evidence of such responsibility can be gleaned from a letter posted to the Boston selectmen on June 7, 1813, and signed by sixty-two homeowners on North Street, including Paul Revere.

> We the Subscribers of Properties of the Common Sewer in north St. do understand that there has been application for Liberty of Cleaning and Replacing said Common Sewer. We the Subscribers being a large majority of the Proprietors do think it very unnecessary at this distressing time [likely referring to the war of 1812], and as our Cellars are Perfectly Dry. There was water in some of the Cellars last spring after a very heavy rain. Partly owing to the Cellars being lower than the Drain, as we understand, the Drain appears to answer as good a purpose now as it has done for many years past, and the Street is new and handsomly paved. Therefore, Gentlemen, we the Subscribers Do Pray that you will not grant any such request.[43]

The two-man team that the selectmen sent to investigate the situation reported that a few houses on the lower part of North Street had experienced some flooding in the past but were dry at present, and that the owners of those homes believed that fixing as little as 150 feet of the common sewer would solve the problem. The repairs were subsequently approved by the selectmen and carried out at a cost of $159.60. Apparently, this solution was acceptable to all because none of the original sixty-two complainants objected to paying their share of the assessment.[44]

Sewering the New and Growing City

On February 23, 1822, the town of Boston incorporated as the city of Boston. With more than 43,000 residents, Boston had outgrown the town form of government. Providing services for such a large and growing population required a more extensive network of administration and professional management. Josiah Quincy, who became Boston's mayor in 1823, made improving the sanitation of the city a key goal of his administration. "No subject had been pressed upon the Mayor," Quincy wrote, recalling his entry into office, "with more earnestness, by private citizens, than the state of the streets and the importance of adopting systematic plans for effectually removing the various accumulations and nuisances in them, which are incident to a populous city."[45] Quincy launched a street-cleaning program that was as extensive, if not more so, than that of any other city in the country. These efforts bore fruit soon after they were instituted, enabling Quincy to write a letter to Philadelphia authorities on July 20, 1825, in which he boasted, "So well regulated are our city teams and operations that, notwithstanding the excessive heat of last week, the whole number of complaints for neglect in carrying away the household dirt in the whole city for that week was but *four*. I do not believe it is possible for any city of equal population to carry into effect this species of cleaning at a less expense, or more thoroughly or to more general satisfaction."[46]

Quincy and his successors in office also focused on the sewers. In 1823, the city took over the cost and responsibility for laying and repairing common sewers, with the proviso that any person who entered "his or her particular drain into such common sewer, or shall otherwise be benefited there by," would have to pay the city that amount of money deemed "just and reasonable" by the mayor and the aldermen. Furthermore, the authorities could now require an owner to connect his "house, yard, or lot" to the common sewers whenever such a connection was felt to be in the best interest of the city.[47] An 1824 ordinance required "that all waste water shall be conveyed through drains under ground to the common sewer," or if such a sewer were lacking, that the wastewater be sent to an underground reservoir.[48] The same law dictated that privy vaults be "boxed, or made tight, so that the contents thereof shall not escape therefrom." Before emptying such a vault, an owner had to obtain a permit from the city marshal. In 1833, the health ordinances were expanded, requiring that all "tenements" be provided with sufficient drains and privies, and that vaults be connected, via drains, to the common sewers, but that only liquid and not solid human waste be allowed through such drains.[49] In 1834, the city allowed persons to "carry the rain water from the roofs of said buildings, into any common sewers, free of any charge."[50] With these changes, Boston's loose network of sewers expanded, reaching its tendrils out to more of the city year by year.

Apparently, having the city take over the responsibility for sewer construction and then charging users was not much of an improvement over the earlier system of individual initiative and financing. In 1837, a city committee called on to investigate the matter found that "the present system of assessing and collecting debts due the City on account of Common Sewers, is so exceedingly defective and so injurious to the interests of the City, that the government are called upon imperatively to effect some alteration in it."[51] The report noted that from 1823 through 1836, the city had spent $121,109.52 on sewers, but had collected only $26,431.31, leaving a shortfall of $94,678.21, the majority of which could be properly assessed to individuals benefiting from the city's actions. In the present year, the report added, nothing had been collected, causing the level of debt to rise further. The current system of having the city auditor and city marshal collect the dues had failed, the report said, primarily because those officers were too busy with other work. The solution offered and quickly adopted by the city was to appoint a Superintendent of Common Sewers, whose sole focus would be overseeing the construction of sewers and assessing fees, with the responsibility for collecting fees being left to the city treasurer. In line with the importance of this new job, the new superintendent's salary was set at $1,000 annually, which was $400 more than the annual salary for the city solicitor. Still, the issue of sewer assessments caused controversy. Some wanted the city to pay for all construction costs out of the general taxes because sewers were a "public and general good."[52] Others wanted the city to bear most if not all of the burden. The city responded in March 1838, when it passed an ordinance making it liable for one-fourth of the costs of sewer construction, with the balance being assessed to the usual property owners.

In his inaugural address in 1847, Boston mayor Josiah Quincy Jr. offered a snapshot of how the city was faring with its sewage. "Another great expenditure of the city is for sewers," he said. "During the past five years, there have been constructed 34,115 feet of drain, at a cost of $52,180.26." He pointed to increasing problems in the Back Bay, which was an inlet near the confluence of the Charles River and Boston Harbor, noting that "more than 2,000 tenements deposit the contents of their sewers" into that body of water, which, "consisting principally of stagnant water, is of itself almost a nuisance" that would soon require a remedy. One possible remedy that the mayor discussed was using the sewage from the Back Bay as fertilizer. "This experiment has been made, on a small scale, during the past year, in the public garden, and from the result, I cannot but believe that the contents of these sewers might be converted into valuable manure, which would more than reimburse the whole cost of its collection, and which might be removed without giving the slightest offence to the inhabitants." Quincy was especially excited about this option because it would obviate the need for the major expenditures that would be required to build a sewer

high that it was necessary to approach the bedside of a patient by means of a plank, which was laid from one stool to another; while the dead body of an infant was actually *sailing* about the room in its coffin!

Many of the inhabited cellars in this vicinity are inundated by the back-water of the drains during high-tides; and being entirely below the level of the sidewalks, they are necessarily, therefore, almost entirely without light or ventilation.[57]

This report showed quite clearly what had always been true—namely, that the poor of Boston often lived in wretched and unsanitary conditions and were much worse off in this regard than their counterparts in the middle or upper classes. Those who had the money to pay for new privies, sewers, and sewer connections had, at least, the opportunity to have such services provided. The poor were not so fortunate. According to one physician, lacking ready access to privies and sewers, the poor threw their "excrement . . . into the yard, and even under the lower floor of the houses."[58] In many cases, it was not the poor who were to blame but their landlords, few of whom felt compelled to provide services that would take a bite out of profits, even if the law required that they take action.

The Boston Health Department report also clearly indicated that the miasmic theory of disease transmission, in which gaseous emanations were causative, still held sway. "The general opinion of physicians in this city seems to be against the contagious nature of the disease, and we have seen no reason to differ from their opinion."[59] At the time of this report, the seminal work of the English anesthetist Dr. John Snow, in which he argued that cholera was contagious and could be transmitted through excreta and vomit, was less than a year old and had yet to be widely accepted. Indeed, the miasmic theory of disease would not truly die until the end of the century, well after Robert Koch discovered the bacterium responsible for cholera, *Vibrio cholerae*, in 1883.[60]

The report's heavy focus on the Irish and their living conditions lent support to the commonly held perception among physicians and others that, to some degree, intemperance, including immorality, gluttony, alcoholism, and lechery, provided a firm foundation for the spread of the disease. The report found that, "in nearly all these localities, an over-crowded population, bad ventilation, insufficient and unwholesome diet, *intemperance*, and the entire absence of cleanliness, have been the most efficient adjuvants in assisting the operation of other causes."[61] It further stated, "An examination of the habits of the victims of Cholera, shows with how much discrimination they were selected for its attack; *while* the rate of mortality, among those who were intemperate, is still more remarkable."[62] As Charles E. Rosenberg noted in his excellent study of cholera in America, "Cholera still seemed a disease of poverty and sin. . . . The deaths of the moral, the prudent, the respectable were usually ignored."[63] In the minds of many, the poor had only themselves to blame for their predicament. The idea that poverty alone, and not the moral fiber of individuals, placed the poor in horrid and unhealthful situations where disease could flourish was not yet as potent of an idea.

The report gave a concise description of why the lower parts of the city, in particular, were in such a wretched sanitary state. "There are many streets, courts, and lanes which are exceedingly contracted, ill ventilated, and dirty; without any proper grade and with no, or very insufficient sewerage. This state of things is mainly owing to the fact of their having been originally laid out by private speculators, whose only object was to make a profitable investment for themselves, and who paid but very slight attention to the health or comfort of those who have to reside upon them."[64] The report concluded, "The experience of this epidemic has certainly given most satisfactory evidence of the power and value of sanitary measures: for, as we have stated in the early part of this report, while no person was attacked without some obviously exciting cause, so, in every case in which those much exposed were removed from these deleterious influences, and provided with cleanly, airy apartments, and suitable food, an attack of the disease was averted. . . . Modern science has demonstrated that the most malignant epidemics may be greatly controlled by efficient sanitary reforms."[65] To that end, the committee recommended that existing statues pertaining to the "width, ventilation, grade, and drainage" of streets and ways be thoroughly enforced and new laws be passed as needed. With respect to tenements, where the worst conditions existed, the committee also argued that the laws should be enforced, noting, "Great public considerations seem to them to demand, that every dwelling-house should be provided with sinks, drains, and privies, that are adapted, in size, number, and construction, to the number of individuals who shall occupy it," and that the owners of such houses be compelled to provide such amenities.[66]

2

The Sanitary Awakening

The Boston Health Department report's recommendations and the steps that Boston had taken to improve its sewerage since its incorporation were all reflective of a growing national and international awareness of the intimate relationship between improved sanitation and improved health. The epidemics that had swept through Europe and the United States focused increased attention on the need to keep people and their waste away from each other or, at least, to get the waste away from the people before it putrefied and gave off supposed disease-causing fumes. The earliest and most complete consideration of the need for a revolution in the way sewage was handled came from England, primarily from the hand of Sir Edwin Chadwick, a lawyer who in the late 1830s headed up an effort to investigate the relationship between sanitary conditions and poverty. The *Report on the Sanitary Condition of the Labouring Population of Great Britain*, published in 1842, focused considerable attention on the connection between poor sanitation and disease. According to Martin V. Melosi, an eminent U.S. public works historian, "what made the report so radical was its denial of disease in fatalistic terms, as God's will, and also its rejection of a more current view that poverty was the main cause of ill health."[1]

Chadwick focused on the situation in London and didn't like what he saw. "The sewerage of the Metropolis, though it is a frequent subject of boast to those who have not examined its operations or effects, will be found to be a vast monument of defective administration, of lavish expenditure and extremely defective execution."[2] On the subject of the more than 200,000 cesspools in London, the report quoted the findings of a civil engineer who had inspected a couple of houses before doing repairs. "I found whole areas of the cellars of both houses were full of nightsoil to the depth of three feet, which had been permitted for years to accumulate from the overflow of the cesspools."[3]

Drawing a correlation between filth and sewage and disease, the report called for a range of reforms to cleanse the city and to improve the health of the citizenry. These focused on upgrading various public works, including sewers and water supply. According to Melosi, Chadwick "proposed a hydraulic (or arterial-venous) system that would bring potable water into homes equipped with waterclosets [toilets], and then would carry effluent out to public sewer lines, ultimately to be deposited as 'liquid manures' onto neighboring agricultural fields."[4] Although Chadwick's ideas received a mixed and not altogether positive reception in England (at least in the years immediately following the report's publication), the report can arguably be cited as one of the seminal documents, if not the seminal document, of the sanitary awakening that swept over Europe and the United States beginning in the middle of the nineteenth century. From this point forward, the move to install efficient sewers in cities and towns took on added urgency and purpose.

Chadwick's work found a ready acolyte in Lemuel Shattuck of Massachusetts. In 1849, the General Court of Massachusetts authorized a sanitary survey of the state, and Shattuck, who was in the state legislature, was appointed the head of a three-person commission to carry out the survey, the two other members being Nathaniel P. Banks Jr. and Jehiel Abbott. The commissioners' charge was extremely broad and vague—namely, "to prepare and report, to the next General Court, a plan for a Sanitary Survey of the state embracing a statement of such facts and suggestions as they may think proper to illustrate the subject."[5] Although three men were named as authors, the survey was really the work of Shattuck, whose efforts yielded a report that was monumental not only for its length, which was over five hundred pages, including appendices, but also for its scope. It laid out a comprehensive plan for vastly improving the sanitary laws and condition of the state, and in that, echoed many of the major themes that were highlighted in Chadwick's report nearly a decade earlier. Shattuck honored Chadwick, stating that he was "the individual to whom, perhaps, more than to any other, the cause is indebted. . . . His name should be handed down to posterity as one of the greatest and most useful reformers of his age."[6]

Shattuck was an excellent choice to head up the sanitary survey of the state. Born in Ashby, Massachusetts, on October 15, 1793, Shattuck was a man of considerable intellect and insatiable curiosity, with an especially strong interest in history and genealogy. In 1835 he published a history of the town of Concord, and his pursuit of genealogical studies led him, in 1844, to help found and then became the first vice president of the New England Historic and Genealogical Society. Shattuck was also very interested in vital statistics. He helped to found the American Statistical Association in 1839, and was one of the prime movers in the successful effort, in 1842, to get the state to establish registries for births, deaths, and marriages. Shattuck's considerable statistical skills helped him conduct the census of Boston in 1845, which included a sanitary survey of the city that exposed him to the horrible conditions the city's poor and immigrant populations faced; this survey helped prepare him for performing the much larger state survey.[7]

The sanitary survey of the state began with a ringing declaration of Shattuck's beliefs based on the data collected.

> WE BELIEVE that the conditions of perfect health, either public or personal, are seldom or never attained, though attainable;—that the average length of human life may be very much extended, and its physical power greatly augmented;—that in every year, within this Commonwealth, thousands of lives are lost which might have been saved;—that tens of thousands of cases of sickness occur, which might have been prevented;—that a vast amount of unnecessarily impaired health, and physical debility exists among those not actually confined by sickness;—that these preventable evils require an enormous expenditure and loss of money, and impose upon the people unnumbered and immeasurable calamities, pecuniary, social, physical, mental, moral, which might be avoided;—that means exist, within our reach, for their mitigation and removal;—and that measures for prevention will effect infinitely more, than remedies for the cure of the disease.[8]

In the pages that followed, Shattuck marshaled a mountain of statistics to make the case that the health of the inhabitants of the state was not as good as it should be and that mortality rates were clearly influenced by sanitary conditions. Unlike Chadwick, Shattuck adopted the predominant view of the day that the poor, especially immigrants, who had particularly high rates of disease and mortality, were partly to blame for their predicament because through their behavior and intemperate living they had, in effect, invited poverty and disease and allowed it to spread.[9] Still, regardless of the specific cause of the problem, in Shattuck's view, as in Chadwick's, it was the state's responsibility to improve sanitary conditions through direct action.

The report laid out fifty detailed recommendations constituting a plan that, if instituted, would have been revolutionary in its impact. For example, Shattuck called for a complete revision of the state's laws regarding public health and the establishment of something yet unknown in the United States, a state board of health. Each city and town was called on to convene its own board of health. Annual reports on the health of the citizenry were to be produced. The registration of births, marriages, and deaths was to be placed on firmer footing, with one of the benefits being that public health officials would have data available to help detect and analyze trends on mortality that might be used to establish cause-and-effect relationships between activities and disease. The report called for a proactive approach to health that focused on prevention rather than treatment. It advocated the construction of "better accommodations" for the poor so that they not be subject to the horrid, unsanitary conditions so prevalent in the tenement houses of Boston and beyond. Pointing out that the "smoke of furnaces, manufacturers, and other establishments" is deleterious to health, the report argued that measures must be taken to minimize the smoke nuisance, thereby likely making Shattuck one of the first Americans to call for curbs on air pollution.

Of the report's fifty recommendations, only two focused on sewers and sewage, but they were an important part of the overall plan. One of those was number 17, which read, "We recommend that, in laying out new towns and villages, and in extending those already laid out, ample provision be made for a supply, in purity and abundance, of light, air, and water; for drainage and sewage, for paving, and for cleanliness."[10] Under the subheading of "drains and sewers," Shattuck said that they "should be made to carry off water introduced in any way into cities and villages. If the surplus be permitted to remain, it often becomes stagnant and putrid, and is then a fruitful source of disease."[11] Under cleanliness, Shattuck stated: "The only safe rule is, to remove out of a town, and out of a house, all refuse as soon as it is produced. Refuse matters, either animal or vegetable, are constantly undergoing change, and giving out vapors and gases which, even in extremely small quantities are injurious to health, especially if they are constantly inhaled." He added that those who allow the atmosphere to be contaminated with such vapors "should be looked upon as worse than a highway robber. The latter robs of us property, the former of life."[12] Recommendation 40 urged "that, whenever practicable, the refuse and sewage of cities and towns be collected, and applied to the purposes of agriculture."[13] In support for this recommendation, Shattuck pointed to studies abroad that had indicated the pecuniary values of waste, particularly human excrement.

Two thousand copies of the report were printed and Shattuck had high hopes that the power of his arguments would launch a sanitary revolution in Massachusetts, but it did not. The report was ignored. As one contemporary observer remarked, it "fell stillborn from the hands of the state printer."[14] Just eight years later, Banks, who had become governor, did not even remember he had signed the report. Many reasons have been offered for this neglect, all of which likely played a role. Some have argued that the report was too overwhelming in scope to be readily absorbed by politicians or the medical community.[15] Others pointed to the widely held belief that poverty and disease were retribution for intemperance and sinful behavior. If this were the case, then why should the state take a stand in reforming the habits of such people if their afflictions were, in part, the will of God? Even if the politicians of the time believed the proper role of the state was to enforce cleanliness for the sake of communal health, doing so could be politically dangerous. The mid-eighteenth century was a time of massive immigration to Boston, and many of these immigrants voted. Similarly many of the non-immigrant poor also voted. As Barbara Gutmann Rosenkrantz argued, Massachusetts's politicians were "more concerned with the voting behavior of the immigrant and the urban poor than with their hygienic habits."[16] Telling such a large voting bloc that they must, in effect, clean up their act might not have been well received.

Although Shattuck might have taken some comfort from the fact that in 1850 Boston had roughly thirty-two miles of sewers—a more extensive system than most other U.S. cities had—he could not have been happy with the quality of sewerage or the deplorable conditions that still existed within many parts of the city, where human and other organic wastes could be found putrefying in overflowing privies, in the streets, and in the sewers. The divide was deep between the type of effective and efficient sewerage system that Shattuck's report called for and the haphazard, unplanned, and often shoddy system that Boston had. If one ventured outside the confines of Boston to other cities and towns in Massachusetts, the sewage situation was worse, with many localities having such rudimentary sewer systems that they made Boston's look quite advanced. Although Shattuck's report fell on deaf ears, a range of societal forces were inexorably pushing Boston to the point where dramatically improving its sewage system would become not an option but a necessity.

Made Land

By the middle of the nineteenth century much of Boston was standing on what one engineer of the time called "made land."[17] Bostonians were not willing to let the diminutive size of the real estate that nature had originally bequeathed keep them from expanding. They looked to the marshy lowlands and shallow intertidal areas surrounding Boston Neck and started filling them in with soil and rocks. Year by year, the surface area of Boston expanded. Although this provided for an ever-increasing population, it also created major sewage problems. Because the new lands were just barely above sea level, many of the cellars and other parts of the buildings constructed on those lands were below sea level. Thus, underground sewers necessarily exited those buildings also below sea level. When the tide was out, the waste in these sewers had at least a fighting chance of slowly flowing from the building, through the sewer pipes, and out the end that lay at the water's edge. But when the tide rolled in, the terminuses of the sewer pipes were often underwater, and that meant that instead of flowing away from the buildings, the waste in the sewers was pushed back into the buildings by the force of the rising waters.

Some building owners installed flaps on their pipes to keep the waste from backing up, but as many or more did not, and even the flaps that were installed often failed to work well or got stuck in the open position. The net result was that many residents of Boston's made lands were subject to diurnal, subterranean dousings of raw sewage. Making matters worse was that a significant number of the sewers were too big. The bigger the pipe, given the same amount of liquid wastes, the slower the velocity of the liquids that flow through it, because of increases in friction and drag. The shape of the sewers themselves in many instances exacerbated this problem. Although rounded pipes were arguably the best for transporting liquid waste, many of Boston's sewers were flat-bottomed or square. Because the slugs of sewage traveling through these overly large and often unfortunately shaped pipes moved so slowly, the larger solid materials tended to settle and to decay in place. This not only increased the production of sewer gases, which often seeped back into the buildings, it also created a situation in which the solids at the bottom of the sewers further reduced the flow of the sewage, which in turn increased the deposition of solids. This vicious circle, if left unchecked, could eventually completely plug up the sewer. And the underground sewers were not the only problem. Street-level drains constructed on these low-lying, made lands did not have the same declivity as the drains that were constructed on the hills of Boston. Therefore, the helpful hand of gravity was all but muted, and the sewage and runoff flowing on the streets in the flatter parts of the city had a difficult time making its way expeditiously to the harbor and its tributaries.

Various engineering solutions were employed during the mid-nineteenth century in an effort to ameliorate the sewage problems associated with made lands. In some areas, such as the Back Bay, houses were raised at considerable expense. Tide flaps were installed on the many sewer outlets at the edge of the harbor to keep the ocean from flooding back into the buildings. Although such engineering solutions helped to alleviate these problems, they did not eliminate them. The tide flaps, for example, did not always perform as expected, and when stuck in the open position, were essentially useless. When the flaps did function properly, other problems arose. Until the next low tide, the sewage stagnated in the pipes, transforming them into temporary cesspools. When the flaps opened, no sooner had the accumulated waste started to exit the sewers than the incoming tide would push the sewage onto the shorelines of the city, making the areas in close proximity to the outlets most objectionable. A city Board of Health report during this period complained,

> Large territories have been at once, and frequently, enveloped in an atmosphere of stench so strong as to arouse the sleeping, terrify the weak, and nauseate and exasperate everybody. . . . It visits the rich and poor alike. It fills the sick-chamber and the office. . . . The sewers and sewage flats in and about the city furnish nine-tenths of all the stenches complained of. . . . The accumulation of sewage upon the flats and about the city has been, and is, rapidly increasing, until there is not probably a foot of mud in the river, in the basins, in the docks, or elsewhere in close proximity to the city, that is not fouled with sewage.[18]

Not surprisingly, the disposition of sewage, especially in the areas of made land, remained a topic of controversy for many years.[19]

Water, Water Everywhere, with No Place to Go

Today it is impossible to imagine having a system that supplies water without also having a system that can take the used and excess water away as part of a larger stream of sewage. After all, input with little or no output makes for a real mess. In the mid-1800s this connection, apparently, was not as clear, or, at least, people felt less of a need to solve the input/output problem before rather than after it arose. During this time, many cities and towns in the United States implemented ambitious waterworks programs that provided fresh, potable water to a citizenry who had grown tired and angry about having to rely on cistern-collected water or well water, both of which often became polluted in heavily populated areas or just tasted awful. But these same cities and towns commonly failed to construct sewers and gutters to efficiently take this new water away. Boston fell into this category.

In the early 1800s, many Bostonians still relied on wells and cisterns for their water supply. The Aqueduct Corporation, which incorporated in 1796, piped water from nearby Jamaica Pond to certain parts of the city, but the system was neither extensive nor completely reliable.[20] On October 24, 1848, this all changed, for that is the day that the $4 million Cochituate water system, capable of delivering 18 million gallons of water per day from Lake Cochituate to Boston, began operations. So great an event was this that the mayor proclaimed a holiday. An account of the day's festivities offers a glimpse of the excitement.

> [The day began with] the simultaneous roar of 100 cannons and the ringing of every church bell in the town and beyond. There would be no commerce that day, nor work, nor learning. . . . The parade terminated at the Common where a crowd estimated at between 50,000 and 100,000 were gathered around a fountain placed at the center of the famous Frog Pond. . . .'Do you want the water?' Mayor Quincy shouted to the . . . people as . . . dusk fell. 'Yes!' they roared back and with a mighty pull on the lanyard, the sluice shot open and a geyser leaped 70 feet into the air. Beyond the Common on the crest of Beacon Hill rockets burst into the air, setting off a display of multicolored fireworks of intricate design. . . . It was, all in all . . . a wonderful party in the end.[21]

The famed poet James Russell Lowell read a poem he had written for the occasion, "An Ode on the Introduction of Cochituate Water," part of which reads,

> My name is Water: I have sped
> Through strange, dark ways, untried before,
> By pure desire of friendship led,
> Cochituate's ambassador:
> He sends four royal gifts by me
> Long life, health, peace, and purity.[22]

Bostonians had every reason to be excited. Fresh and plentiful water was a cornerstone of a healthy and prosperous city, and the residents of Boston made ample use of this new resource. By 1852 per capita water consumption in Boston was estimated at fifty-eight gallons per day. Five years later it had risen to seventy-three gallons. And, in 1860, with the population of Boston at roughly 200,000, per capita water consumption averaged almost one hundred gallons a day.[23]

But plentiful water was not an unmitigated blessing. Boston was already a city that was having great difficulties draining its lands and getting rid of liquid waste. Now that the volume of water coursing into the city had become a virtual torrent, as compared with what had trickled into it before, the problems of getting rid of the water and the waste worsened manyfold. The increased burden was often more than the existing sewers and drains could handle. Indeed, many of them had never worked very well before the introduction of the Cochituate water. To make matters worse, this was also the time when many Bostonians of means were trading in their privies for indoor plumbing and flush toilets that were, appropriately, called water closets. According to one estimate, in 1863 there were 87,000 Boston households that had piped-in water, and 14,000 of them had water closets.[24] As time progressed, the volumetric disconnect between water coming into the city and water efficiently leaving it grew worse.

The Sanitary Awakening Here and Abroad

Even though Shattuck's report was essentially ignored in Massachusetts, the concepts he and others before him promoted found fertile ground in many places in the United States and internationally. The ever-present concerns about epidemics and the supposed link between atmospheric emanations from putrefying organic waste and sickness, as well as the desire to create more pleasant living conditions, propelled a growing number of large cities to take steps to improve their sewerage systems. Among these were Paris (1833), Hamburg (1843), Brooklyn (1857), Chicago (1859), and Frankfurt am Main, Germany (1867).[25] The most famous contemporary effort to improve sewerage was in London. For many centuries the waste of London flowed to the Thames River. In 1357, in an address to the mayor and sheriffs of the city of London, King Edward III touched on complaints that were similar to those that would come from Bostonians many centuries later. "Whereas now," the king said, "when passing along the water of the Thames, we have beheld dung and other filth accumulated in diverse places in the said City upon the bank of the river aforesaid and also perceived the fumes and other abominable stenches arriving therefrom . . . [we] do command you that you cause as well the banks of the said river, as the streets and lanes of the same City, and the suburbs thereof, to be cleaned of dung and other filth without delay and the same when cleaned to be so kept."[26]

The situation had gotten much worse by the mid-1800s. After centuries of building sewers and drains throughout the city, and with significant population growth, London was virtually saturated with sewage, both on its lands and in the sluggish river Thames that meandered through its heart. The famed scientist Michael Faraday recorded the following observations in a letter to the *Times* on July 7, 1855.

> Sir, I traversed this day, by steam boat, the space between London and Hungerford Bridges. . . . It was low water. . . . The appearance and the smell of the water forced themselves at once upon my attention. The whole of the river was an opaque, pale brown fluid. . . . The smell was very bad . . . the whole river was for the time a real sewer. . . . The condition in which I saw the Thames may, perhaps, be considered as exceptional but it ought to be an impossible state, instead of which, I fear, it is rapidly becoming the general condition. If we neglect this subject, we cannot expect to do so with impunity, nor ought we be surprised if, ere many years are over, a hot season give us sad proof of the folly of our carelessness.[27]

Faraday's last comment was prescient. The summer of 1858 became famous for the Great Stink, when the rising mercury transformed the polluted Thames into a decomposing organic stew that generated a stench so bad that legislators in Parliament were forced to hold handkerchiefs over their faces and retreat to rooms in the Parliament building that were as far from the river as possible. The Great Stink did a wonderful job of forcing the legislators to confront the sewage issue head-on. Observing the subsequent Parliamentary deliberations, a London newspaper noted that "gentility of speech is at an end—it stinks; and whoso once inhales the stink can never forget it and count himself lucky if he live to remember it."[28] Another local newspaper reported that "the Thames, which had become more and more heavily used as a sewer, finally made its point by stinking out the Commons Committee."[29] With the public demanding the elimination of the stinking conditions, Parliament launched an ambitious program of sewerage construction that over subsequent decades produced a system of intercepting sewers, pumping stations, and treatment works that greatly ameliorated the sanitary problems in the city, and which still serves London today. Finally, Chadwick got his due. The success of London and other cities in confronting their sewage problems placed pressure on other cities to follow suit for the benefit of their citizens and offered extensive precedents on which to base similar efforts.

The Health of Boston's Citizens

In the mid-nineteenth century the proposition that sewage, especially sewage gas, could threaten human health was widely accepted within the medical community. But although the medical community of Boston had often raised concerns about the health implications of sewage, not until the 1870s did doctors take an extremely active and leading role in arguing that the city needed to be much more aggressive in properly disposing of its sewage. On April 14, 1870, the Consulting Physicians of the City of Boston delivered a report on the status of public health and what could be done to improve it.[30] As expected, given the city's tempestuous history of dealing with its own waste, the issue of sewage was a major focus of the physicians. After noting that "The death-rate of Boston has been for some years past so high as to excite the attention of the medical profession," the report went on to list the various causes for this alarming trend. The physicians argued that

> Among the first requirements for public health in a crowded city are sewerage and pavement—such sewers as will cause all the foul liquids to flow away by force of gravity, and such pavement as will prevent all soakage into the soil. To obtain these in perfection is a work of time, of great cost, and of the highest engineering skill. . . . There are, in all parts of Boston, filthy back-yards, alleys and passageways, broken down and overflowing vaults, and, in the older portions, disused wells and cisterns which are receptacles for dirt. All these nuisances should be reformed.

The report concluded with clarion call for the city fathers to overcome any hesitation they might have to invest the considerable amounts of money necessary to undertake the reforms the physicians had presented.

> . . . we believe they [the reforms] would prove to be good investments, and that a true economy demands them.
>
> The money value of human life to a community is real. A destructive epidemic is expensive. Moreover, a clean and unquestionably healthy city, such as Boston might be made, would have attractions for permanent residents & transient visitors which could not fail to favorably affect its commercial interests. It might also well be an object of pride with every citizen to furnish in Boston an example of public cleanliness & public health which other American cities would imitate.

Any confidence that the consulting physicians had that their words would precipitate reform was slowly strangled by official silence. In the ensuing months, the physicians repeatedly contacted the city's committee on health to find out what, if any, actions were being taken to secure the reforms outlined in the report. These inquiries were either ignored or responded to politely but without much substantial information about the progress, or lack thereof, of sanitary measures. By the end of the year, three of the five consulting physicians had had enough and quit. Their letter of resignation stated, "They had hoped that this office might be one of active usefulness, but they find it a sinecure."[31] The three claimed that the sanitation of the city had not improved during the past year, and they ended their letter with a ringing condemnation of Boston's lack of responsibility on this issue.

> When public property is at stake professional advice is sought for its protection; when public health is in danger there seems to be equal reason for taking counsel of the medical profession, and this policy is recognized in nearly every great city of the world. In Boston alone the interests of public health are made a branch of the business of street-cleaning, and the advice of its Consulting Physicians is not asked, and when volunteered is rejected as of no value. A continuance in office under such circumstances would seem to the undersigned to be wanting in respect to the profession to which they belong.

The resignations were accepted. If the city fathers thought that they had heard the last from the medical community on the need for improved sewerage, they were mistaken. In 1873, the newly established Board of Health of the City of Boston weighed in with its own thoughts on the sewage situation, in its first annual report.

> The promptest attention should be paid by all our citizens to stagnant and waste water, defective drainage and sewerage. As to the troublesome question of sewerage, or what to do with our sewage, the problem has not yet been solved. . . . Yet the time must come sooner or later, when sewage, properly so called, must be disposed of in some manner independent of and disconnected from the sewers, or something must be added to our present sewers. Vienna, on an elevated site with the Donau at its base, having three times the rapidity of current of the Hudson or the Rhine, may for years to come send her sewage through that channel to the sea, but Boston cannot always avail herself for this purpose of her sewers, as they now are, or the river Charles. Our sewers must be extended, or some large one take the contents of all those which now fail to go there, into the deep tidal currents of the river or the sea, and the vexed problem may be saved for us for a long time, if not forever.[32]

Sewage was again a major topic in the second annual report of the city's board of health.

> The whole system of sewerage is clearly wrong. Our beautiful city is almost encircled by the mouths of sewers discharging their contents into shoal water or upon flats, the sewer gases rendering the atmosphere for some distance about the wharves absolutely dangerous to breathe. . . . There are large neighborhoods in the city entirely destitute of sewers, or any proper means of getting rid of their vault, sink, or cesspool drainage, and much sickness exists in these places in consequence. . . . We are satisfied that all sewers should discharge their contents into deep water, and as far out into the harbor as possible, and in no instance should the mouth of a sewer be exposed, even at the lowest tide.[33]

On December 17, 1874, the city's board of health wrote to the city council on the sewage issue, noting that, although the board had already raised this issue in the first two annual reports, the issue was so important that it should be raised again. The board was especially concerned about the connection between "summer diseases" and the "poisoned atmosphere" caused by rotting sewage.

> The best remedy for the evil complained of may not be so apparent as the evil itself. We beg to suggest, however, that whatever disposition is ultimately made of the sewage, whether carried inland and utilized, or seaward and lost, it should not be discharged at all points in the circumference of our city. If it is to be discharged into the sea—and this for Boston seems the most practicable—there should be the least possible number of outlets, and those well out into the channel of the harbor. We believe that the time has come when large main sewers, which can be relied on for the next century to collect and convey the sewage of all others to a proper place for disposal, or to the sea, should be laid. We believe that the very best interests of the city, public economy, and the public health would be well served by beginning this work with the least necessary delay.[34]

This same letter to the city council also gave voice to the serious problems posed by the supply of fresh water to the city.

> There are many places within the limits of the city . . . where, although a supply of water has been furnished, there are no means of getting rid of it after it has done its service, and the result is a perfect saturation of the soil about the dwellings, etc., by the vast overflow of cesspools and vaults. Typhoid fever and other preventable diseases are frequent in these places, and we fear must continue until proper sewage is instituted.

While it is regretted that water-pipes have anywhere preceded the laying of sewers, it is but fair to say that the supply of pure water from the pipes, in some of the sections referred to, had become a necessity, and the people would have suffered, but in a little different way, without it.[35]

In the third annual report of the city's board of health, delivered in 1875, the sewage issue again took center stage.

During the past year we have been constantly reminded, by the just complaints of suffering citizens, of the many defects to be found in the sewerage. In many sections of the city the foul odors arising from the sewage have been at times almost unbearable. Many of the sewers are so foul as to emit from the manholes, when opened, stenches so offensive as to become a nuisance to the whole neighborhood. Moreover, the discharge of the sewage at various points surrounding the city, on the flats or in shoal water, is rapidly causing the formation of a grand cesspool, in the centre of which we are living.[36]

While the city's board of health was making a strong case for sewage reform by pointing out the gross defects of the current system, the Massachusetts State Board of Health, established in 1869, was exploring the sewage issue from a broader perspective, focusing on the current state of sewage science and what Massachusetts and, to some extent, foreign countries were doing to handle their sewage problems. The second annual report of the state board of health, in 1871, included a letter from Dr. Henry Ingersoll Bowditch, the first chairman of the board, remarking on the results of investigations during his residence in London in the summer of 1870. "The great sanitary question throughout Great Britain," Bowditch argued, "is the economic removal from houses of what is deleterious to man, and the proper use, as a source of income, of what has heretofore been wholly wasted. There is no single subject that is attracting more attention in England, and which excites more heated partisanship than the vast questions looming up under the various names of 'earth-closet,' 'water-closet,' 'sewage,' 'its danger to health,' 'its widespread and fatal waste,' 'its utilization as manure.'"[37] Bowditch also visited the Thames, where he observed the working of London's new sewage outfalls. He was amazed to find that the sewage issuing from these outfalls had no odor. He was also pleased to learn "that at present there was no proof that this deodorized sewage water of London does actual harm to those dwelling near it."[38]

The fourth annual report of the state board of health, in 1873, offered an extensive survey of the options for dealing with sewage. On the subject of whether sanitary sewers and stormwater sewers should be combined or separate, the report said the following:

> Sewers may be used (1) for the exclusive removal of excremental and waste fluids; (2) for the removal of rainfall; (3) for the removal of superfluous water in the soil. . . . There are those who strongly advocate the separation of the first two from each other. The rainfall to the river, the sewage to the soil is an alliterative saying which has had great currency in England. It however involves the construction of a complete double set of sewers in every case, and it sacrifices the advantage of occasional flushing and the complete washing out of these conduits by occasional storms. Our best engineers do not advise this separation, except to provide storm-water overflows as a measure of economy.[39]

On the subject of ocean discharge, the report was equally clear. "We believe that, in the present state of human knowledge and experience, no better receptacle than the ocean can be found, provided the sewage is delivered where deep currents can disperse it so that it can be no more seen, and can prevent its deposit in the settling-basins of docks and the mud flats of estuaries."[40]

The report also noted that "the utilization or '*beworthing*' of waste material of every sort is of equal interest to the political economist and to the sanitarian. To the one it is a direct saving of money; to the other a saving of health and of life, both of which have true money value. . . . It is no exaggeration to say that this problem of conversion of the excremental waste of towns and people and the refuse of factories, into useful materials, is now engaging as much of the attention of intelligent minds throughout the world as any social question."[41] Nevertheless, the authors didn't hold out much hope for successfully utilizing Boston's sewage in this manner. The value of the city's sewage was reckoned to be, at most, a mere one cent per ton. And the likelihood of extracting profit from the waste was scant considering the investment that would be necessary to transport Boston's sewage to the farms where it could be applied. According to the superintendent of sewers for the city, "to utilize by irrigation the dry-weather sewage of only Boston, would require its collection by a large encircling sewer, the raising of 100,000 tons of water daily, to a height of twenty or thirty feet, the construction of a covered channel, sufficient for its carriage to a suitable district, and its continuous discharge upon a farm of 2,000 acres." The problems associated with the transport and use of sewage would only be worse during rainstorms when the volume of wastewater would greatly increase, while the concentration of manurial elements would be more dilute.[42]

The state board of health praised the lowly sewer. "Hidden, and consequently but little thought of, they are, in crowded cities, our constant and faithful servants, removing from among our dwellings, yards and streets, not only superfluous rain, but every fluid and semi-fluid form of refuse matter, which if allowed to accumulate, would pollute the air and cause pestilence, as it did in European cities centuries ago."[43] Sewer gases were highlighted as the cause of much disease, but the specific causal factor remained a medical mystery. "What the specially noxious element in them is, no one can define. It is evidently neither carbonic acid, nor sulpheretted hydrogen, nor any other of the gases with which chemists are familiar in the laboratory. There is something beyond all this, coming from the decay of organized substances in a closed, pent-up position, without the free access of light and air, which at times gives rise to the most virulent poison, and to the most destructive forms of disease."[44]

The report also presented the results of a recent survey of Boston's sewer system, indicating that there were "five miles of stone-masonry [sewers], sixty-seven miles of brickwork, two miles of cement-pipe, fifteen miles of wood submerged at high-water, ten miles of Scotch pipe, one mile of other earthen pipe, and twenty miles built with dry-brick sides, covered with slate."[45] It was estimated that about one-half of the city's annual load of ten thousand cords of human excrement was removed through sewers, while the other half was deposited in privy vaults, from which it was taken by carts at night to the countryside beyond the city limits. Most of the other components of sewage, such as kitchen slop, were transported to local waterways through the sewers.[46] In considering the state of Boston's sewers, the report concluded that the city needed to appoint a competent engineer to survey Boston and the surrounding communities and to suggest "a comprehensive and harmonious" system of sewerage.[47] It was not long before this was done.

"Future Wants of the City"

By the early 1870s, the weight of evidence in favor of overhauling Boston's antiquated sewer system was so great that the subject became a major focus of local debate. Boston politicians could not ignore the many sewage-related problems facing the city or the rising chorus of complaints from the medical community and the citizenry. The reports of the city and state boards of health were particularly powerful in overcoming political inertia. As a result, on July 14, 1873, the city council requested that its committee on sewers examine the system of sewerage in the city and recommend any improvements necessary to protect the public's health. The committee's conclusions, delivered on September 1, were surprising, to say the least. "Our system of drainage is as perfect, though not so complicated, as that of any other city," the report stated. "We are favored by location with generally good grades and outlets to deep water; and though we have no long lines composed of huge sewers with their many branches, with pumping works and flushing apparatus, yet the removal of the sewage from the house to the ebbing tide in the harbor is rapid and complete; and *that* is a perfect system." Of the five thousand or so cellars that lay below extreme high water, the report said that, "with few exceptions, [they] are perfectly drained; but after a heavy storm the newspapers invariably report the flooding of cellars in the low parts of New York, Brooklyn and Baltimore. In the drainage of the surface of streets and in the appliances for protecting cellars from tide-water, our system is probably better than that of any other city."[1] The report ended by stating that "Everything which appears necessary to the public health or convenience will be carried out by the Department as soon as it is possible or expedient." The state of mind and the motivations of the three aldermen who penned this report is lost to the mists of history, but there is no doubt that their optimistic and reassuring tone was out of step with reality. While Boston's sewers certainly compared quite favorably with the sewer systems of other large U.S. cities, that had more to do with the sad state of contemporary sewerage than with the supposed "perfection" of Boston's sewers. The bar was not set that high.

In 1875, at the urging of a subsequent city committee on sewers, the mayor appointed a commission to "report upon the present sewerage of the city" and to "present a plan for the outlets and main lines of sewers for the future wants of the city."[2] The commission was to consist of two civil engineers and one person skilled in sanitary science. The two engineers were E. S. Chesbrough, who had gained fame designing the sewage system of Chicago and had served as the chief engineer of the Cochituate water works, and Moses Lane, the city engineer of Milwaukee. The third member was Charles F. Folsom, M.D., a member of the Massachusetts State Board of Health. At the commission's first meeting, on April 23, 1875, Mayor Samuel Cobb was reported to have told the assembled crowd that "the subject of the sewerage of Boston was the most important which he had been called upon to consider."[3]

The Commission's Recommendation

The commission's report, delivered early in 1876, began with the observation that "for many years past there has been a growing feeling among the more intelligent of our community, and particularly among physicians, whose habits of study lead them especially to watch the public health, that our high death-rates are connected more or less directly with the defects and evils of our sewerage-system, more especially in the low-lying and originally tidal districts,—evils which are increasing from year to year, and which have been and are so manifest to the senses that it is not necessary here to more than allude to their existence."[4] The commission concurred with the findings of the fourth annual report of state board of health, stating, "The Board had daily evidence of the connection between decomposing matter from our sewers and disease, and the experience of the rest of the world confirmed that of Boston. London, Paris, Brussels, Hamburg, Dantzig, Frankfort-on-the-Main, and many other cities have had their sanitary condition so remarkably improved by better sewerage that Berlin, Stuttgart, Munich, St. Petersburg, and many others of the cities of Europe are fast following their examples. In all these places, the cardinal principle is to get their sewage away, far out of reach, *before putrefaction begins*."[5]

A review of Boston's sewerage system followed. Noting that they had not had time to examine all sewers in the city, the commissioners nevertheless were able to examine many of them and over four hundred manholes. "The modern sewers in Boston are," the report said, "most of them, well-constructed and of good material. . . . There are now in the city proper thirty-two independent drainage-districts, the principal sewers of which were built in different years, often widely apart, discharging by separate outlets." Despite the encouraging state of many of the sewers, the commissioners found much that troubled them. The sewers in made lands, particularly in the Back Bay, were a continuing source of vexation. Many of the catch basins underneath the manholes were full of putrefying waste. "They cannot ever be properly cleaned, and must always of necessity be full of sewage; the annual or semi-annual clearing-out only serving to remove the sand and other solid matters. There are thus several hundred literal open-mouthed cesspools connected with the houses in all parts of the city." One such catch basin near Haymarket had a solid deposit five feet in depth that was "so hard that it was difficult to thrust a pole through it." The outlets of many of the sewers also earned the commissioners' scorn. "It is certainly a very serious objection, in a sanitary point of view, that twenty million gallons of sewage are discharged at forty different points, completely skirting our city and polluting the atmosphere throughout most of its length and breadth." Many of those outlets released "directly into the docks, or upon large surfaces or impervious dock mud. Under the influence of the moisture and heat in summer, this highly putrescible organic matter gives forth such offensive gases as to render it impossible to remain with comfort in some of the most costly houses in the city. . . . Great as these evils are, they can only increase as the city grows and the population becomes more dense."[6]

In summary, the commission found that "the evils which exist in our system of sewage in Boston chiefly arise from additions being constantly made to the territory of the city, and from the sewers being necessarily extended through these low districts, and on very flat grades, without a definite comprehensive system."[7] There was a pressing need, the commissioners argued, for getting the waste "out of the way" before it could cause harm. The commissioners even put a limit on the amount of time that sewage could fester before becoming a nuisance—twelve hours. Noting that the city's present system failed miserably at getting waste "out of the way," the commissioners explored potential remedies to this situation. Raising as much as half of the city, as a means to improve drainage, was "entirely out of the question" because of the great cost.

Having dispensed of this scheme, the commissioners presented their preferred alternative.

> There are in use now in various parts of the world three methods of disposing of the sewage of large cities, where the water-carriage system is in use.
>
> 1st. Precipitation of the solid parts, with a view to utilizing them as manure, and to purifying the streams.
>
> 2d. Irrigation.
>
> Neither of these processes has proved renumerative, and the former only *clarifies* the sewage *without purifying* it; but if the time comes, when, by advance in our knowledge of agricultural chemistry, sewage can be profitably used as a fertilizer, or if it should now be deemed best to utilize it, in spite of a pecuniary loss, it is thought that the point to which we propose carrying it will be as suitable as any which can be found near enough to the city, and at the same time far enough away from it.
>
> The third way is that adopted the world over by large cities near deep water, and consists in carrying the sewage out so far that its point of discharge will be remote from dwellings, and beyond the possibility of doing harm. It is the plan which your Commission recommends for Boston. The work will require a large sum of money, but no larger than has been expended by other cities for the same purpose; only two-thirds as much as the city of Frankfort-on-the-Main has lately appropriated for their sewers, and a small sum when we consider the benefits that will come from it.[8]

What they proposed, in short, was that two sewerage systems be built. One would collect and carry off the sewage from the part of Boston located between the Charles and Neponset Rivers as well as Brookline, the other would service the areas north of the Charles River, including Charlestown, East Boston, and the cities of Cambridge, Somerville, and Chelsea. The two systems were almost identical in their design and would include intercepting sewers, which would receive the flow of existing sewers, and main sewers, which would collect sewage from the intercepting sewers. The main sewers would then transport the sewage to the pumping stations that would, in turn, lift it roughly thirty-five feet into outfall sewers that fed into large reservoirs on the coast where the sewage would be held and then released during the first two hours of the ebb tide. For the system south of the Charles River, the outlet point would be off Moon Island. For the system lying north of the Charles, the release point would be Shirley Gut, a narrow channel of water between Point Shirley and Deer Island. The cost of the southern system was estimated to be $3,746,500; the northern system, $2,804,564.

The commissioners' proposal was firmly in line with much of the established thinking of the day. Although the thought of utilizing sewage for its manurial content sounded good, the idea was economically and practically infeasible. The ocean disposal of wastes was an accepted practice and in fact worked quite well as long as the dilution of the waste into the receiving waters was great enough. Combined sewer systems, which handled both sewage and stormwater runoff, were very common abroad and were the standard in the United States where a double or separate system of sewers had never been constructed. For many years, all of the sewers constructed in and around Boston had been the combined type, and that practice continued for the balance of the nineteenth century, when most of the combined sewers in the area were built.[9] If a double system were required sometime in the future for sanitary reasons, Chesbrough noted, "the previous existence of an ordinary system need not prevent the introduction of the other, although it would then be more difficult and expensive to arrange some of the details, than if both were planned in connection."[10]

During their eight-month investigation, the commissioners heard from many individuals and received many correspondences. One letter appended to their report, which clearly reflected the general sentiment of the medical community, came from a physician, J. P. Reynolds. "I am most deeply convinced," he wrote, "of the importance of an immediate improvement in the system of sewerage. Immense as the outlay for any substantial change must be, that outlay is nothing in comparison to the cost in lives and in the resources of the community, which a continuance of the present evil entails. In the presence of an hourly poisoning such as the air undergoes, the death-rate cannot fail to be raised, and medical measures for the preservation of the public health will have but little effect."[11]

The commission's report was referred to a special joint committee composed of aldermen. During their deliberations the joint committee received a variety of letters from concerned citizens, the most amazing of which came from George B. Emerson et al., who worried that the plan would "prove not only ineffectual, but destructive to the health and prosperity of this city." This project, like many other public works, they feared, would cost far more than was estimated, thereby placing a massive burden on local taxpayers. Emerson et al. called the project a "mere experiment," and wondered "whether the more glutinous and heavy portions of this matter will drift, float, or be carried to the ocean. What assurance can be had that it will be taken or take itself even so far as the light-house?"[12] They worried about operational issues and odors as well.

> It will likewise be borne in mind that the thick mass of liquid corruption within the sewers and drains must be drawn along to their up-hill or final ascent of thirty feet and over, and kept in motion, and delivered at the distant outlets on the bay, by means of enormous pumps and machinery worked by steam engines. . . . for a stoppage in the operation of such an extensive system for only a day or two, along the low lands and other parts of the city, would almost inevitably result in serious maladies and other evil consequences. Is it possible that no system can be devised less expensive, difficult or dangerous as this? It is also obvious that the existence alone of wide and deep sewers and drains of so many miles in length, filled with organic matter constantly decomposing, must yield poisonous emanations enough, aside from stoppages or outbursts. . . . At each outer terminus of the main sewers there are to be erected capacious reservoirs and outlets, into which the miscellaneous contents of the drains and sewers are to be pumped or impelled. . . . Now these contents must accumulate and remain in a fermenting state, with more or less of agitation, for all the time between ebb and flow of the tides. Will not the exhalation and odor blown by every changing wind here and there along the wharves, upon the shipping, and back upon the land, on nearly every side, create a nuisance so offensive and unhealthful as to become intolerable?[13]

Perhaps the most unusual concern that this group expressed pertained to the possibility of attack.

> As to the sites of such refuse-reservoirs and works near them, so important for the proposed system, if in spite of all objections it can be carried out, none could perhaps have been selected so completely exposed to assaults and destruction in time of war as those designated in the report; and when it is borne in mind what submarine vessels, torpedoes for water and torpedoes for land operations have been invented and made, to say nothing of 'infernal machines,' it will not be difficult to foresee how instantly such reservoirs and outlets might be reduced to ruins in any future day of hostilities,—either foreign or domestic,—should such hostilities ever occur; the effects of which ruins would be the fatalities of the plague.[14]

This and other objections were vastly outweighed by petitions in favor of the plan, and the joint committee recommended its adoption, but with a major twist. Instead of proceeding with the construction of the sewer systems north and south of the Charles River, the committee voted in favor only of the latter, noting that constructing the system to the north would "require the cooperation of adjoining municipalities, and, as the necessities are not so pressing in that locality, it may be deferred for the present."[15] The city council agreed and ordered that $40,000 be appropriated for a preliminary engineering study of the sewer system proposed for the area south of the Charles River. Only one city councilor opposed the plan, fearing that the proposed discharge of waste would cause the harbor's islands to become enveloped in sewage and "sooner or later . . . cause trouble."[16]

The Engineering Study

Mayor Frederick O. Prince, in his inaugural address to the city council on January 1, 1877, made it clear that effectively dealing with sewage was of critical importance to the city.

> No subject at this time claims so large a share of your serious consideration as that of sewerage. The health, prosperity, every interest, in fact, of our people depend on it. Do you expect Boston to maintain its present position among other cities in the country? Do you wish her to increase in wealth, in commercial importance, in political influence, to be what we claim she is, the model metropolis? See to it, then, that she shall have *pure*, as well as *free*, air for the lungs of her people. The importance of perfect sewerage and good drainage, cleanliness, and ventilation cannot be overstated. Boston is now one of the most unhealthy of the large cities. . . . If this plan should be adopted, it would, without doubt, give us a perfect system of sewerage for an indefinite time, however large our population may be. The cost of the works, or of any works which would secure the desired result, would be great; but I am sure that any additional taxation which they might require would be cheerfully submitted to by our tax-payers, because adequate sewerage is NECESSITY; and whatever necessity demands it vindicates.[17]

The engineering study was completed that July. It considered four possible locations for the sewage reservoir and discharge—Spectacle Island, Thompson's Island, Castle Island, and Moon Island—and ultimately settled on the latter, the choice included in the original plan. According to the study, the sewage of the city would be collected by the new interceptor and by main sewers and would be transported by gravity to the pumping station at Old Harbor Point. At the station, the sewage would pass through a filth-hoist where it would be screened by grates to take out large objects that might foul the engines. The pumping engines would then raise the sewage thirty-five feet to get it high enough so that it could flow by gravity two-and-a-half miles farther to the sewage reservoir on Moon Island. For the transit from Old Harbor Point to Squantum Neck, which lay between the Point and Moon Island, the sewage would travel through a large, lined tunnel dug through the clay, slate and conglomerate underlying the navigable waters of Dorchester Bay and running just over seven thousand feet.[18] The sewage would then travel from Squantum Neck to Moon Island through a constructed embankment. The reservoir on Moon Island would be designed to hold twenty-five million gallons of sewage, which would be discharged on the outgoing tide through outlet sewers extending roughly six hundred feet out into the sea. The cost of the system was virtually identical to what had been estimated a year and a half earlier, and came in at $3,712,700.

The Joint Special Committee appointed to review the engineering study delivered its verdict on July 12, 1877, recommending that the city proceed with construction.

> Your committee believes that it is unnecessary to present any argument to prove the necessity of adopting a comprehensive system of sewerage for the city. . . . if the mass of testimony which has been presented from time to time be reviewed, it will be seen that the evils arising from defective sewerage are discernible in this city to an alarming extent.
>
> While it is not assumed that an improvement in the system of sewerage will secure to us complete immunity from disease, it is believed that it will remove a powerful agency for evil. . . . The plan for an improved system of sewerage which is now presented has the endorsement of the best engineering talent in the country.[19]

A month later the city council voted 52 to 5 in favor of constructing the so-called main drainage system; the aldermens' vote was 9 to 1. "The public have accepted the belief, as one needing no further evidence," observed one of the aldermen, "that our sanitary condition is so bad that it must be improved by a radical change in our system of sewerage."[20]

Boston's Main Drainage

Boston's main drainage system was built between 1877 and 1885. It was a massive public works project, using fifty million bricks and 180,000 casks of cement, and one that presented many engineering challenges. With so many of the city's existing sewers being at or below sea level, the new intercepting sewers, some of which were ten-and-a-half feet in diameter, had to be built lower still, to an average depth of twenty-one feet with the bottoms of the trenches generally resting several feet beneath the level of low tide.[21] Many of these trenches filled readily with water, especially at high tide. This meant that most of the construction took place during low tide. Because the laborers had a relatively brief window of opportunity, they had to work fast, and that meant using wood instead of bricks to form the outer shell of the sewers. Wood was no cheaper than masonry, but it could be built more quickly and had the added advantage, if necessary, of being fastened in place while under a couple of feet of water.[22] Wood also was somewhat elastic and could bend slightly, lengthwise, to fit the contours of the trench. But while the longitudinal flexibility of the wood was a plus, its tendency to yield transversely was a distinct problem because that meant it that the wooden shells of the sewers often bowed out on the sides and sunk at their crowns. This flexibility and the imperfection of the seals between timbers allowed water to leak inside the wooden sewer casings. Thus, although using wood facilitated work in wet conditions it also contributed to the creation of wet conditions that made it difficult to finish the sewers by lining them with bricks or cement.

The engineers overseeing the construction were extremely concerned with the problem of infiltration. They knew that if the joints between sewer sections were not well sealed, groundwater would flow in, thereby reducing the capacity of the sewers to handle what they were designed to handle—namely, sewage. To reduce such leakage, the sewer joints were filled with cement, cement mixed with clay or grease, oakum, sheet lead, or dry pine wedges.[23]

Amazingly, many of the streets that had to be ripped apart for the laying of sewers remained open to traffic during construction. The person to thank for this was H. A. Carson, the superintendent of sewers for Boston. He designed and later patented a machine, the so-called Carson's Excavating Apparatus, that ingeniously dug trenches along a relatively narrow tract of land, leaving open for business the surrounding street. Carson's apparatus was a relatively lightweight wooden-framed structure with a revolving series of buckets that moved from the front of the machine to the back, attached as they were to wire ropes and transported by an engine. The men digging the trench would fill the buckets at the front end and the buckets would then take the dirt to the rear of the machine, where it would be dumped in a part of the trench where the sewer had recently been laid. The Excavating Apparatus rested on wheels so that its engine could propel it forward once its work in a particular place was complete. Through such digging and backfilling, this two-hundred-foot, ten-ton machine snaked its way through the streets of Boston, moving in thirty-foot increments.[24] Work did not stop during the winter, except on days when the mercury plummeted to ten or more degrees below freezing. On days less cold but still numbing, the bricks were steamed in boxes before use, and the sand and water that was mixed to make cement was also warmed. Finished work was covered with seaweed or straw for protection from the elements.

The most impressive engineering feat of the entire project was the construction of the tunnel under Dorchester Bay, the average elevation of which was 142 feet beneath low water.[25] Three working shafts, 3,000 feet apart, were built and into them were sunk cast iron cylinders 9.5 feet in diameter and nearly 2 inches thick. With the cylinders in place, tunnel excavation moved outward in both directions from the base of each of the shafts, the plan being that the tunnelers would eventually meet up. Both hand drills powered by compressed air were used to eat away at the rock faces, and the two methods proved fairly equal in their output, with four-foot advances being considered a good day's work. According to Eliot C. Clarke, the principal assistant engineer in charge of the construction, "The chief merit of the air drills seemed to be that they were not demoralized by pay-days, and never struck for higher wages."[26] In some instances a more explosive form of tunneling was employed, courtesy of nitroglycerine. As with the construction of the land-based sewers, building the tunnel was wet work, and at times as much as 64,000 gallons of water leaked into the tunnel per hour. The 25,000 cubic yards of materials taken out of the tunnels were piled around the three shafts, forming small islands. Fortunately, the tunnelers met up in fine fashion during the first half of 1882, and then the lining of the tunnel with multiple layers of brick and mortar began, at a rate of roughly 12 lineal feet per day.[27]

As George Emerson and his co-signers had predicted, the project ran over budget, and in 1882 the committee overseeing the construction requested an additional appropriation of $1.5 million.[28] The reasons cited for the overrun included escalating labor and materials costs, changes in the construction plans to ensure that they accorded with the best engineering practices, and unforeseen engineering difficulties, especially as related to the ambitious tunnel under Dorchester Bay.

Unlike the launching of the Cochituate water works, operations for Boston's main drainage system began without parades. No famous poets wrote odes to the collection of sewage and its safe transit to the harbor. The residents of Boston were certainly relieved to have a better sewage system, and were pleased that sanitary conditions were improved, but it was not a joyous occasion. Nevertheless, Boston's main drainage system did capture the attention of the media. In August 1880, an article in *Harper's Weekly* described the project and placed it within context.

> Until recently, in almost all sewer systems, and still in most American ones, the sewers have been allowed to empty their contents into the nearest water, without reference to its ultimate destination, or the proximity of population. English sanitarians first announced that sewage was a constant source of danger unless discharged remote from habitations at points whence it could not return. Most foreign cities have already expended sums, often amounting to many millions of dollars, in constructing works to convey their sewage to safe places of deposit, miles beyond their limits. Boston is the first large American city to institute similar reform, and . . . the works in the process of construction at that place will doubtless furnish a model for other cities. . . . Short siphons, as that under the Seine in Paris, and others, have heretofore been constructed in connection with sewerage-works, but a tunnel of such magnitude as the one now building at Boston for conveying sewage is a novel and bold engineering conception. . . . if the results confidently expected are attained, it will prove a wise expenditure of time, labor, and money.[29]

A few months later, an article in the *Manufacturer and Builder* stated that "the city of Boston will have, when the works now in course of construction are completed and in operation, a very complete and intelligent system for the disposal of its sewage, and which cannot but have a most beneficial influence on the health of her population. We commend the example of Boston to the careful consideration of the authorities of other cities as an excellent one to imitate in its general features."[30] *King's Handbook of Boston Harbor*, written by M. F. Sweetser in 1882, observed that the Old Harbor Point, "after ages of neglect, has recently become a centre of great activity, on account of the works of the great sewer, the *Cloaca Maxima* of Boston, whose works are being constructed on a scale of magnitude and munificence worthy of ancient Rome or Modern London."[31]

On January 1, 1884, although not quite finished, the main drainage became operational with the opening of the first connections between the common and intercepting sewers. A month later all such connections were complete, and the city's sewage was successfully routed to Moon Island and on into the harbor. A year later, when virtually all parts of the main drainage were completed, Mayor Hugh O'Brien lauded the work in his inaugural address. He stated that "the water in the bays and docks around the city has again become pure, as evidenced by its being frequented by fish, which for years have been unable to live in it on account of the sewage contamination."[32] A later chronicler claimed that the new sewage system immediately benefited the city— "the death rate diminished; . . . the offensive odors had disappeared; and the cellars were no longer periodically flooded."[33]

One Sewer System Is Not Enough

Although the city fathers had earlier agreed to put off building a new sewer system for the areas north of the Charles River, the necessity for such a system soon became apparent. In the early 1880s various sewage commissions along with the state board of health offered compelling testimony in favor of affording the areas above the Charles the same sanitary benefits that would be realized by Boston proper by virtue of the main drainage. Still to be faced was the thorny issue of how to construct and to pay for a sewerage system that would cut across so many jurisdictions. The only feasible alternative, according to most observers, was for the state to step in and to offer a solution that could overcome these political obstacles. The job of handling the region's sewage was simply too large to be addressed unilaterally by individual cities and towns. To that end, in 1887 the state legislature ordered the state board of health to consider the issue. In 1889, the board recommended that a new metropolitan sewerage district be created and separated into two parts. The larger portion would lie to the north of the Charles and would discharge near Deer Island Light at the mouth of the harbor. The other part, referred to as the Charles River District, would drain areas including part of the Back Bay and a few towns situated along the Charles River. Instead of having its own outlet to the harbor, the Charles River District would have a large intercepting sewer that would hook into the main drainage and be discharged off Moon Island.[34]

The legislature approved the board of health's plan the same year it was presented and appointed a Board of Metropolitan Sewerage Commissioners to "construct, maintain, and operate" the works described in the plan, as well as to take over responsibility for Boston's main drainage.[35] This commission represented the first instance of an American city vesting a special district with the responsibility for providing public services.[36] This transfer of power away from elected officials to a semi-autonomous board ran against contemporary deep-seated suspicions about regionalism and the diminution of local autonomy.[37] But given the magnitude of sanitary problems being addressed and the belief that such problems could best be handled by experts that were somewhat insulated from the vagaries of politics, little opposition arose to the establishment of the Metropolitan Sewerage Commission. The Charles River Valley and the Northern Metropolitan Sewerage systems were constructed simultaneously, with the former reaching completion in 1892 and the latter in 1896. The engineering obstacles and feats related to these two systems were similar in magnitude if not exact in nature to those faced by the builders of Boston's main drainage.

The Metropolitan Sewerage Commissioners were not through building yet, however. In the years since the main drainage had commenced operations, the areas serviced by this new system had expanded to include communities in the Charles River District the Neponset River District, primarily west and south of Boston. This meant that with each passing year the main drainage was being asked to carry an increasing burden of the regions' sewage load. A report of the Metropolitan Sewerage Commissioners laid out the problem as follows. "The territory whose sewerage systems, so far as they are developed, are now tributary to the Boston main drainage works comprises an area of about 121 square miles. This is about double the area which these works were intended ultimately to serve. . . . The officials in charge of the sewer division of the street department have already recognized the need for relief."[38] One concern was that the pumping facilities that enabled the sewage in the main drainage to make the trip to Moon Island were being overtaxed. Another concern was stormwater, as noted in a report by the state board of health.

> The quantity of rain water that can be received from tributary districts provided with combined sewers is already less than was intended to be received when the works were constructed; and, as the quantity of the ordinary flow of sewage in the main drainage and tributary systems increases with the growth of population in the districts which these systems now serve, the capacity of the main drainage system for removing storm

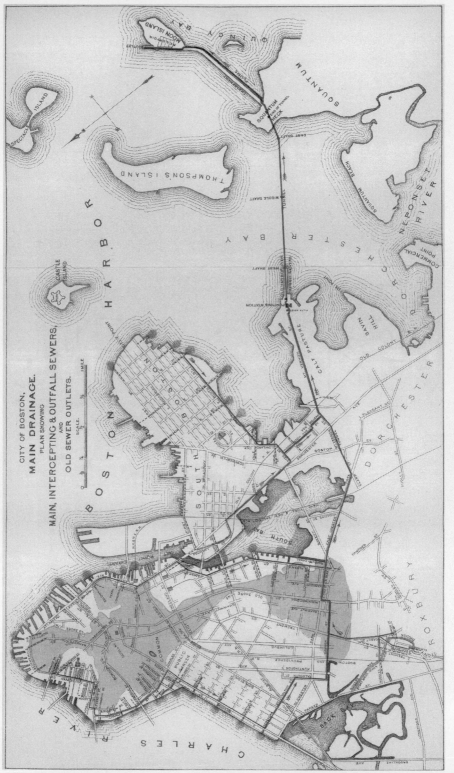

Plan of the main drainage. From Clarke, plate V.

A map showing the vast areas of Boston that were filled in over time.

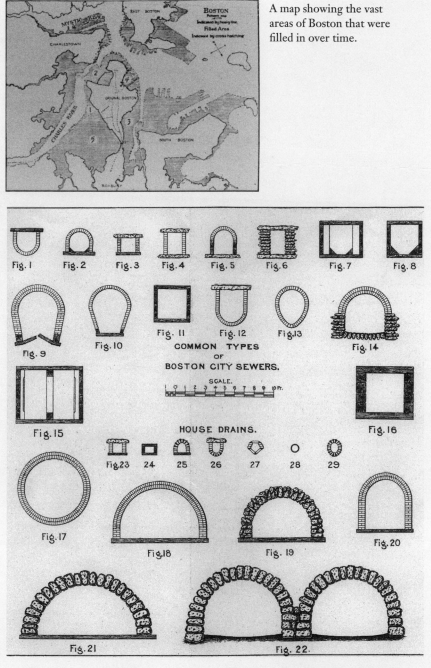

COMMON TYPES
OF
BOSTON CITY SEWERS.

SCALE.

HOUSE DRAINS.

Cross-sectional views of the types of sewers in use at the time of the main drainage construction. From Clarke, plate II.

Main drainage pumping station, front view. From Clarke, plate XVI.

Interior of engine house, showing Worthington pumping engines. "The two pumping engines for storm service were built at the Hydraulic Works, Brooklyn, L.I., by the firm of Henry R. Worthington, of New York, from their own designs, and cost $45,ooo each. . . . The capacity of each double engine is 25,000,000 gallons of sewage a day raised against a total head of 43 feet." From Clarke, page 59 and plate XV.

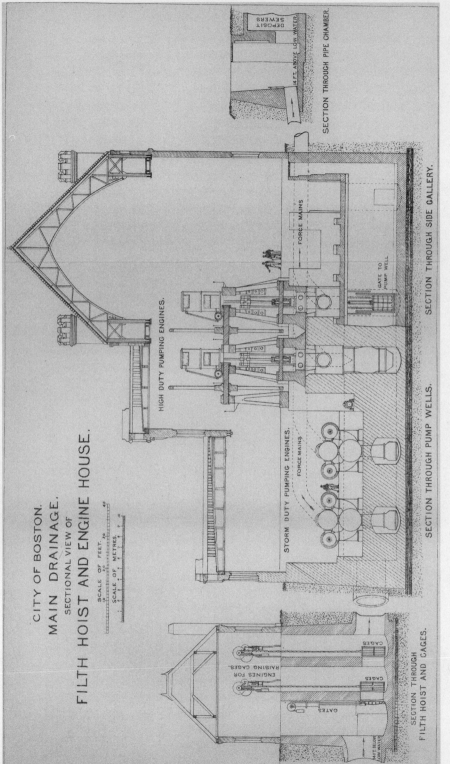

Schematic of the main drainage filth hoist and engine house. From Clarke, plate XI.

Interior of a filth hoist with one pair of cages raised. This is the filth hoist that was located in the main drainage pumping station situated at Old Harbor Point on the seacoast of Dorchester. According to Clarke, the filth hoist is "where the sewage passes through screens to remove solid matters which might clog the pumps." It is a "solid masonry structure, extending from the surface of the ground down to below the main sewer." From Clarke, page 53 and plate XII.

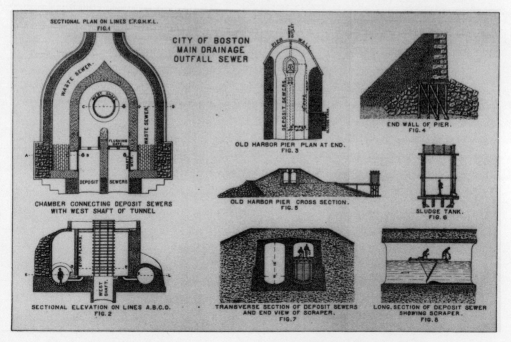

Schematic of the main drainage outfall sewer. From Clarke, plate XIX.

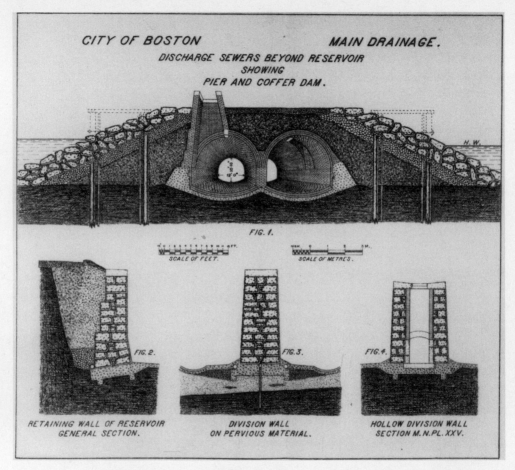

Schematic of the discharge sewers. From Clarke, plate XXVI.

Storage reservoir at Moon Island. From Clarke, plate XXIV.

Construction on Causeway Street, 1884. According to Clarke, "Causeway Street is one of the most crowded thoroughfares of the city. It contains two lines of track for horse-cars and one for freight-cars. . . . It was with some apprehension of trouble that work was begun on this section. The most difficult feature of the work was to conduct it that travel should not be seriously impeded. Owing to the skill and care of the superintendent and his subordinates, and to the appliances used for handling the earth and other material [including the famed Carson's Excavating Apparatus], the sewer in this street was built within four months, without closing any portion of the street to travel, and with the minimum of inconvenience to the public." From Clarke, pages 51–52 and plate IX.

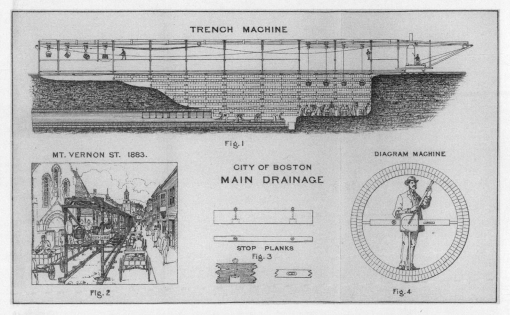

TRENCH MACHINE

Fig. 1

MT. VERNON ST. 1883.

Fig. 2

CITY OF BOSTON
MAIN DRAINAGE

STOP PLANKS
Fig. 3

DIAGRAM MACHINE

Fig. 4

Schematics of the Carson's Excavating Apparatus, in cross section for illustrative purposes and in use on Mt. Vernon Street. The diagram machine in the lower right corner was used to examine the loadings on the sewers and to check for signs of weakness in the sewer walls. According to Clarke, "In the case of the main drainage sewers such examinations were made graphically, by taking diagrams of their inside shape. . . . [The diagram machine] consisted of a light frame, which could be so fixed against the masonry that its centre should be in the axis of the sewer. A moveable arm was then rotated radially from the centre, with its outer end bearing lightly against the inside perimeter of the sewer. At the centre of the machine was a disk, on which was placed a piece of paper. A pencil point, attached to the rotating arm, traced upon the paper a diagram, showing the shape of the sewer and its variation, if any, from the established form." From Clarke, page 91 and plate XXVII.

Construction of the main sewer, section 4, near Taft's Hotel, Winthrop, centers and supports in place, diameter 9 feet, 1 inch, August 4, 1890. From Board of Metropolitan Sewerage Commissioners, *Fourth Annual Report*, Public Document no. 45 (January 1893), page 54.

Old sewage pumping station on Deer Island around the turn of the nineteenth century.

A sight that used to be quite common along the shores of the harbor.

Planning and Reality

Despite the construction of three extensive sewer systems, the sewage problem in the Boston area was by no means solved. Sanitation in the area did dramatically improve, but that was to a large extent because the conditions the new systems sought to alleviate were so horrendous. Problems remained and new ones arose. Many drains from houses and businesses still were so poorly constructed that their ability to get the sewage to the street sewers remained suspect. The efforts of the engineers notwithstanding, many joints in the new sewers leaked, especially those below the water line. Heavy precipitation often forced into service the sewer overflows dotting the harbor. A few towns in the area were not connected to one of the three systems, and their sewage entered the harbor and its tributaries in tidal areas through multiple outlets. As the population grew, the sewers were placed under increasing strains. And the new outlets, serving to concentrate waste that had formerly been dispersed more randomly throughout the harbor, created problems of their own. On calm days determining the location of the sewer discharges was easy. All one had to do was look to the broad expanses of the harbor's surface, extending from the outlet points for a mile or more, that were covered with a greasy film or "sleek."[1] Sailors moving through these areas not only were assailed by pungent smells, but they also found that the hulls of their boats were encircled by a ring of filth where the water's surface lapped the sides. The people who lived closest to the discharges also knew of their existence, for although the tidal currents were supposed to quickly transmit the waste out to the open sea, a considerable amount of it sloshed back in with the returning tide, and some of the sewage found its way onto the nearby shores.

The Legislature Focuses on Sewage

The issue of sewage and, in particular, the state of Boston Harbor was the subject of five studies initiated by the state legislature between 1915 and 1939. A 1915 House report noted:

> The sanitary condition of South Bay [a part of the inner harbor, some of which has since been filled in] has always been a grievance with the people living around it; protests against its odors and alarms concerning its dangers to the public health have bombarded the ears of legislation for three quarters of a century; and there has hardly been a year since 1837 that some committee, commission or board has not investigated its condition and reported remedial plans to the legislature.[2]

Although the report indicated that problems persisted in this area of the harbor, it also expressed confidence "that the so-called nuisance in South Bay is a rapidly diminishing evil" that the appropriate city authorities would soon remedy.[3]

A 1918 House report noted that

> aside from the main sewer outlets there are many other sources of pollution of Boston Harbor. . . . Most important among these sources of pollution are the overflows from the sewer systems in the cities adjacent to the harbor . . . Separation of the systems of sewage and storm water already begun in parts of the district tributary to the harbor will, if continued, eventually remove this source of pollution.[4]

The report made the following observation concerning conditions in the vicinity of Moon Island.

> So far as can be judged from numerous careful examinations, the conditions about this outlet have shown no noticeable change since the works were first established. . . . The pollution of a considerable area of the sea to such an extent as to be offensive to sight and smell, as happens in the neighborhood of this outlet at the time the sewage if discharged, especially on calm days, is objectionable, and no doubt the objections to this condition will increase with the rapidly increasing use of the harbor as a place of recreation in the summer season and the undoubtedly increasing attention that is paid by the public to objectionable conditions caused by offensive odors.[5]

In 1931 a Senate report found "the most notable evidence of pollution . . . in the inner harbor and in some of the estuaries thereto," and in comparing current findings with those of previous studies, concluded that there had been "a gradual but very slight deterioration in the gen-

eral character of the harbor waters, but at such a slow rate . . . there is
no reason to anticipate any very serious deterioration in the harbor
waters for years to come."[6] A 1936 House report admitted problems
but concluded that "the condition of the Boston Harbor has not
reached such a state as to be dangerous to public health, and the Special
Commission [appointed by the legislature] cannot therefore recommend that [sewage] treatment works be provided at this time." Despite
the commission's belief that a new sewage treatment plant was not necessary to protect public health, it took stock of the political situation
and proposed that treatment works nevertheless be built because "the
population residing in the vicinity of Boston Harbor will soon demand
a change."[7] Specifically, the commission urged the legislature to consider constructing facilities that would provide "partial treatment" of
the sewage coming from all three sewerage systems before it was discharged into the harbor. "Such consideration," the report continued,
should "include the possible future extension of the outfall sewers beyond the harbor limits."[8] Another Special Commission, whose findings
were published by the House in 1939, made it clear why it was essential
that the legislature act on the sewage issue soon.

> During the hearings, residents of shoreline communities expressed alarm
> at conditions in Boston Harbor. They did not request—they demanded
> correction. . . . The Commission was repeatedly told that conditions in
> Boston Harbor are revolting to the esthetic sensibilities and violate all
> public health requirements. . . . when mothers, physicians and health of-
> ficers—all of whom testified before us—believe disease can be traced to
> polluted water, then steps must be taken to stop pollution. . . . the public
> is entitled to correction of this nuisance.[9]

The report presented a compelling case.

> The commission was alarmed by the discharge of raw sewage into the
> waters of Boston Harbor [over 250 million gallons every day]. . . .
>   It was pointed out to us that recreation is "big business" in Massachu-
> setts, and particularly along the seacoast. We were bluntly told that un-
> less steps are taken to correct present conditions to rid the harbor of
> pollution, this much sought recreational business will be seriously hand-
> icapped, with a subsequent depreciation of property values along our
> beach fronts.[10]

As for the possibility of transforming the Boston area's sewage into
fertilizer, the commission concluded that it "would be of such low quality and value that it would not be justifiable to install the necessary

works for its processing."[11] The report ended with a clarion call. "We urge immediate correction of pollution. We must not evade our responsibility. Public property must be free of pollution."[12] Contending that the public had waited long enough for a remedy to these problems, the commission recommended that treatment works be constructed on Deer, Nut, and Moon Islands, the discharge points for each of the three sewage collection systems.[13] Noting that the harbor afforded the opportunity for substantial dilution of waste flowing into it, and therefore would greatly enhance the degradation of organic matter, the commission argued that a high degree of purification was not necessary.

Sewage Treatment Plants for Boston

In 1952 and 1968 respectively, sewage treatment plants were built on Nut and Deer Islands. Construction of a plant on Moon Island, however, remained only a recommendation. Instead, Moon Island's old facilities continued to hold and to discharge untreated sewage through 1968, when the main drainage system was rerouted to feed into the Northern Metropolitan Sewerage system, discharging off Deer Island.

The Nut Island facility was designed to handle a flow of 112 million gallons per day (mgd) and a peak flow of 280 mgd. Its effluent was discharged through underwater outfalls located between Long Island and Paddock's Island. Deer Island's facility was designed to handle an average daily flow of 343 mgd and a peak flow of 848 mgd, and its effluent was discharged through underwater outfalls located between Deer and Long Islands. Although the plants on Nut and Deer Islands differ in size, they were both designed to provide primary treatment, broadly defined as treatment that removes nearly all settleable solids and reduces the concentration of total suspended solids by 60 percent and biochemical oxygen demand by 30 to 35 percent.[14] These two measures are important for a variety of reasons. High levels of suspended solids increase turbidity, reducing the transmission of light through the water column, which can, in turn, inhibit the growth of aquatic plants and plankton necessary for a healthy ecosystem. Biochemical oxygen demand indicates the approximate amount of oxygen that will be required to decompose the waste present in the treatment plant's effluent.[15] The higher the biochemical oxygen demand of the effluent, the more dissolved oxygen needed for decomposition, and the more dissolved oxygen needed for decomposition, the less of it that is available to the organisms living in the water. If the levels of dissolved oxygen are reduced too much, those organisms can suffocate.[16]

At the Nut Island and Deer Island plants the incoming sewage first entered a sedimentation tank where the scum and grease floated to the top and heavy settleable solids, along with a significant amount of suspended solids, sank to the bottom. The floating material and that which sank to the bottom, high in biochemical oxygen demand and collectively referred to as sludge, was mechanically removed from the sedimentation tank and was placed in digestion tanks, where it was partially decomposed by microorganisms. A by-product of this decomposition, methane gas, in turn was siphoned off and was used to generate electricity for the treatment plants. Both facilities discharged their effluent, including the sludge generated by the treatment process, into the harbor.[17] This last step in the supposed treatment of the sewage was certainly the most bizarre and counterproductive. By simply discharging the sludge generated by the treatment process in the harbor, the treatment plants negated most if not all of the benefits of primary sewage treatment. Even at a later date, when chlorine was added to the sludge effluent for disinfection purposes, the actual treatment of the sludge was minimal.

During the 1950s and through the mid-1960s the water quality in Boston Harbor did not improve much, if at all. Only the small primary plant on Nut Island was operating, and it was having problems maintaining the exceedingly minimal levels of treatment it was able to afford. Hundreds of millions of gallons of raw sewage were still being discharged into the harbor from Deer Island, and the holding tanks on Moon Island were still doing what they were originally designed to at the turn of the century—discharging untreated waste on the outgoing tide. Unfortunately, when the tide came in again it brought back much of the waste. In addition, the combined sewer overflows (CSOs) throughout the harbor were still discharging millions of gallons of untreated urban runoff and sewage into the harbor whenever it rained. Thus, the Nut Island facility, by itself, worked as well as a Band-Aid on a ruptured artery. The state of the harbor was reflected in newspaper articles of the time. One noted that "the harbor closeup is a . . . slimy, polluted body in places. Oil and sewage smear its surface . . . [and in the air] is the unmistakable stench of man's wastes and the corrupt odor of stagnant water."[18] Another called the harbor "a floating garbage can," adding, "Millions of gallons of raw waste are discharged into the harbor every day. And industrial effluent, pumped into rivers and streams, eventually flows into the harbor."[19]

The passage of the federal Water Quality Act of 1965, an amendment to the Federal Water Pollution Control Act of 1948, brought with it the promise of change for waterways around the country, including Boston Harbor.[20] Prior to 1965, the federal government had been involved in water pollution control, but only in a limited fashion, providing grants for the construction of sewage treatment plants but leaving virtually all pollution management decisions in state hands.[21] With the 1965 act, the federal government not only increased its sewage construction grants to the states, it also took on a greater management role, requiring the states to develop and to implement water quality standards. Under this approach, states had to establish acceptable standards of water quality for interstate, navigable waters and then devise an implementation plan, including monitoring and enforcement actions, to ensure that industrial and municipal polluters controlled their pollutant discharges so that the standards were met.[22] As one knowledgeable observer noted, "There is a great deal of theoretical merit to the water quality standard approach. You establish the level of water quality you seek in the water, and then you backtrack to the respective sources that contribute the pollutants that are subject to that water quality standard and then apply the necessary control."[23] The 1965 act also authorized the secretary of the newly created Federal Water Pollution Control Administration, located within the Department of Interior, to convene enforcement conferences if pollution was found to be adversely affecting shellfish beds in interstate or navigable waters. The purpose of these conferences was to recommend steps that could be taken to reduce pollution. On September 6, 1966, Massachusetts passed its own water pollution control legislation, the Massachusetts Clean Waters Act, and roughly a year later the state's newly created Division of Water Pollution Control devised state water quality standards.[24] Under the state's implementation plan, the level of sewage treatment required in the harbor was clear. For the Nut Island and the soon to be completed Deer Island plant primary treatment was determined to be adequate to maintain water quality.[25]

Continued Problems and Debate

On paper, the harbor cleanup was moving forward, but the water told a different story. On May 20, 1968, the Federal Water Pollution Control

Administration convened an enforcement conference on the "Pollution of the Navigable Waters of Boston Harbor and Its Tributaries." According to one of the Administration representatives in attendance, the greatest source of pollution was the 460 million gallons of raw or partially treated sewage, coming from the Metropolitan District Commission's (MDC) two sewerage systems, that were discharging daily into the harbor. (The Deer Island plant had just become operational.) This and other pollution entering the harbor, including industrial waste and sewage from other nearby communities, had forced the commonwealth to restrict or to prohibit shellfishing in 89 percent of the shellfish-growing areas. In only 500 out of 4,492 acres of shellfish beds was shellfishing approved without restrictions.[26] At the conclusion of the conference, the conferees agreed to form a technical committee that would further investigate pollution in the harbor and possible remedial actions.

Two more enforcement conferences were held in the following years, one in April 1969, and the other in October 1971.[27] The third conference was particularly interesting because of the debate over the need for secondary sewage treatment in Boston Harbor. Four months prior to this conference, the newly created Environmental Protection Agency (EPA), which had assumed responsibility for the nation's water pollution control program, promulgated regulations that required publicly owned treatment works (POTWs) receiving federal grants to implement secondary treatment. Secondary treatment involves taking primarily treated sewage and subjecting it to bacteria in an oxygen-rich environment to speed up the decomposition of organic wastes. This process achieves greater reductions of biochemical oxygen demand and total suspended solids than that which is achieved by primary treatment alone. The regulations essentially defined secondary as treatment resulting in the complete removal of all floatable and settleable solids and at least 85 percent of the biochemical oxygen demand. There was, however, a potential exception to this blanket requirement. The administrator of EPA could waive the secondary requirements for POTWs discharging into "open ocean waters through an ocean outfall" if he determined that such a discharge would "not adversely affect the open ocean environment and adjoining shores."[28]

The waiver option was primarily the result of lobbying efforts on the part of municipal discharges from the West Coast.[29] Throughout the late 1950s and 1960s the federal government had been encouraging POTWs, most of which used primary treatment, to install secondary treatment in order to improve water quality. West Coast dischargers, however, argued that the secondary requirement should not apply to them because they were discharging into deep ocean waters that, because of strong currents and mixing, had great assimilative capacities for sewage effluent. The West Coast dischargers believed that requiring them to upgrade to secondary, therefore, would not result in improved water quality. Furthermore, upgrading to secondary was expensive, not only in capital costs, but also in operation and maintenance costs, both of which were roughly double that of primary treatment. Thus, the West Coast dischargers argued that it was both environmentally and economically unsound to require them to apply secondary. They were aided in their argument by the conclusions of many water quality professionals, engineers, and biologists, who agreed that the indiscriminate application of secondary to ocean discharges was improper. Secondary levels of treatment were important for inland freshwaters, where assimilative capacities were limited, but, continued the argument, the oceans were a totally different environment and should be treated appropriately, literally and figuratively.

One of the most ardent supporters of this concept was A. M. Rawn, former general manager of the Los Angeles County Sanitation Districts and chairman of the California State Water Board, who said the following at the First International Conference on Waste Disposal in the Marine Environment in 1959.

> The great economy inherent in the discharge of urban sewage and industrial wastes into nearshore water for final disposal is apparent to all who will investigate. It is doubly apparent to those charged with the responsibility of disposing of such wastes without excessive cost to the public or menace to the public health. If the ocean, or one of its arms, can be reached by sewer outfall, within the bounds of economy, the grim spectre of an expensive complete [secondary] treatment plant grows dimmer and dimmer until it fades entirely and, to the great satisfaction of those who have to gather funds for the public budget, as well as they (you and I) who have to pay the bill, the good old ocean does the job for free.
>
> And small wonder that we look to the ocean for this assist. Its vast area and volume, its oxygen-laden waters, its lack of potability or usefulness for domestic and most industrial purposes, present an unlimited and most attractive reservoir for waste assimilation.
>
> To be able to relegate the entire job of secondary sewage treatment to a few holes in the end of a submarine pipe and the final disposal of the effluent to the mass of water into which the fluid is jetted, and to accomplish this without material cost or maintenance and none for operation,

presents a picture of such great allure as to capture the imagination of the dullest and justify extensive exploration into ways and means of satisfactory accomplishment.[30]

At the end of his paper, Rawn said he had some concern that primarily treated sewage might have a negative impact on the marine ecosystem, and concluded that we would have to wait and see what scientists discovered. Then, in what would prove to be a prophetic statement in light of the controversy over ocean waivers beginning in the 1970s, Rawn said that "those of you who are responsible for the disposal of sewage and industrial wastes from seaboard cities, prepare for critical associates in your efforts, associates who will have a good deal to say about such matters in the future."[31] At the same conference, Roger Revelle, director of the Scripps Institution of Oceanography, presented a similar perspective on ocean disposal of sewage. "I am convinced that if due care is exercised, based on adequate scientific knowledge and with generous respect for other people's uses of the oceans, very large amounts of wastes can be safely disposed of at sea."[32]

Reading the waiver language in the EPA's regulations, MDC officials assumed that the MDC might well qualify for an open ocean waiver for the Nut Island and Deer Island plants and, therefore, would not be required to upgrade them to secondary. But during the enforcement conference, John R. Quarles Jr., assistant administrator for enforcement and general counsel for the EPA, made it clear that secondary treatment would likely be in Boston's future.

The time is here I'm sure when it's necessary for the Metropolitan District Commission and the Commonwealth of Massachusetts to face up to the very real prospect that secondary treatment will be required in the Boston Harbor disposal system. Around the country there are few, if any, cities which are comparable in size to the Massachusetts situation where they do not already have secondary treatment or, if they don't have it, are not at least on a program to install it. In many places they are moving to much higher levels of treatment.

Those situations are not directly comparable, I recognize perfectly clearly, as to the need for the treatment, but the national policy is developing very clearly and very strongly that minimum reasonable treatment is required without in all cases having to complete the uncertainties of proof as to where the line lies. Certainly secondary treatment for municipal wastes is one of the clear rules of thumb that is emerging. . . .

While I am not by any means here saying that secondary treatment now could be decided upon, I think that delay in facing that question and delay in making a decision on it can't help but be contrary to the best interests of this State and Boston Harbor.

My personal feeling is that I will be—again speaking clearly only personally—quite surprised if a conclusion is ever reached that secondary treatment is not necessary in this situation.

We have in Boston Harbor one of the most serious situations of urban pollution in the country—with an antiquated system for collecting the wastes and bringing them into the treatment plants, with primary plants, unsatisfactory sludge disposal practices, and a lot of work that needs to be done which in many cases is well behind the schedules that have been established. . . .

The real burden in this situation in my judgment clearly falls with the general public. I don't believe the general public has any understanding at all of the inadequacies in the present system and the need for vigorous action.[33]

John W. Sears, commissioner of the MDC, responded to Quarles:

It is true that the MDC has a problem with secondary treatment. For 82 years we have assumed that we were providing open-ocean disposal. And we are startled really to learn that standards that are applied to inland communities may also be applied perhaps without some sophistication to us.

Secondary treatment for us is on the order of $40 or $50 million. If we are to attack the combined sewage problem, we are talking of $600 million. And we are dealing with 43 rather strapped Eastern communities [the number of communities serviced by the MDC's sewerage system].

We need your pressure. We need your vigor. We need your spirit. And we are going to need your help. It will not work otherwise.[34]

The State Division of Water Pollution Control director, Thomas C. McMahon, then argued that, contrary to popular belief, Boston Harbor was not so bad. Indeed, he pointed out that a recent report commissioned by his agency indicated that there was no need for additional treatment at Deer and Nut Islands through 2020, though alternative methods of sludge disposal were recommended.[35] McMahon continued:

I think we have made the point reasonably clearly that as far as secondary treatment is concerned, this would have to be a fairly low priority item in the face of other serious problems within the harbor. . . . [The research of our consultants] indicates that it will be the year 2020 basically before secondary treatment is needed. . . .

The biggest besetting problem [sic] confronting the Boston Harbor area is solving the combined sewer discharge problem, and I hate to see us getting off the track and not coming up with programs that are basically going to solve this problem. . . .

Lest one think I am not interested in secondary treatment, we have quite an interest in secondary treatment. It is the policy of our division to require secondary treatment on all of the freshwater treatment facilities and its equivalent as far as industrial wastes within the Commonwealth. On coastal areas our requirement is the degree of treatment necessary to meet the water quality standards.

Our point here is that on a priority basis we do not believe that secondary treatment at this time is anywhere near as important as many of the other things I have outlined. . . .

So that again we're throwing in another input of $40 to $50 million for what I would consider a very low priority in contrast to the treatment plants we would need in Springfield, in Lowell, and in Lawrence, at the South Essex Sewerage District, because of a regulation and because of basically a policy decision that you should have treatment for treatment's sake. I think that this is incorrect. I don't think it's based on good engineering judgment. And, frankly, I think our priorities are completely out of kilter.[36]

In the end, the conferees agreed to disagree. Nevertheless, the conference did result in the initiation of two very important studies. In October 1971, the MDC and the Division of Water Pollution Control reached an agreement whereby the former would prepare a sludge management plan. And in July 1972, the MDC, the Division of Water Pollution Control, and the EPA signed an agreement in which the MDC would be the lead agency for a comprehensive study of the region's sewage system and the need for improvements over the next fifty years. In the latter agreement, the MDC, at the strong urging of the EPA, grudgingly put aside its aversion to secondary treatment, pledging to upgrade the Nut Island and Deer Island plants by December 31, 1980.[37] The MDC also agreed, under the threat of an EPA lawsuit, to stop discharging sludge into the harbor's waters by May 1, 1976.[38] In late 1972, Congress amended the Federal Water Pollution Control Act again. The 1972 amendments ushered in a new era in water pollution control that would have a profound impact on Boston Harbor.

Where to from Here?

Before considering the impact of the 1972 amendments, it is important to reflect on how things stood with respect to the harbor on the eve of the act's passage. From the planning perspective, there was cause for optimism. The enforcement conferences had highlighted many of the pollution problems in the harbor, and major studies addressing those problems were getting under way. The information provided by those studies was intended to aid the MDC in moving forward with whatever remedial actions were deemed necessary. With respect to the latter, the state had already consented to upgrade the two sewage plants to secondary by 1980 and, regardless of the debate over whether secondary was necessary, the upgrade would, at a minimum, mean less pollution flowing into the harbor. Similarly, the state's pledge to cease the discharge of sludge by 1976 meant that one of the worst sources of harbor pollution would soon be cut off. From another perspective, however, there was significant cause for concern. Despite the planning efforts and the promise of future pollution abatement actions, the harbor was still grossly polluted. The two sewage treatment plants continued to discharge roughly sixty tons of sludge daily into the harbor. During wet weather, the flow of sewage and stormwater runoff transported through combined sewers exceeded the capacity at Nut and Deer Islands, causing the numerous CSOs to discharge raw sewage at various points in and around the harbor. Even during dry conditions, some CSOs would discharge raw sewage directly into receiving waters. Many Boston area beaches and shellfishing beds remained closed because of pollution. And to the chagrin of those who believed that the opening of the Deer Island plant would solve many of the harbor's pollution problems, that is not what happened.

When the Deer Island plant opened in August 1968, it looked great. According to former Governor Francis Sargent, the plant was "as polished and clean as the engine room of an aircraft carrier."[39] Unfortunately, it did not work properly. The major culprits were the nine Nordberg engines, installed to pump sewage into the treatment tanks. They were the wrong machines for the job.[40] Although they were designed to run at a continuous speed, the engine's rate had to fluctuate in response to the changing flow rates for sewage, resulting in numerous breakdowns and subsequent discharges of raw sewage. Repairs were made difficult by the fact that the Nordberg Manufacturing Company was bought out just as the Deer Island plant opened. The new company continued to supply replacement parts, but delivery of those parts often took a significant amount of time.[41] Compounding the equipment problems was a lack of adequately trained staff to run the plant and to deal with operational and maintenance problems. From day one, Deer Island was understaffed. Finding workers proved difficult, in part because the salaries offered were regulated by the state's civil service system and were relatively low compared with private industry, reducing the financial incentive for trained individuals to work for the MDC.[42] And even when staff could be found, their skills were often questionable. The MDC had long had a reputation as a place for patronage jobs, and there is no doubt that some of the Deer Island employees were there because of connections, not qualifications.[43] Sargent once described the MDC as a place that "employed everybody's cousin."[44]

Deer Island was not alone in having operation and maintenance problems. Nut Island, too, suffered from poor performance. Part of this was to be expected. In 1972, the Nut Island plant was already twenty years old and at the end of its operational life expectancy. One of the most serious problems at the plant was the uneven settling of the sedimentation basins, which greatly reduced the plant's efficiency. And Nut Island was as poorly staffed as Deer Island, for the same reasons. The sewage system's problems extended beyond the plants themselves, however. Many of the pipes that brought sewage to the plants were quite old, some over one hundred years, and in need of repair.

Thus, on the eve of the passage of the 1972 amendments, the divergence between plans for improvements in the sewage system and the status of the existing system and the harbor was apparent. Although planning was moving ahead, full of promise, the sewage infrastructure was falling into disrepair, and, in many cases, untreated sewage continued to be discharged into the harbor. How the 1972 amendments would affect the split between planning and reality, and whether they would move the harbor cleanup forward, remained to be seen.

5

From Bad to Worse

With Earth Day (April 20, 1970) and the publicly supported and successful battle for the Clean Air Act (1970) still fresh in mind, Congress was eager to move ahead aggressively on the water pollution issue in the early 1970s, and it did. Many observers described the 1972 amendments to the Federal Water Pollution Control Act, more commonly referred to as the Clean Water Act, in watershed-type terms, as "a major change in environmental and intergovernmental policy";[1] "the most sweeping environmental measure ever considered by the Congress";[2] "a landmark of environmental legislation";[3] and "one of the most significant bills of all time."[4] Although one may disagree with the superlatives chosen, the general thrust of these comments is true. The Clean Water Act did usher in a new era of water pollution control. As signed into law on October 18, 1972, the Clean Water Act ran to eighty-nine pages of fine print covering many issues, including pretreatment standards for industry, inspections and monitoring requirements, oil and hazardous substance liability, and standards for thermal discharges.[5] For the present purposes it is sufficient to cover the main sewage-related provisions of the act, for more than anything else, it is around the issue of sewage that the cleanup of Boston Harbor has revolved.

The main objective of the 1972 amendments was "to restore and maintain the chemical, physical, and biological integrity of the Nation's waters."[6] To achieve this objective the amendments established two national goals. The first was to eliminate the discharge of pollutants into the navigable waters of the United States by 1985, usually referred to as the "zero-discharge" goal, and the second was to achieve, "wherever attainable," a level "of water quality which provides for the protection and propagation of fish, shellfish, and wildlife and provides for recreation in and on the water" by July 1, 1983, the so-called "fishable-swimmable" goal. To help achieve these goals the act established a wide-ranging policy structure for sewage management. POTWs had to provide a minimum of secondary treatment by July 1, 1977. The EPA subsequently defined secondary treatment as removing at least 85 percent of both biochemical oxygen demand and suspended solids from the POTW's effluent, and not exceeding certain levels of coliform bacteria and pH.[7]

Congress imposed technology-based effluent limitations on POTWs, in large part because of the difficulties presented by the water quality standards approach. Although the standards approach had theoretical merit, in practice it was extremely difficult to enforce. Under the Water Quality Act of 1965, before the government could initiate any pollution abatement action it had to prove that a specific polluter was causing a specific problem. Technical expertise at the time was not sophisticated enough to infer from pollution in a particular body of water the level of control required for an individual discharger in cases where more than one source was discharging into the water.[8] The government would thus find it impossible to prove that discharger X was causing pollution problem Y, especially if discharger X claimed that some other discharger was causing the problem. Establishing a technology-based effluent limitation made enforcement much simpler, for one could clearly determine whether a violation had occurred.

Despite the reliance on technology-based effluent limitations for POTWs, the amendments did not eliminate water quality standards altogether. POTWs that complied with the technology-based limitations but still violated the water quality standards for the receiving waters were required to take steps, including the installation of additional treatment technologies, to ensure that such violations ceased.[9] Thus, the amendments' technology-based limitations served only as a pollution floor, not a ceiling. To aid the states and localities in constructing required facilities, the sewage construction grants program was greatly expanded, to $18 billion over three years, with the federal government covering 75 percent of the costs of sewage treatment (up from 55 percent); the remaining 25 percent was picked up by state and local government.[10]

The requirements with which POTWs had to comply are spelled out in National Pollutant Discharge Elimination System permits. These permits include not only the effluent limitations for specific pollutants, but also a schedule that details the dates by which time the discharger must comply with the limitations. If violations of the permit

are discovered, the regulating agency, the EPA or the state, can take a
variety of enforcement actions, including issuing a notice of violation
or an administrative order requiring that certain remedial actions be
taken, levying fines, or initiating a civil action in federal district court.
Private individuals and groups, too, can also bring a civil action, in
federal district court, under the amendment's citizen suits provision.
Such suits can be brought against any government or private institution
alleged to be violating effluent standards or an administrative order
issued by the administrator of the EPA or a delegated state agency. Suits
may also be brought against the administrator for failing to perform
nondiscretionary duties under the act.

CSOs and sludge were also regulated by the amendments. The statutory language on CSOs left some unanswered questions about how
such pollution sources should be managed. In line with subsequent EPA
regulations and supporting court cases, CSOs were defined as point
sources, meaning that they discharged to receiving waters through a
single point or pipe, and it was up to the EPA or the delegated state
agency to establish, on a case-by-case basis, appropriate technology-
based and water-quality-based effluent limitations in accord with the
best professional judgment of the permit writer.[11] Such limitations, in
turn, were written into the permit. As for sludge, the amendments forbade its discharge into navigable waters.

The waiver issue made only a brief appearance during the extensive
debates over the 1972 amendments. Appearing before a Senate subcommittee, Charles V. Gibbs, head of Seattle Metro, the regional sewerage
agency in Seattle, and president of the Association of Metropolitan
Sewerage Agencies, a group representing many of the nation's largest
sewerage agencies, including the MDC, pleaded for flexibility in applying standards. "Because we do not have absolutely unlimited funds,"
said Gibbs, "the Federal government must not enact legislation providing for national effluent standards. To do so would cause a waste of
taxpayers' money because the use of such standards by the Administrator will result in treatment costs far exceeding those required to meet
and maintain the state and Federal water quality standards."[12] In a
follow-up letter to the Senate Subcommittee on Air and Water Pollution, Gibbs amplified his remarks and made clear that his association
was particularly concerned with the fate of ocean dischargers should
national minimum standards be enacted. "To use a hypothetical illustration," Gibbs said, "it may be absolutely essential to limit drastically
the amount of BOD [biochemical oxygen demand] that could be con-

tained in water passing from a plant in Cleveland in to Lake Erie because of the condition of that Lake. To apply the same restrictive standard to a plant in San Diego where the effluent discharges into the Pacific Ocean [and] is quickly assimilated into water with a very low level of BOD and which contains more than the universally acceptable amount of dissolved oxygen would be a great waste of money and resources."[13]

The call by the Association of Metropolitan Sewerage Agencies for ocean waivers, which was echoed by a few other groups and individuals, had virtually no impact. As Phil Cummings, staff member on the Senate Committee on Public Works, commented, once it was decided that the concept of zero discharge was acceptable, "it was easy to say the least we could do is require uniform secondary treatment."[14] According to Bill Corcoran, staff member on the House Public Works Committee at the time, there was "no way you could crack the Senate on the secondary requirement."[15] And, indeed, Senator Edmund Muskie of Maine, the driving force behind the 1972 amendments, had made it clear that there should be no regulatory distinction between the levels of treatment for sewage discharges into the ocean and inland waters.

Another key factor in favor of uniform secondary treatment was money. According to Joe G. Moore, former head of the Federal Water Pollution Control Administration, "Secondary treatment got into the 1972 act because the formulators of the act in effect raised the construction grant participation to a sufficiently high position so as to muffle the opposition to secondary. I won't say it was an absolute quid pro quo, but the increase in construction grants from 55 percent federal to 75 percent federal was surreptitiously, at least, referred to as the federal funding necessary to provide secondary treatment. To put it more bluntly, the opposition was bought off with federal money." Corcoran agreed, noting that "there was a big buyoff here of all kinds of people with that number."[16]

The Downward Slide Continues

Despite the combination of the strong directives contained in the 1972 amendments and the agreements reached prior to the passage of the amendments on long-range sewage planning and sludge management, the situation with respect to Boston's sewage system and water quality in the harbor became worse, not better. Indeed, by 1982, when the city of Quincy filed a lawsuit in a state court case aimed at cleaning up

Boston Harbor, the Deer Island and Nut Island plants were even more dilapidated than they had been ten years earlier, with breakdowns and the subsequent discharge of raw sewage a common occurrence. Most of the pipes leading to the plants were ten years older and were leaking more than ever. The plants remained seriously understaffed. Tons of sludge were still pumped into the harbor daily.[17] With the exception of a couple of CSOs—which were receiving some form of treatment, such as chlorination—the vast majority of the CSOs emptying into the harbor and its tributaries continued to do so without any form of treatment, during wet and, on occasion, dry weather.[18] Given this, the obvious question is, why? There is no one answer. With large and multifaceted problems, involving numerous actors, there never is. Instead, a suite of factors contributed to the failure to adequately address the region's sewage management needs and the continued degradation of the harbor between 1972 and 1982.

At one level, the failure was the result of what Jeffrey L. Pressman and Aaron Wildavsky term the complexity of joint action.[19] The implementation of a governmental program of any consequence requires coordination among many actors, often with differing perspectives, and the clearance of numerous decision points. The more decision points, the more time expended and, hence, the greater the likelihood for delay in reaching implementation goals. As conflict among the various actors increases, the potential for delay increases as well.[20] In the present case, before planned sewage improvements could become actual improvements, numerous administrative hurdles had to be overcome. The planning process established by both federal and state law was extremely involved, presenting many decision points and requiring the input of numerous actors, each of whom had to review the plans and give approval before the next step could be taken. The delays inherent in such a complex situation were exacerbated by the magnitude of the projects envisioned and controversy over some of the decisions reached.

Although the complexity of joint action is a characteristic that inevitably slows government action in any societal context, it is a particularly prevalent element of the government in the United States. As James Q. Wilson notes, "America has a paradoxical bureaucracy unlike that found in almost any other advanced nation. The paradox is the existence in one set of institutions of two qualities ordinarily quite separate: the multiplication of rules and the opportunity for access. We have a system laden with rules. . . . We also have a system suffused with participation."[21] At each step of the way we stop, consider, debate, reflect, reformulate, and proceed. The implementation process moves along in fits and starts because we have designed it that way.

At another level, implementation problems were the result of changing federal law. As Daniel A. Mazmanian and Paul A. Sabatier argue, "much of bureaucratic behavior may be explained by the legal structure (or lack of such structure) imposed by the relevant statutes."[22] A necessary corollary of this is that as that structure changes, so too do the dynamics of the implementation process. As the implementation of a particular program proceeds under one set of statutory guidelines, the various actors make assumptions about what actions are within the confines of the law, and thus acceptable, and act appropriately. When the rules change, so too do the assumptions and the actions of those involved. Changing legal imperatives can throw into doubt the usefulness of past planning efforts, as well as require additional plans and the clearance of new administrative hurdles, all of which adds to the complexity of joint action. In Boston, changing law significantly impacted the movement toward improved sewage management. The 1977 amendments to the Clean Water Act presented the MDC with the opportunity to apply for a waiver from the secondary treatment requirement, and the MDC took it. This change in direction added a significant element of uncertainty to the implementation process: while the EPA's decision on whether to grant a waiver to the MDC dragged on for years, the ultimate goal of a major part of the MDC's planning efforts—the choice of primary or secondary treatment—remained unclear. Lacking a clear goal, the MDC planned for both the possibility of getting a waiver and being denied, and, as long as the waiver decision was pending, planning continued to be a substitute for action.

At still another level, movement toward improved sewage management in the Boston area was affected by the EPA's enforcement posture. In 1976, the EPA issued the MDC a permit that required the latter to comply with various Clean Water Act requirements by certain dates. For example, the permit required the MDC to complete a series of projects by July 1, 1977, including upgrading the Nut Island and Deer Island plants to secondary, and constructing sludge and CSO management facilities. In light of such requirements, one might assume that, as those deadlines passed, the EPA would have used its enforcement powers to pressure the MDC to comply with the terms of the permit. The delays resulting from the complexity of joint action and the EPA's review of the waiver application, however, constrained the agency's ability to enforce compliance with many of the permit's deadlines in the years following its issuance. Instead, the EPA chose to extend deadlines and to work with the MDC in moving the various projects forward. Not until 1980 did the agency decide to compel compliance with some of these extended deadlines by issuing an administrative order. Although the order was partially effective in moving projects forward, by 1982, when the state court case began, they were still in the planning stage.

One particularly important permit condition was not affected by the delays resulting from the complexity of joint action or the waiver review. The MDC's permit required it to properly operate and maintain its sewage facilities. Although the EPA was well aware that this condition was being grossly violated, even before the permit was issued, the agency chose to pursue a nonaggressive enforcement strategy, encouraging the MDC to voluntarily take action to address its operation and maintenance problems. This approach failed, and in 1981 the EPA issued an administrative order designed to compel compliance. This order, followed by another in 1982, however, barely touched on the numerous infrastructure problems that needed to be addressed.

Although the EPA can be faulted for not taking stronger enforcement actions against the MDC to get the agency to improve operations and maintenance at the sewage plants, the main reason that the sewage infrastructure continued to fall apart between 1972 and 1982 was political. Throughout the 1970s and into the early 1980s, neither the legislative and executive branches in Massachusetts nor the public championed the cause of sewage infrastructure, despite the fact that the problems with the system were widely known. And since the MDC's operations and maintenance budget was set by the governor and the legislature who, in turn, reacted to public cues, the budget remained woefully underfunded. Furthermore, the MDC's position as a politically weak institution limited its ability to fight its own battles and, therefore, compounded its financial problems.

The following sections illustrate how these different, yet interconnected, factors combined in a way that enabled things to go from bad to worse between 1972 and 1982. Ironically, the dynamics and failures of this ten-year period helped to create the forces that ultimately would lead to the cleanup of Boston Harbor.

Complexities of Joint Action

The main examples of the delays resulting from the complexity of joint action during this period concern the Boston Harbor–Eastern Massachusetts Metropolitan Area Wastewater Management and Engineering Study (the EMMA study), CSOs, and sludge management.

The 1972 amendments required the MDC to upgrade its Deer Island and Nut Island treatment plants to secondary by July 1, 1977. Before that could be done, however, the MDC had to prepare plans for the upgrade. That preparation was under way even before the passage of the amendments. An outgrowth of one of the agreements reached after the enforcement conferences was the initiation of the EMMA study, which was intended to provide guidance for needed sewage improvements over the next fifty years. This was an enormous task, given that the MDC sewerage system was immense, handling hundreds of millions of gallons of waste daily, coming from forty-three cities and towns, and was composed not only of the two treatment plants but also thousands of miles of sewers.

The study began in late 1972 and was conducted by the MDC and the U.S. Army Corps of Engineers. EMMA was completed in October 1975. From its twenty-five volumes came fifty-two recommended projects which, if completed, were expected to cost $855 million in 1975 prices. These projects included the rehabilitation, repair, and expansion of the sewage treatment facilities on Deer and Nut Islands and, in accord with the 1972 act, the upgrade of those facilities to secondary; the construction of two advanced (beyond secondary) satellite sewage treatment facilities in the Southern Metropolitan Sewerage District; and the building of facilities designed to manage sludge through incineration and to control pollution from CSOs.[23]

The process used to produce EMMA was extremely open. From the moment the study began, the public was asked for input and kept abreast of developments through numerous public meetings, many of which were well attended. In addition, a Citizen Advisory Committee was established, and its members included representatives from a variety of public interest groups.[24] Through this form of involvement, the public became quite aware of the MDC's planning efforts, and with this public awareness came controversy. Communities in the Southern Metropolitan District objected to the placement of satellite plants in their area. Concerns focused on the ultimate location as well as the expected impacts on water quality and public health. The citizens of Quincy were equally angry. EMMA recommended that part of Quincy Bay be filled to make room for an expanded treatment facility.[25] Opposition to this idea was strong enough to result in the legislature's passing a bill that forbade filling the bay for that purpose.[26]

EMMA was not the end of the planning process; it was only the beginning. Since EMMA was designed as a preliminary engineering report, the projects it outlined still needed to go through formal facilities planning before moving on to facility design and ultimate construction. The EPA determined that an environmental impact statement was needed before the MDC could proceed with facilities planning for the EMMA projects.[27] The EPA's environmental impact statement, which began in September 1976, focused on the rehabilitation and expansion of the Nut Island and Deer Island plants, the upgrade to secondary, the two satellite sewage facilities, and the construction of facilities to manage sludge associated with secondary treatment and advanced treatment.[28] Like EMMA, the draft environmental impact statement, which came out on August 4, 1978, generated controversy. Although scrapping the satellite plant concept, to the relief of the communities in the southern system that had been exerting political pressure to that end, the EPA called for the consolidation of all sewage treatment facilities on Deer Island. This last change caused an uproar in Winthrop, the town that included Deer Island, where residents argued that they had already suffered enough from the negative impacts of public projects. Not only did the town house the sewage treatment plant and a prison, but it was also in the flight path of Logan International Airport.[29]

It took three years to complete EMMA and then another two years for the EPA to finish the draft environmental impact statement on the major EMMA projects. This delay was due to the normal workings of a large-scale environmental planning-and review process that had to clear a variety of decision points, was open, provided for significant public involvement, and generated controversy. For example, the MDC held roughly seventy meetings during the drafting of EMMA to solicit public opinion.[30] And although EPA's environmental impact statement review, which involved public review opportunities, was long, it was not out of line with the review time for other environmental impact statements on projects of this magnitude.[31] The completion of the draft environmental impact statements, of course, was not the end of the planning process. More planning still had to be done before the actual facilities could be built. That planning, however, would not be completed prior to the initiation of the lawsuit in 1982.

The EPA did not require an environmental impact statement to be completed on EMMA's CSO projects prior to the initiation of facilities planning. Therefore, in June 1978 the MDC applied for and received more than $3 million in federal funding to begin CSO facilities planning.[32] With roughly one hundred CSOs throughout the Boston area, determining what type of facilities were needed to comply with the CSO effluent limitations spelled out in MDC's permit was a major task that was not finished until mid-1980.[33] The MDC's recommended plan then went to the EPA and to the state for review, whereupon the latter required the MDC to prepare another evaluation of the plan that was completed in 1982. Thus, on the eve of the state lawsuit, planning for CSO management facilities was still the order of the day.

Another outgrowth of the enforcement conferences was an agreement to study sludge disposal alternatives and to cease the discharge of sludge by May 1, 1976. The MDC hired a consulting firm that, in 1973, recommended the incineration of sludge on Deer Island.[34] After subsequent EPA evaluation, the plan was slightly modified. When the facility plan was presented at a public hearing, in April 1975, the plans for incineration on Deer Island were quite controversial. Because of the controversy and ongoing concerns about the potential environmental impact of the incinerators, the EPA and the state decided that another study was needed. In March 1979 the EPA issued its final environmental impact statement on primary sludge management, which recommended dewatering and incineration on Deer Island. Not surprisingly, the plan generated considerable and loud public opposition. The Boston Harbor Interagency Coordinating Committee, which included various state environmental agencies, also expressed reservations about the environmental impact statement and recommended further study of certain issues.[35] As with EMMA and the CSO projects, sludge management facility planning went on and on. After seven years and a range of studies, more studies and planning were yet to come; these also would not be completed prior to the state lawsuit. The process had been delayed by the magnitude of the task, the need for multiple reviews, controversy over certain options, and changing laws.

The Waiver from Secondary Treatment

Although the ocean discharge waiver was almost a nonissue during the debates over the Clean Water Act, it became a major topic soon thereafter. Everyone knew that the Clean Water Act would come up for reauthorization in 1977, and those who supported the waiver began working toward ensuring that this time it would be high on the congressional agenda. Serious congressional attention to the issue of ocean dischargers began in 1974. By that time disillusionment over the implementation of the Clean Water Act was widespread. President Richard M. Nixon had impounded a significant percentage of the construction grants money, setting off a battle between the administration and Congress that would ultimately be resolved by the courts and congressional action. The EPA had created a complex and time-consuming grant application process that the states disliked intensely.[36] The impoundment and the application process created a situation in which the states were getting less money than they had hoped for, at a slower pace. In addition, the states and the EPA were understaffed in the water pollution control area. It was clear that all POTWs were not going to be able to make it to secondary by the July 1, 1977, deadline. The Clean Water Act was suffering from the twin problems of underestimation of the magnitude of the problem and an unrealistic expectation of what could be achieved. These factors combined to make fertile ground for those who argued for exceptions from secondary for ocean dischargers. Not only were they offering Congress a way to save public funds, but they were also presenting scientifically based, albeit inconclusive, arguments that such savings would not be at the environment's expense.

During House hearings on the implementation of the Clean Water Act in February 1974, it became clear that the EPA had doubts about the need for secondary treatment in all cases. Among the issues taken up during the hearings were the resolutions of the New England Water Pollution Control Association's "Town Meeting of New England." One resolution, written by McMahon, still head of the Massachusetts Division of Water Pollution Control, read, "Be it resolved, That the Congress and the Environmental Protection Agency take due note of the experience already achieved in the attempted application, without exception, of a national standard, the secondary treatment of public wastewater treatment plant effluents, without regard to the degree of beneficial improvement in the quality of the receiving waters; and the Congress is urged to amend the law to assure that priority consideration will be given where significant water quality improvement can be practicably demonstrated in the receiving waters."[37]

The EPA responded that it

in general supports the concept of technology based effluent limitations unrelated to water quality and feels that it is important to achieve the national secondary treatment standard. We recognize, however, that the imposition of such a national standard may not affect any beneficial improvement in the quality of the receiving waters in certain instances. For example, some have pointed out that in some cases, the ocean discharge of effluents treated to less than secondary treatment would apparently not deteriorate the water quality. We feel that this might be the case in Los Angeles and Honolulu. At the same time, however, such a policy would not be appropriate in places such as New York *and Boston where there is little seaward motion and where there is a real threat of shore pollution* [emphasis added].[38]

Over the next few years, Congress held numerous hearings on the issue of ocean waivers to secondary treatment. The proposals ranged from not modifying the treatment standard, to allowing only certain West Coast dischargers the opportunity to apply for a waiver, to allowing any municipality that thought it could make a case for a waiver to make it and have it be reviewed on its merits by the EPA. By 1977 it had become fairly clear that a waiver provision would be included in the amendments to the Clean Water Act. The forces in favor of such an addition were simply too strong to ignore. The content of the waiver was still subject to debate, however, and that debate was so messy and so filled with opposing agendas that the waiver provision that passed was virtually guaranteed to be extremely difficult to implement.

The problems started in the Senate, where the main force behind a waiver provision was Senator Mike R. Gravel, a member of the Committee on Environment and Public Works. He argued that Alaskan cities such as Anchorage and Seward should not be required to go to secondary because it would be a waste of money for limited, if any, environmental gain.[39] Gravel tasked Dem Cowles, one of his staff members, with crafting waiver language that would allow dischargers such as those in Anchorage and Seward to get a waiver. Cowles, in turn, approached Leon Billings for assistance in writing the amendment. Billings worked for Senator Muskie, the chairman of the Committee on Environment and Public Works. By asking Billings for help, Cowles was, in effect, walking into the lion's den. Muskie and Billings both strongly opposed the granting of any waivers.[40] Nevertheless, they realized that wishing that Gravel would drop his insistence on a waiver provision was no use. Gravel not only wanted the provision, but he was also willing to risk a lot of political capital in getting it into the bill. Rather than fight an all-out battle with another member of the committee, the outcome of which would be in doubt, Muskie decided to give Gravel his waiver provision, but to make it restrictive to the point of essentially being unusable. Billings took up the task and, he said, "wrote that provision so that it would be virtually impossible for any municipality to successfully gain a waiver from secondary treatment."[41] According to Joan Bernard, a staff member on the House Public Works Committee at the time, Cowles was "basically being led down a primrose path by others on the staff who were solidly aligned with their chairman who was adamantly opposed to any waiver." It was, Bernard notes, a classic legislative game, "allowing a member to politically say he got his provision so he gets a political win, but then letting the technicians write it in such a way that when the process plays out there will be no change in result."[42]

The waiver provision that came out of this process was included in a Senate bill that passed the Senate on August 4, 1977, by a vote of 96 to 0. The amendment read as follows:

> The Administrator, with the concurrence of the State, may issue a permit under Section 402 which modifies the [secondary treatment] requirements of subsection (b)(1)(B) of this section with respect to the discharge of any pollutant in an existing discharge from a publicly owned treatment works into marine waters, if the applicant demonstrates to the satisfaction of the Administrator that—
>
> (1) there is an applicable water quality standard specific to the pollutant for which the modification is requested which has been identified under section 304(a)(4) of this Act [the section requiring the administrator to publish water quality criteria];
>
> (2) such modified requirements will not interfere with the attainment or maintenance of that water quality which assures the protection of public water supplies and the protection and propagation of a balanced, indigenous population of shellfish, fish and wildlife, and allows recreational activities, in and on the water;
>
> (3) the applicant has established a system for monitoring the impact of such discharge on a representative sample of aquatic biota, to the extent practicable;
>
> (4) such modified requirements will not result in any additional requirements on any other point or non-point source;
>
> (5) all applicable pretreatment requirements for sources introducing waste into such treatment works will be enforced;
>
> (6) to the extent practicable, the applicant has established a schedule of activities designed to eliminate the entrance of toxic pollutants from non-industrial sources into such treatment works;
>
> (7) there will be no new or substantially increased discharges from the point source of the pollutant to which the modification applies above that volume of discharge specified in the permit;

(8) any funds available to the owner of such treatment works under Title II of this Act [Grants for the Construction of Treatment Works] will be used to achieve the degree of effluent reduction required by section 201(b) and (g)(2)(A) or to carry out the requirements of this subsection.

For the purposes of this subsection the phrase "the discharge of any pollutant into marine waters" refers to a discharge into deep waters of the territorial sea or the waters of the contiguous zone, or into saline estuarine waters where there is strong tidal movement and other hydrological and geological characteristics which the Administrator determines necessary to allow compliance with paragraph (2) of this subsection and section 101(a)(2) of this Act [the fishable/swimmable goal].[43]

Define the Waiver My Way

The legislative history that the Senate Environment and Public Works Committee produced to further explain the applicability of its waiver provision was included in the report accompanying the bill and was written by Muskie. The report stated, "Some communities located along the Nation's oceans have argued that there is no need to require secondary treatment for municipalities which discharge into ocean waters. The committee determined, after much analysis, that there should be a mechanism by which communities making this argument can test their case in the administrative process."[44] The report then elaborated on those factors the administrator could use in determining which communities should have an opportunity to "test their case." Depth was listed as a "key factor." The report, however, did not define what the waiver provision's reference to "deep waters" actually meant. Instead, it pointed out that "In some instances, depth of water in the territorial seas or contiguous zone in excess of 200 feet is necessary to achieve sufficiently rapid dispersion (i.e., 45 seconds) of waste water and waste water constituents. In some instances, depth of 200 feet is insufficient to provide adequate dispersion."

Additional factors cited that influence the rapidity of dispersion were degree of tidal movement and other geological and hydrological characteristics. The report went on to state that the "distance offshore for location of outfall lines is also a factor which must be considered in many situations," with greater distances offshore possibly providing "the desired protection during adverse conditions of onshore currents and wind." The common thread running through all of these factors was their generality and vagueness. None of them offered the EPA administrator who would have to interpret the waiver's statutory language and intent any clear guideposts to action. For example, the depth description might have led one to argue that two hundred feet was a threshold requirement, but the plain language of the report did not disqualify from consideration those offshore areas that were less than two hundred feet deep. Nevertheless, after laying out the various factors, the report attempted to limit the universe of potential waiver applicants by stating that "areas described by these conditions include most of the coast of the western United States, the coasts of Hawaii, Puerto Rico, American Samoa, the Virgin Islands, and portions of estuarine waters such as Cook Inlet near Anchorage, Alaska, and Resurrection Bay near Seward, Alaska."[45]

Despite Muskie's effort to make the waiver provision very restrictive, the EPA was concerned that the language in the Senate's waiver amendment was not restrictive enough. In testimony before the House Committee on Public Works and Transportation, which was also considering the waiver issue, Tom Jorling, assistant administrator for water and hazardous materials at the EPA, stated:

> We think, however, it is much too loosely written and potentially qualifies areas of the marine environment which should not receive the relief that is desired. . . . with some modification, we can support the Senate amendment, but we believe it has to be tightened, especially in the area of the definition of deep water marine waters, so that only deep water marine waters qualify. The other areas that have an acute problem in this area, I might add, are Hawaii and Puerto Rico. We recognize their legitimate claim to discharge, BOD, and suspended solid[s]. But we want to make sure that it is confined to the area of difficulty and not used as an escape valve for legitimate pollution cleanup needs.[46]

The EPA's efforts to get the language changed were unsuccessful; the dynamics of the Senate-House conference on the amendments to the Clean Water Act illustrate why. House conferees believed that the waiver provision was drafted too tightly. They were specifically concerned that many of the West Coast municipalities that had lobbied most strenuously in favor of a waiver provision might not qualify for one. Senator Gravel, too, was beginning to view the provision he sponsored with some alarm, worrying that Alaskan municipalities might be left out as well. As a result, House conferees worked with Gravel, also a conferee, to figure out changes that would make the waiver provision a bit more flexible.[47] When these changes were presented to the conference committee, strong arguments in favor of and opposed to the suggested changes ensued. In the end, Senator Robert Stafford, who was chairing the conference in Muskie's absence (because of illness), used a parliamentary tactic to end debate. The Senate bill contained a waiver provision and the House bill didn't. In light of congressional rules, the Senate had two options. The senators could either choose to negotiate their language, or accede to the House's position on the waiver, which in this case was nothing. It was clear that Muskie did not want the waiver provision opened up to negotiation that might broaden its applicability. So what Stafford did, at the urging of Muskie and with the support of the majority of Senate conferees, was to say, if you want to make any changes in the Senate provision, we'll just accede to the House position and drop the whole thing. This would have sat well with Muskie and many other Senate conferees, but it was unacceptable to the House side. As Bernard noted, "that was the high stakes poker game that occurred." Rather than drop the provision, "as bad as it was," the House conferees decided that having a flawed provision was better than nothing. Both the House and the Senate conferees also realized that if the waiver issues were pushed any harder, agreement on the entire bill might be jeopardized.

Since the conference accepted the Senate's waiver language, the conference committee's joint explanatory statement simply appropriated the Senate's earlier legislative history that dealt with the waiver provision. The legislative wrangling over the waiver provision, however, was far from over. During the House and Senate debates on the amendments, members on both sides tried to fashion the legislative history in a way that would persuade the EPA to interpret the wavier's language in a manner consistent with their own interpretations. Some House members inserted lists of cities that should be considered likely to meet the requirements for receiving waiver. Others attempted to further define terms in the amendment, such as "balanced, indigenous population," in ways that were in line with a less restrictive view of the waiver's applicability. On the Senate side, Muskie, in particular, attempted to clarify how the waiver provision should be construed. So as to leave no doubt about how the administrator of the EPA should view attempts by other members of Congress, in both Houses, to interpret this and other provisions of the bill as being applicable to specific cases, Muskie noted that

during the course of debate on this conference report in this and the other body, attempts will be made to bind the Administrator by creating legislative history describing specific situations. The conferees did not examine specific cases for exemptions, extensions or modifications.

The conference report provides a general framework for the Administrator to make judgments. The Administrator should be guided by the framework of the statute and the statement of managers and other appropriate legislative history, and should not feel bound by attempts to legislate by colloquy special cases which are contrary to the letter and intent of the law.[48]

After the debates, the Senate and the House passed the amendments on December 15 and sent the bill to President Jimmy Carter, who signed it on December 28, 1977.

EPA Defines the Waiver and Boston Applies

Congress left the EPA with a difficult task when it sent over the waiver provision. The statutory language and the legislative history were ambiguous at best. The EPA had to use considerable discretion in determining congressional intent and in transforming statutory law into regulations that could be applied on a case-by-case basis to municipal ocean dischargers. In performing this task, the agency was placed in the middle of essentially the same forces that had argued for and against the waiver during the legislative process, the difference being that now instead of debating the acceptability of the waiver concept, the focus shifted to how the statutory provision would be interpreted. The environmentalists attempted to make the regulations restrictive, while the coastal municipalities pushed to broaden their scope.

Shortly after the 1977 amendments passed, the EPA established a waiver task force to devise the regulations that would implement the waiver provision. One of the first things that the task force did was to hold a public hearing, on February 22, 1978, in San Francisco. More than one hundred persons attended the hearing and thirty-seven testified, but the comments provided no surprises. In addition to responding to the issues, many of the municipal representatives came to argue that their communities should be granted waivers. David Phillips, from the South Essex (Massachusetts) Sewerage District, argued against limiting waivers to discharges into "deep" ocean waters, contending that this would unfairly exclude East Coast dischargers. He added that the most important factors were strong tidal flushing and circulation, such as was present off the Massachusetts coast. Whereas the municipalities were trying to broaden to applicability of the waiver provision, the environmentalists argued just the opposite. Ken Kamlet of the National Wildlife Federation argued that the waiver provision should be limited to outfalls off the West Coast, Hawaii, Puerto Rico, American Samoa, the Virgin Islands, and certain waters near Anchorage, Alaska. East Coast communities, he added, should not even be allowed to apply.[49]

From the end of February through the middle of March, the task force worked to develop a preliminary concept paper that was, in effect, its first draft of the proposed regulations. Given the ambiguity in the statute and the legislative history, the question was how the task force was going to exercise its regulatory discretion in interpreting the provision. The answer to this question evolved over time, but at the outset there was little doubt as to how the task force would use its discretion. The EPA wanted to limit the waiver's application to very special circumstances.[50]

As the task force looked more closely at the science and the law, what became clear was that certain means of narrowing the eligibility criteria could not be used. Originally, there was some discussion of using depth of the receiving water as a limiting criterion. A number of the dischargers who had been most involved in the development of the waiver provision, including Seattle Metro and some of the southern California sewage districts, discharged into waters more than two hundred feet deep. If there were a depth restriction, huge numbers of potential applicants, especially ones on the East Coast, would be disqualified. Although the legislative history identified the depth of discharge as a key factor is assessing application, the only mention of a specific depth was the two-hundred-feet reference in the Senate and conference reports. That reference merely stated: "In some instances, depth of water in territorial seas or contiguous zone in excess of 200 feet is necessary to achieve sufficiently rapid dispersion. . . . In some instances, depth of 200 feet is insufficient to provide adequate dispersion." Nowhere, however, was there an indication that depths of less than two hundred feet were unacceptable. Indeed, task force scientists, as well as outside experts, argued persuasively that depth was not necessarily a factor of concern—other hydrological and geological characteristics such as circulation and tidal flushing, which were explicitly cited in the statute and the legislative history, could be more important. As a result, the concept paper had no depth restriction.

Geography, too, was considered as a means for reducing the applicant pool. Limiting consideration to dischargers in certain areas, such as southern California or Hawaii, was found to be indefensible for two reasons. First, the legislative history never explicitly excluded any areas from consideration, and Senator Gravel's comments during the Senate debate indicated that geographical restrictions should not be applied.[51] Thus, the task force believed that any attempt to limit applications based on geography would be strongly challenged on legal grounds. There was yet another, more compelling reason not to impose geographical limitations, and it went back to the debate over depth. Geographic restrictions would not reflect best scientific judgment. A conversation that Donald Baumgartner, a sanitary engineer and physical oceanographer with EPA's laboratory in Corvallis, Oregon, and Jorling had at the time illustrates this point. According to Baumgartner, Jorling said, "What about Boston? Is the situation so bad there and generally on the East Coast, or is it too hard to prove, scientifically, that we shouldn't be considering a place like Boston?" Baumgartner responded, "Everybody who thinks they can prove their case, scientifically and technically, ought to be given a chance to do that. Those of us who know oceanography and the biology of both coasts know the differences. We know there is less circulation on the East Coast, and there are more and more discharges closer together. We know the background concentrations [of various pollutants] are going to be higher, so we'll know how to take that into account when we look at their proposals to see if they made a good case."[52] Thus, geographical restrictions were not included in the concept paper either.

The concept paper was distributed to the participants at a San Francisco hearing on March 15, 1978, and the comments received were nearly all negative. An MDC representative expressed concern that the "narrow" interpretation of the provision would eliminate East Coast dischargers from qualifying. California Representative Glenn Anderson was so upset by what was presented in the concept paper that he wrote a letter to EPA Administrator Douglas Costle. "To be perfectly frank," complained Anderson, "this paper contains statements which are personally quite disturbing. To that end I am requesting that our Full Committee Chairman, Harold T. Johnson, authorize our committee staff to make these proposed regulations its number one priority."[53]

The task force considered the comments and prepared proposed regulations that were published in the *Federal Register* on April 25, 1978.[54] Interested parties were given forty-five days to comment on the proposed regulations, and because they were quite similar to the concept paper, many of the comments received were similar as well. A representative from the Massachusetts attorney general's office summed up the frustrations felt by many potential applicants for a waiver. "In 1977 the Congress clearly recognized that secondary treatment had to be changed somehow. I would not propose to tell you that they intended that everyone should get it and I don't think it is fair for you to tell the rest of the world that they intended, as Muskie says, that nobody should get it."[55]

In late May, the EPA was hit from another direction. Representative Anderson's request, two months earlier, to get the staff of the House Committee on Public Works and Transportation to make the proposed waiver regulations its top priority had borne fruit. The staff and the members had been watching and they didn't like what they saw. According to Bernard, then a staff person on the Committee's Subcommittee on Water Resources, "EPA was coming out with regulations that would make it absolutely impossible to comply, they made it even worse than it was in the bill."[56] As a result, the subcommittee held hearings, on May 24 and 25, on the "Modification of Secondary Treatment Requirements for Discharges into Marine Waters." The stated purpose of the hearings was to "hear from scientific experts" on the various issues pertaining to the waiver process.[57] But one look at the list of witnesses made it clear that the testimony would be one-sided, with the evidence presented pointing to the problems with the EPA's approach thus far and to the need for broadly based waiver regulations. Normally, when conducting hearings, the subcommittee would not "rig" the witness list. Sometimes specific witnesses would be invited, but "if you wanted in, you got in. We didn't rig the agenda." According to Bernard, "The only time we did not follow this procedure was on the . . . [waiver] regulations." She described the politics of the situation as follows:

Biz Johnson [committee chairman, from California] was so furious with the way things were being handled that I was instructed to get people who were prominent in their field, who have knowledge on this issue and basically would testify as to why it made sense to do it [have a functioning waiver process]. The whole thing was laid out just to get the information on the record in an effort to do a back push against what was going on at the agency. People at the agency were furious because they wanted to argue against the waiver but we would not allow them in. That was the first and last time we ever did that, and that was simply because Biz Johnson felt so strongly that the whole process was being so badly manipulated in the opposite direction [of what the House had intended] that something had to be done to counterbalance the situation, and this was our only opportunity to do so.

Of the seven scientists testifying, all but one were from California, Washington, and Hawaii, and the vast majority of the discussion focused on secondary treatment and its relationship to Pacific waters. The testimony of Professor John D. Isaacs, director of the Institute of Marine Resources at the University of California, was indicative of the general tone of the hearings:

> With my conviction that the gulf that cleaves action and understanding is a most tragic syndrome of our times, it was with deepening sadness that I reviewed the EPA proposed modifications under consideration. . . . [The proposal] directly or implicitly repeats the same old myths of the bioaccumulation of trace metals, the delicate balance of the marine environment, and all-healing properties of secondary sewage treatment, and many of the other cliches and misrepresentations that already have led us to a serious estrangement from reality.[58]

The task force was not surprised by the nature of the comments it was getting. It had gone with an extremely restrictive approach to the waiver provision, and it expected to get hit hard. The EPA knew that it would have to alter the proposed regulations; the question was how. The task force still had many of its earlier concerns. It wanted to maintain the waiver as a "narrow opportunity for certain dischargers," thereby keeping the number of applicants to a minimum and excluding clearly "unmeritorious" applications that would serve only to tax the agency's limited time and resources and enable unqualified applicants to put off compliance with the act. Concerns about scientific and legal defensibility also remained high on the task force's agenda.

The EPA had hoped to have the final regulations prepared by September 24, 1978, the statutory deadline for application submissions, but the agency missed the deadline. The delay in promulgation created a problem in that, if the statute were directly adhered to, applications would be due before the final regulations were released. The EPA solved this problem by announcing, on September 5, 1978, that applicants would be required to submit only preliminary applications by the statutory deadline. The final regulations came out on June 15, 1979, and they were significantly less restrictive than the proposed regulations. Even so, many people still found much in them to dislike. And as often happens in the United States when individuals or groups are unhappy about a law or regulation, they go to court. Within weeks, the Natural Resources Defense Council filed a petition for review of the waiver regulations, and then a group of municipalities from Alaska and California did the same.

Essentially, Natural Resources Defense Council argued that the EPA "misinterpreted the law to provide too great an opportunity for variance applications," while the municipalities argued "that the regulations are too restrictive and impracticable."[59] The U.S. Court of Appeals, District of Columbia Circuit, handed down its decision on May 7, 1981, basically upholding the regulations, with a few exceptions that were not relevant to the situation in Boston Harbor. Congress responded on December 15, 1981, by passing amendments to the Clean Water Act, which further clarified the applicability of the waiver provision.[60] Finally, almost four years after the waiver provision was first passed into law, the regulations were completed.

In the meantime, Boston had taken the plunge and entered the waiver process. On September 18, 1978, the MDC submitted a preliminary application to receive a waiver from the secondary treatment requirement; the final application arrived at the EPA on September 13, 1979.[61] Boston's waiver application was one of seventy applications that the EPA received by the 1979 deadline. The reasoning behind the MDC's waiver bid was straightforward. Ever since the late 1960s, the MDC had argued that secondary treatment was not a priority for the harbor. As John Snedeker, commissioner of the MDC from 1975 through 1978, noted around this time, "There is no evidence that secondary treatment will benefit the marine environment of Boston Harbor. The construction of combined sewer facilities and the expansion of primary treatment with extended outfalls will, in our judgment, provide ample water quality in the harbor for at least the next two or three decades."[62] But, just as with other municipalities, water quality considerations were not the only ones that prompted Boston-area officials to argue against an across-the-board requirement for secondary. Upgrading to secondary cost a great deal of money. According to the MDC's waiver application, a waiver could "save $144 million in construction costs and about $14 million in annual operation and maintenance costs."[63] Even if the MDC received federal funding of 75 percent of the project costs, the other 25 percent had to come from the state. The MDC argued that spending so much money did not make sense if the benefits were not there.[64] MDC's application requested a waiver of effluent requirements for biochemical oxygen demand and suspended solids, and called for ceasing sludge discharges, upgrading the primary treatment facilities at both Deer and Nut Islands, and constructing one ocean outfall to discharge the effluent from the two plants in one hundred feet of water, roughly 7.5 miles out into Massachusetts Bay.

The task force had hoped to review the applications in relatively short order. Indeed, in a June 1980 letter to the MDC commissioner, the EPA's Region 1 administrator expressed confidence that Boston would learn the fate of its application soon. "I requested that your application be given review as a first priority by our headquarters ocean waiver office. They honored my request and they expect to be able to make a decision by the end of this year."[65] The decision was not made by the end of the year, however, nor were the decisions on any of the applications made by that time. The task force found the review process more difficult than expected. Many of the applications were quite extensive; the MDC's ran to five volumes. None of the applications were summarily dismissed or approved. All had pros and cons, and the task force had to make very difficult scientific and technical determinations in coming to its decisions. As John Lishman, an attorney on the task force, noted, "We had a combination of people agonizing over whether they had enough information to really know [if a waiver should be granted], and you also had people who felt there was enough data, agonizing over what it meant."[66] The task force was also intent on making well-founded decisions. With so much money on the line, the applicants and the politicians who represented them were sure to attack any decision to deny. The task force wanted to make decisions that could withstand scrutiny and any administrative and/or judicial appeals. For these and a variety of common bureaucratic reasons, including scheduling meetings among twenty or more people, some of whom had to be flown in from the regions, the task force made slow progress. It wasn't until September 8, 1981, that the EPA announced its first eight waiver decisions, and Boston's was not among them.[67] The decision to deny Boston's waiver application was not made until June 30, 1983.[68] Thus, when the state lawsuit was filed in 1982, the waiver decision was still pending.

The pendency of the waiver greatly impacted the MDC's movement toward improved sewage management. First, large-scale construction, either of the sewage upgrade envisioned in the waiver application or secondary treatment facilities, was put on hold because of the uncertainty over what the MDC was supposed to build. Second, while the MDC waited on the results of the application, planning became more difficult. Not only were many of the elements of past planning efforts, specifically EMMA and the draft environmental impact statement, now questionable, but the MDC, in preparing for the future, was also forced to pursue double-track planning. This can be seen in the preparation of the *Nut Island Wastewater Treatment Plant Facilities Planning Project Phase 1 Site Options Study*, which was intended to determine the most environmentally sound and cost-effective location for the MDC's sewage treatment plants.[69] In that study, which was completed in 1982, the MDC evaluated both primary and secondary treatment options, to be located on one or more of three harbor islands, Deer, Nut, and Long. This was done for two reasons, one practical and one legal. First, by considering primary and secondary configurations, whatever the outcome of the waiver, the MDC would have already thought through the issue of where treatment facilities should be located. This, in turn, would enable the MDC to begin facility planning earlier than would have been the case had the agency waited until the waiver process was completed.[70] Second, the waiver regulations required all applicants to continue planning for secondary while the waiver was pending, for the same reason—to ensure that the applicant could quickly move forward with planning and construction, regardless of the outcome. Such double-track planning cost the MDC in both time and money.[71] Finally, in addition to making planning for sewage treatment facilities more cumbersome, the pendency of the waiver affected efforts to plan for sludge management because of the disparity, in both tonnage and character, between the sludge produced by secondary as opposed to primary treatment. Secondary treatment creates roughly twice as much sludge as primary, and secondary sludge contains higher concentrations of certain toxic materials.[72] Not knowing what type of sludge had to be managed added a great element of uncertainty to decision making, and made the state reluctant to commit to a specific plan of action.[73] But according to Jeffry Fowley, who would later be the lead EPA lawyer on the Boston Harbor case, the pendency of the waiver need not have stalled the MDC's movement toward more effectively dealing with sludge. Fowley argues that the MDC could have sequenced the construction of sludge facilities, first building facilities to deal with primary sludge, then later adding those for secondary sludge if the waiver was not successful. Fowley believes that the state's contention that the pendency of the waiver made it impossible to move ahead on the sludge front was "just an excuse used by state officials . . . to avoid dealing with the hard issues involving even primary sludge." Indeed, Fowley points out that at one point in the late 1970s, the EPA and the MDC reached agreement to end primary sludge discharges through incineration, but that plan was "in effect vetoed by the Massachusetts Secretary of Environmental Affairs."[74]

EPA Enforcement

During the 1970s and early 1980s, the planning, reviews, and decisions for sewage management in the Boston area were motivated and structured by the requirements embodied in the Clean Water Act. Those requirements, in turn, became part of the Clean Water Act permit issued to the MDC on August 12, 1976.[75] Along with the permit, the EPA issued an enforcement compliance schedule letter, which stated that

> EPA and MDC concluded that it [the Permittee, MDC] cannot, despite all reasonable best efforts, achieve the limitations from the discharge between the final effective date of the Permit and July 1, 1977.
>
> The compliance schedule contained in the Permit notwithstanding, this Agency, in the exercise of its prosecutorial discretion, will not take [enforcement] action against the Permittee . . . with respect to the Permittee's failure to achieve the limitations on and after July 1, 1977, until the date specified herein for the achievement of the limitations provided that the Permitee complies with the following conditions.[76]

Those conditions extended the time that MDC had to comply with the various deadlines established in the permit. For example, the compliance letter required the MDC to complete construction of secondary treatment at Deer Island by May 1, 1984, and at Nut Island a year later, and to construct facilities for the disposal of primary sludge by May 1, 1980, and for secondary sludge by May 1, 1985. It also included a variety of interim deadlines, concerning facility planning and design that would have to be completed prior to the actual construction of facilities.

That MDC would be unable to meet the construction deadlines in its permit was not surprising. When the permit was issued, the environmental impact statement process for EMMA had not begun and, thus, the potential construction of the facilities envisioned by EMMA was still relatively far off in the future. Similarly, sludge management planning was still at the early stages of development, with the draft environmental impact statement having only recently come out. When EMMA was completed, in 1975, the general feeling at both the EPA and the MDC was that the tide was turning in the fight for improved sewage treatment in the Boston area.[77]

From a national perspective, the fact that the MDC would not have secondary on line by 1977 was not unusual. By that date, only about 30 percent of the POTWs in the United States had upgraded to secondary.[78] The $18 billion sewage construction grants program turned out to be much too small. The 1974 EPA construction grants national needs survey came in at $342 billion; the 1976 survey, based on a different accounting mechanism, dropped to $96 billion, still much higher than envisioned in 1972.[79] President Nixon's impoundment of $9 billion of the $18 billion right after the passage of the Clean Water Act and through 1975, when the Supreme Court overturned the impoundment, limited funds even further. Even if unlimited funds had been available from the start, however, compliance with the 1977 deadline would still have been poor. It simply took longer than five years for regulations to be promulgated, sewage construction plans to be developed and approved, money to be dispersed, contractors to be hired, and construction to be completed. In the 1977 amendments to the Clean Water Act, Congress took stock of these problems and extended the deadline for achieving secondary to July 1, 1983, for those POTWs that either couldn't complete construction by July 1, 1977, or for which the federal government had failed to make funds available in time to meet the original deadline.[80]

The year after the issuance of the permit and the enforcement compliance schedule letter, sewage planning for the Boston area progressed. By the summer of 1977, however, the EPA enforcement staff became concerned about the slippage of some of the enforcement compliance schedule letter's deadlines and were eager to enter into a consent decree with the MDC governing various sewage projects, thereby creating a court-enforced schedule for the completion of those projects.[81] When the proposed consent decree was transmitted by the EPA to the MDC, on August 18, 1977, and backed up by threats of litigation, it provoked a sharp response. The MDC, supported by the secretary of the Massachusetts Executive Office of Environmental Affairs and the state's attorney general, not only refused to sign a consent decree; they filed a suit against the EPA, essentially alleging that it was EPA's fault, not the MDC's, that certain projects were not being completed on time. The MDC also prepared a script for a press conference that would pin the blame for the delay in the harbor cleanup on the EPA. Wanting to avoid open confrontation with the state, the EPA agreed to reconsider its suit, and the MDC, in turn, withdrew its suit and canceled the press conference. In reconsidering legal action, the EPA determined that litigation was not appropriate, especially since the main reason that many of the deadlines had been missed, or were in danger of being missed, was delays in the EPA's environmental impact statement work on

EMMA and primary sludge management, not recalcitrance on the part of MDC. Thus, the EPA decided to forgo any legal action and, instead, to work cooperatively with the MDC in trying to complete environmental reviews quickly and to move forward with the various projects.[82]

In the following year it appeared as if the cooperative relationship between the EPA and the MDC was working. On September 27, 1978, Rebecca Hanmer, EPA deputy regional administrator, Region 1, concluded that "it can be stated that the cleanup of Boston Harbor's water pollution is gathering momentum. Comprehensive facilities planning is underway to find cost-effective solutions for combined sewer overflows, and similar planning is about to start for the collection, treatment, and disposal of sewered wastes. When this planning is complete, design and construction of the necessary facilities will begin immediately."[83] At the same time these comments were made, the MDC was entering into the waiver process. According to Richard Kotelly, deputy director of water management at EPA, Region 1, while the waiver decision languished, planning efforts were "knocked into a cocked hat."[84] Despite this uncertainty, the EPA continued to have conversations with the MDC concerning the progress of the implementation and administrative review process and the possible next steps that could be taken even though the waiver issue had yet to be decided. As a result of those conversations, additional planning efforts, including the Nut Island options study, were begun.

It was not until late 1980 that the EPA decided that the cooperative approach alone was not working. On August 8 the EPA issued an administrative order that required, among other things, that the MDC complete facilities planning for CSO projects and primary sludge management by new deadlines. The order was partially effective, and over the next couple of years, the MDC had produced some of the required plans, such as a CSO facilities plan. Yet, however effective the order was, one fact remained—on the eve of the Quincy suit, planning was still the order of the day.

The administrative order notwithstanding, throughout the late 1970s, and through the initiation of the Quincy suit in 1982, the EPA was reluctant to pursue enforcement actions against the MDC for missing deadlines relating to the planning and ultimate construction of new sewage-related facilities, in large part because many of the violations were due to delays resulting from the complexity of joint action and the EPA's review of the waiver application—causes that were largely outside the MDC's control. One permit condition, however, was unaf-

fected by all of these delays. The MDC was required to properly operate and maintain its sewage treatment facilities.[85] This was a basic
requirement and would have to be complied with regardless of what
future improvements or changes in the MDC's sewage system might be
mandated by federal law. When the EPA issued its permit to the MDC,
the agency already knew that this permit condition was being violated.

The operation and maintenance problems in evidence at the Nut
Island and Deer Island plants prior to the passage of the Clean Water
Act worsened in the following years. For example, the Nordberg engines at Deer Island, which began breaking down as soon as the plant
opened in 1968, became even less reliable. The company that had
bought out Nordberg Manufacturing in 1968 discontinued supplying
engine replacement parts in 1973.[86] After that point, new parts were
either specially fabricated at the plant, a process that was both difficult
and time-consuming, or inoperative engines were cannibalized to keep
others running. Equipment breakdowns were common at Nut Island as
well. And both plants were still poorly staffed. Graphic evidence of
these problems came in January 1976, when all of the generators at Nut
Island broke down, resulting in the discharge of hundreds of millions of
gallons of raw sewage into the harbor. The EPA task force that convened in the wake of the spill to look into the plant's problems painted
a disturbing picture. Nut Island was understaffed by 21 percent, the
equipment in the plant had passed its life expectancy and needed repair
or complete restoration, and there was no preventive maintenance program and no spare parts for the three major engines.[87] Later that year,
an EPA audit of the MDC concluded that a "lack of funds . . . was the
most significant factor contributing to the breakdown of Nut Island as
well as other operational problems [at the MDC's sewerage division]."[88]

The operation and maintenance problems continued in the years
following the issuance of the permit. With respect to staffing, for example, a 1978 EPA inspection report on the Nut Island plant noted that
there were sixteen staff vacancies, eight of which were on the maintenance crew. In 1981 the EPA reported that fifty million gallons of
chlorinated, raw sewage were discharged at the plant "because no 'qualified' diesel operators were available that day." The same year, the Massachusetts Department of Environmental Quality Engineering reported that the Nut Island plant did not have "adequate, qualified,
certified" staff. These last two reports highlight the fact that the MDC's
staffing deficiencies concerned not only the quantity of staff but also
the quality. The civil service salaries that the MDC offered were much

less than the salaries offered for comparable work in the private sector; therefore, the MDC continued to lose out in the competition for highly trained personnel. Similar staff deficiencies were to be found at Deer Island. In 1981, for example, only 190 of the necessary 236 positions at the plant were filled, and many of those employees were not well qualified. According to Noel Barrata, the former chief engineer of the MDC's sewerage division, having too few staff made for a situation in which "you have a preventive maintenance program that is never adhered to because you don't have enough men. Therefore, repairs take place on a crisis basis."[89] In addition to the problems involving the quantity and quality of staff, another problem emerged. Starved of money, the sewerage division was often unable to buy needed tools, forcing some of the workers in the sewage plants to bring in their own just so they could do their job.

Although there was no arguing that the sewage treatment plants were understaffed, and in many cases were staffed with people who were not highly qualified, there were a number of competent workers. Those employees, however, were limited in their ability to succeed by the system in which they operated. Paul F. Levy, the third executive director of the MDC's successor agency, the Massachusetts Water Resources Authority, labeled this situation the "Nut Island Effect." He described the effect as what happens when a dedicated group of hard-working and skilled individuals, motivated to succeed but virtually ignored by upper management and starved for resources, works in increasing isolation, eventually running into problems by creating its own rules and procedures that jeopardize the group's ability to effectively do its job. According to Levy, at the Nut Island treatment plant, especially during the 1960s, 1970s, and early 1980s, there was a core of very competent workers whose requests for help in addressing the continued deterioration of the plant were largely shrugged off by upper management. This dynamic was illustrated by an oft-told story about the time in the 1960s when the Nut Island superintendent asked the MDC commissioner for funds for much-needed maintenance. The commissioner's response: "Take some money and get rid of the dandelions off the lawn. The place looks terrible." In such a scenario, according to Levy, eventually the workers' abilities to solve the plant's problems on their own are overwhelmed by the magnitude of those problems and catastrophe strikes. In one instance cited by Levy, this dynamic led to a six-month period in 1982 when problems at the plant caused the release of 3.7 billion gallons of untreated sewage into the harbor.[90] Although

Levy's analysis focused on the situation at Nut Island, the dynamic he highlighted was no doubt at work across the harbor, at Deer Island, as well.

As for the condition of the facilities themselves, they continued to wear out and to break down. Indeed, the equipment problems at Nut Island were so bad that Commissioner Snedeker stated in November 1977 that "only a complete reconstruction of the Nut Island Facility will allow the plant to achieve adequate capacity, reliable performance, and improved water quality."[91] The combination of inadequate staff and old and faulty equipment led to numerous breakdowns that, in turn, meant more raw sewage was discharged into the harbor. When the pumps at Deer Island failed, for example, the MDC had to close the gates at the headworks that regulated the flow of sewage into the plant. The backed-up sewage then overflowed into the harbor via CSOs and the holding facility on Moon Island. As a result of pump failures at Deer Island, the number of raw sewage discharges via the Moon Island facility rose from twelve to 144 from 1980 to 1981.[92]

After issuing the permit, the EPA responded to the operation and maintenance problems at the plants by encouraging the MDC to voluntarily improve conditions. On August 12, 1981, the agency lost its patience with the MDC's lack of progress in remedying these violations, however, and issued an administrative order requiring the commission to take actions to ensure that at least five of the eight pumping units at Deer Island were in good working order.[93] Roughly a year later, on June 30, 1982, the EPA issued another order, requiring the MDC to maintain the power generation equipment at Nut Island in good working order and to improve its maintenance programs.[94] These orders resulted in some improvements, but in light of the magnitude of the operation and maintenance problems at the plants, they were merely "Band-Aid measures."[95]

Infrastructure Politics

The operation and maintenance problems that plagued the MDC were representative of the larger problem of infrastructure neglect. There are numerous examples of governments building expensive public works projects and then allowing them to fall into disrepair.[96] In the case of the MDC's sewage infrastructure, the main reason for such neglect was political. Annually, the MDC used a statutorily based method to allocate the sewerage costs to the cities and towns within the district. The cities and towns, after having the opportunity to review and to comment on their assessments, would pay the proper amount to the general fund of the commonwealth, not to the MDC. The legislature would then fund the MDC's sewage budget out of the general fund. Thus, MDC funding was totally dependent on the state budgeting process, which culminated in a legislative appropriation—and that was the problem.

Each year the MDC developed an in-house budget. During that process the sewerage division competed with the other divisions in the commission, such as the police department and the parks department, for limited resources. Sewerage was not considered a "sexy" issue at the time, and there was much more of a constituency for the MDC's other services. As a result, the sewerage division, sometimes referred to as the "stepchild" of the MDC, often lost out in the battle over limited resources.[97] The MDC's budget was next sent to the state Executive Office of Environmental Affairs, where it competed with other state agencies for funds. Once again, the sewerage division's piece of the MDC budget usually did not fare well in relation to higher-profile programs, such as air pollution and hazardous waste. Then the Executive Office of Environmental Affairs budget would be sent to the state administration to be woven into the overall state budget that was submitted to the legislature. More often than not, the sewerage division's funding was cut again at one or both of these last two stops of the budget process.[98] The result of all this was that the MDC's sewerage division was chronically underfunded. The dynamics that led to this situation are best understood by analyzing why those actors who could have helped generate the political climate necessary to improve the sewerage division's funding did not.

The first question one can ask is, Where did the public stand on the sewage infrastructure issue? This must be answered from the perspective of the general public and the organized public, such as interest groups. Between 1972 and 1982, the average citizen in the MDC's service area knew little, if anything, about the operation and maintenance problems besetting the agency. The primary source of such information was the media, especially newspapers. Although occasional articles documented sewage infrastructure problems, most of the articles that went into any detail did not appear until the end of that ten-year period. Instead, the vast proportion of sewage-related coverage involved the planning efforts taking place under the auspices of the Clean Water Act.

The other route via which the average MDC customer might have become engaged in the infrastructure debate was through personal experience. If the problems with the plants and the pipes leading to them had resulted in sewage backing up into people's houses, people would have demanded solutions. But despite the problems at the plants, the toilets still worked, and most people at the time had an "out of sight, out of mind" mentality when it came to sewage. As an MDC spokesman in the early 1980s commented, "When a bridge is stuck in the up position, there's a huge public outcry. But when the sewage system breaks, everyone can still flush and it goes away. The problem is in Boston Harbor."[99] To the extent that any citizens made the conscious connection between the degradation of Boston Harbor and infrastructure decay, they could still focus on the flurry of planning taking place as an indication that those problems would eventually be resolved. This is not to say that average citizens were totally disengaged from the sewage debate. Not all citizens viewed the planning efforts in a detached manner or as an indication that things would get better. Those citizens who perceived planned improvements as threats to their communities' health and well-being rose up in protest. Still, the focus was on the future, not on the current deterioration of the sewage system.

As would be expected, public interest groups were much better informed about the operations and maintenance problems at the MDC and about the resulting infrastructure decay. They knew how bad the problems were as a result of both formal and informal interactions with the state and federal agencies involved in sewage planning. For example, one component of the EMMA project was the establishment of a Citizen Advisory Committee, which was intended to act as a conduit between the planning agencies and the public, helping to inform the public about the planning process and the planners about public concerns. Among the groups represented on the Citizen Advisory Committee were the Sierra Club, Charles River Watershed Association, League of Women Voters, Massachusetts Audubon Society, and the Neponset Valley Conservation Association. Through their involvement, the citizens groups became familiar with planning efforts as well as with the current status of MDC's operations. The latter type of knowledge was supplemented as a result of informal contacts that citizen group representatives had with the staff from various agencies and their review of agency documents. Knowledge, however, does not necessarily translate into action. According to one of the representatives on the EMMA Citizen Advisory Committee, "there wasn't as much discussion as you might think" about the MDC as an institution and the management of its existing infrastructure. "We spent much more time focusing on planning for the large-scale, system-wide improvements . . . as opposed to addressing current problems."[100] Other public interest groups reflected this position. However concerned they were about infrastructure problems, these groups never effectively used their voice to demand change. As for the Conservation Law Foundation (CLF), which would later play such a critical role in the harbor cleanup, prior to the Quincy suit its efforts focused on the issues of land use and offshore oil drilling, not the harbor or the sewage that flowed into it.[101] In December 1978, the Boston Harbor Association, one of the few groups that did try to focus attention on the disgraceful state of the harbor, published a report titled "Boston Harbor—An Uncertain Future." In it the group noted that *"In spite of countless studies and millions of spent dollars, little progress has been made in the water cleanup effort.* The future of boating, swimming and other recreational activities in the Harbor remains in doubt. . . . It is now clear that implementation of any solution is a long way off."[102] The Boston Harbor Association also had hosted a conference in 1975 with the evocative title "Boston Harbor . . . Who Cares?" Unfortunately, the answer was, not many people.

The stance of the average citizen and the organized citizens groups meant that there was no active, broad-based, public constituency in favor of improving the sewage infrastructure. Thus, one of the major forces behind political change—public pressure—was nowhere to be found. Elected officials did not pick up where the public left off. Rather, they chose not to give the MDC the resources necessary for proper operation and maintenance. Neither the three governors elected during the 1972–82 period nor the legislative officials fought for increasing the MDC's budget so that these problems could be adequately addressed. As Chester Atkins, former chairman of the state Senate Ways and Means Committee, noted in the early 1980s, "It is a very difficult thing to appropriate public money for the invisible infrastructure."[103] Whereas public officials often reap electoral dividends by getting highly visible public works projects off the ground, building something new, putting people to work, and pumping money into the local economy, such dividends are usually absent or, at least, much reduced when those officials support improvements in the existing infrastructure that is out of sight. As one MDC commissioner in the early 1980s noted, "Sewers do not have a built-in constituency like parks, where you see something demonstrable for what you spend, where you can sit on the swings."[104]

Thus, it is no surprise that the MDC commissioners were able to get legislative appropriations for politically popular parks, skating rinks and pools, while they were being squeezed on the sewage side of their operations.[105]

Not only was there no political payoff in funding operations and maintenance; there was an explicit disincentive. From 1972 to 1982, the ratepayers in the MDC service area paid among the lowest sewage rates in the country, and for good reason. The ratepayers were, in effect, being partially subsidized to the degree that the MDC was not spending money on properly operating and maintaining its sewage systems. If politicians significantly increased the MDC's budget, they would have had to increase assessments to the cities and towns. Increased assessments would have meant increased rates for individual users. Raising rates, like raising taxes, would have been extremely unpopular among the voters, especially since the politicians were receiving no signals from the electorate that increasing the MDC's budget was something they favored. As Douglas Foy, the executive director of the CLF, later noted, the cities and towns in the MDC's service area were "addicted to running their pipes into Boston Harbor because . . . [it was] cheap."[106]

In light of this political atmosphere, getting funding was always a struggle for the MDC. In 1980, for example, the Senate Ways and Means Committee decided to cut $1.5 million from the revolving maintenance account for Deer Island. Only after Atkins toured the plant and saw how bad things had become was the money put back. According to Barrata, "That's what it took—$1.5 million dollars, which is peanuts. If we didn't have that, we wouldn't have kept the Nordbergs running. The point is: nobody cared. Nobody was out there saying, 'I want sewerage.' . . . Let's be honest about it."[107] The MDC was also poorly equipped to fight for increased funding. It just did not have political clout. Between 1973 and 1983, ten commissioners came and went at the MDC.[108] This lack of stability and continuity hampered the MDC's ability to defend its budget requests. Before the commissioners could get up to speed on the issues and build political support, they were out the door. The MDC also continued to be perceived as a patronage dumping ground, further reducing its credibility and clout within the political establishment.[109] Yet another obstacle to properly funding the sewerage division of the MDC was Proposition 2½, which was passed by the state legislature in 1980 and capped local tax increases to 2½ percent annually. Although overriding the cap was an option, it was politically difficult. Thus, even if the state and/or the MDC had wanted to dramatically increase sewer assessments to cover the costs of properly maintaining the sewage system, the possibility of doing so became less likely after 1980.

Things could have been different if state and federal planning and decision making had taken less time and been less contentious; if Congress had created a clearer waiver provision; if the EPA had established waiver regulations and reviewed applications more quickly; if the MDC had not applied for a waiver; if sludge discharges had been addressed; if enforcement had been more effective; and if increased public and political concern had resulted in improved funding, staffing, operations, and maintenance of the MDC's sewage treatment plants. If all or even most of these actions had come to pass, Boston's sewage system would have been in better shape and Boston Harbor's waters would have been cleaner. But these things did not come to pass. As a result, the stage for the state lawsuit was set, and the judiciary was about to begin what was to become a starring role in the cleanup of Boston Harbor.

6

The "Ultimate Remedy"

With so much partially or untreated sewage going into the harbor during the early 1980s, it was no surprise that some of it was washing onto local beaches. One of those was Wollaston Beach, where William B. Golden, city solicitor for Quincy, was running on a summer's day in 1982. At some point he looked down and saw that the surface of the beach was covered in what appeared to be jellyfish. But, according to Golden, "they weren't jellyfish. They were little patties of human waste, and patches of grease."[1] He recalled that he "stood there for a moment looking down at this gelatinous mass covering my sneakers. As I realized what I had stepped in, I felt nauseated. Then I got angry."[2] That human waste and grease, he surmised, probably came from one of the MDC's sewage treatment plants. Still clad in his running clothes, Golden marched down to Quincy City Hall to speak with Mayor Francis X. McCauley about the problem on the beach. McCauley asked him, "What do you want to do about it?"[3] Golden's response came on December 17, 1982, when he filed a civil suit in state Superior Court, on behalf of Quincy, against the MDC.[4] Among the suit's claims were that the MDC had violated the conditions of its joint federal/state discharge permit by discharging partially treated and raw sewage into Boston Harbor and that the MDC had violated the state law prohibiting the discharge into coastal waters of sewage or other substances which might be injurious to public health or contaminate shellfish.

Golden and Peter Koff, an attorney hired by Golden to work on this case, had not hidden their intentions. Before filing suit, they had spoken with the EPA as well as with the recently elected Massachusetts governor, Michael Dukakis, about their planned action. Dukakis was first elected governor of the state in 1974 but then had lost his bid for reelection in 1978, only to win again in 1982. During his first term, he had focused little, if any, attention on the harbor's pollution problem. But now he argued that things would be different, and the governor, who knew Golden, was particularly interested in keeping the matter out of court. On the day before the suit was filed, Dukakis lobbied Golden against taking legal action while the two of them rode in the governor's car and talked between public appearances. Dukakis said that his new administration would make sewage treatment and cleaning up the harbor a priority.[5] Such assurances, however, were not good enough for Golden. As he later commented, "We knew that cleaning up the harbor was going to be a ten- or fifteen-year process. We wanted a court order to assure continuity for the program."[6]

Quincy invited the EPA to join as plaintiffs to no avail. According to Ralph Childs, assistant U.S. attorney representing the EPA, for the agency to become a party to a state court suit would "be inconsistent with the whole federalist system and would raise lots of difficult issues of jurisdiction. . . . We do not want to be a party in state court."[7] Although the EPA did not want to get involved in the state case, the CLF soon thereafter brought the EPA into the legal fray. On June 7, 1983, the CLF, "shocked" by the allegations in the Quincy suit, brought its own suit in federal district court against the MDC and the EPA, asking for "injunctive relief against the state and federal officials responsible for the chronic, unauthorized, and massive discharge of partially treated, often raw sewage into the Boston Harbor and its adjacent waters . . . [which is] in violation of federal law [Clean Water Act], MDC's Federal permit and even the weak administrative orders issued by EPA."[8] According to Peter Shelley, senior attorney at the CLF, "We assumed that everything was working at the sewage treatment plant, and if it wasn't, we'd be hearing a large outcry. Then, in early 1983, the Quincy suit came to our attention. The allegations were so extraordinary that we looked at federal and state files and, well, we were shocked into action. I mean, the shit was going into the ocean and no one had noticed, us included. It was the damnedest thing."[9] The CLF requested that the court establish a schedule requiring the MDC to implement a plan designed to remedy the violations of the Clean Water Act. Judge A. David Mazzone was assigned to the case.

The venue of the Quincy suit was driven by an explicitly legal strategy. As Koff noted,

> The relief we were looking for was a judicial assertion of responsibility and control over the way the MDC was operating. We thought this more likely would happen in state court rather than federal court in light of the

reluctance of some federal judges to assert themselves in control of state political institutions that weren't doing their job. . . . We just made a judgment that political institutional concern would be better dealt with in state court, where it would be a state judge dealing with a state agency, as opposed to having to deal with the question of federal intrusion coming into play.[10]

Not only did Golden and Koff want to stay in state court; they also wanted a particular judge, so they waited six months until Paul Garrity rotated into the city of Quincy's district before filing suit.[11] According to Koff, "We felt Garrity would be best because he wouldn't be afraid of asserting himself, as a judicial activist, to take over and prod the agency."[12] Certainly, Garrity's background indicated as much. Appointed to the superior court by Governor Dukakis in October 1976, Garrity, a registered Democrat who often referred to himself as "an Irish street kid," was described by one commentator as being "rumpled, walruslike behind a handlebar mustache, opinionated in a way that is more mercurial than dogmatic . . . [and having] an activist, populist attitude about government, courts, and, most of all, himself."[13] In July 1979, after finding that an earlier consent decree had failed to eliminate widespread violations of the Massachusetts Sanitary Code by the Boston Housing Authority, Garrity appointed a receiver to take over the day-to-day operations of the authority.[14] This action reflected Garrity's remedial philosophy that when other branches of government failed to carry out their legal duties, it was necessary for the court to step in to ensure that the law was upheld.

Summer Moves

In June 1983, Quincy amended its suit in a number of ways. Three parties were added as defendants—the director of the Division of Water Pollution Control, the commissioner of the Department of Environmental Quality Engineering, and the secretary of the Executive Office of Environmental Affairs. Quincy alleged that these defendants, as representative of the state agencies with the legal responsibility for enforcing state law and overseeing the MDC's operations, had failed to take action to remedy the violations of law cited in the original suit. Quincy also made its request for relief more specific by asking the court to grant preliminary injunctive relief in the form of either a moratorium on new connections to the sewage system or a system-wide reduction of two gallons of extraneous flow for every new gallon of wastewater

added. In addition, Quincy requested that the court appoint a receiver
to manage and operate, subject to court supervision, the sewage division
of the MDC.

Garrity held a hearing on Quincy's motion for a preliminary injunction in mid-June. As a result of that hearing and the submission of
plaintiff and defendant affidavits, Garrity found that

> Boston Harbor is significantly and visibly polluted primarily because of
> the discharge of inadequately treated and untreated sewage into it and
> adjoining waters. The current and potential impact of that pollution
> upon the health, welfare and safety of persons who live and work near-by
> Boston Harbor and who use it for commercial, recreational and other
> purposes is staggering. . . . Moreover, the damage to that environment
> and to the creatures who live in it may very well become irreversible
> unless measures are taken to control and at some point preclude the
> pollution and consequent destruction of that very valuable resource.[15]

Garrity determined that, as a result of such discharges, conditions of
the MDC's state/federal permit had been violated, but he failed to spec-
ify which conditions those were. For example, Quincy's complaint had
alleged violations of a variety of permit conditions, including the ones
prohibiting the exceeding of effluent limitations for various parameters,
such as biochemical oxygen demand, and prohibiting discharges that
caused visible discoloration of the receiving waters or caused state water
quality standards to be violated. Garrity's ruling gave no clue as to
which of these had occurred. Garrity also determined that there had
been violations of the state law prohibiting sewage discharges that
threatened public health and shellfish. Although Garrity implied that
the MDC was to blame for such violations, he stopped short of assign-
ing liability.

Noting that "plaintiffs must not be relegated to have rights without
a remedy," Garrity further determined that Quincy was entitled to preliminary injunctive relief. Such relief is not intended to fully remedy
legal violations. Instead, preliminary injunctions are designed to maintain the status quo until a trial on the merits of the case can be completed and liability determined, after which time more complete remedial relief can be decided on.[16] To support his contention that
preliminary injunctive relief was necessary, Garrity argued that the record gave no indication that the violations of law would cease in the near
future if the existing situation were allowed to remain unchanged. Garrity stated that the defendants had no plan in place, the implementation
of which would result in the discontinuation of raw sewage discharges

to the harbor. Furthermore, Garrity had little confidence that things would change by virtue of Governor Dukakis's recent appointment, in May 1983, of a committee, headed by former Governor Sargent, to establish a cleanup plan for the harbor.[17] The committee's mandate, Garrity contended, "appears to contemplate what committees do best, i.e., study."[18] Garrity decided to hold another hearing on July 6, at which time the parties could present their arguments as to the appropriate form of preliminary injunctive relief. Garrity indicated that he was inclined not to appoint a receiver and instead was considering appointing a special master and giving him thirty days to consult with all the parties and "come up with the most effective remedy and to prepare a comprehensive order."[19]

The state defendants, who were collectively represented by the state attorney general, expressed great concern about Garrity's findings and his tentative plan to appoint a special master. They argued, among other things, that Garrity's conclusions were based on extremely limited and, in some cases, incorrect information. Noting that the court's findings were based on only a single hearing and on "untested affidavits and colloquies with counsel," the state believed that before any remedial decisions were made it should have the opportunity to more fully explore the accuracy of the plaintiff's claims and the court's findings.[20] The state questioned the need for judicial intervention, arguing that it did have plans in place to improve the operation of the sewage system and, furthermore, that it was moving ahead with the development of more comprehensive remedies, as indicated by the governor's appointment of the special committee on Boston Harbor.

Instead of having the court devise a remedy, the state believed that it should have the opportunity to develop the political consensus necessary to draw up a schedule of remedial actions and to generate the political and financial support required to implement such a schedule. The state also worried that the court had something besides preliminary injunctive relief in mind. Garrity's inclination to appoint a special master for thirty days and to have him "prepare a comprehensive order" suggested to the state that the master's task would go beyond determining preliminary relief and instead would establish a long-term remedial regime, an approach the state felt was clearly unwarranted at this juncture in the case.[21]

Garrity discounted the state's concerns. He was especially unconvinced by the state's claim that the court should defer to the political branches of government to allow the state to reach political consensus on appropriate remedies. Garrity cited two reasons in arguing that the court could not afford to wait for the other branches to act.

> First, the history of political consensus building, leading to a rectification of the extensive pollution of Boston Harbor which has been and is permitted to continue and regrettably increase in violation of the law is bleak. That history has been characterized by commission after commission and study after study which both always fade from sight when the appropriations crunch is reached. Second, and most significantly, any effective remedy requires federal, state and local municipal cooperation which needs to be accomplished much more quickly than appears to be possible voluntarily in order to address the issues of health, welfare, safety and the environment referred to above. In sum, there is an urgency about this that the political branches of government just do not seem to be responding to appropriately considering what is occurring is, again, in violation of the law.[22]

On July 8, Garrity appointed one of his mentors, Charles M. Haar, the Louis D. Brandeis Professor of Law at Harvard Law School, as special master and gave him thirty days to hear evidence, make findings of fact, and propose injunctive relief.[23] Garrity decided that the special master was necessary for two reasons. Although he did not view the case as being scientifically complex, Garrity agreed with the plaintiffs that it posed other legal, governmental, and political complexities.[24] A legally and politically savvy special master, like Haar, could help the court develop remedies to address these issues. Garrity also believed that appointing a special master would increase the efficiency of the proceedings by enabling the court to avoid the "time consuming and obviously delay-causing evidentiary hearings [requested by the defendants] to resolve disputed issues of fact and their claim that much of Boston Harbor's pollution comes from sources beyond their control."[25] As Garrity noted later, "The special master was a very creative idea. If I had taken evidence in court, it would have taken half a year."[26]

Haar was an experienced special master who held very similar views to Garrity's on the role of courts in remedial adjudication, especially the need for the court to intervene, as the option of last resort, when the politically responsible branches fail to remedy legal violations on their own.[27] Haar's expertise is in urban policy and land and property law.[28] With the court's permission Haar appointed Steven G. Horowitz, a former student and local attorney, to assist him.[29] Haar also got permission to consult with three environmental experts and to hire research assistants.

During the next month, the special master and his staff read through numerous documents, heard the testimony of thirteen witnesses over two and a half days, consulted various experts and public officials, and toured Deer, Moon, and Nut Islands as well as Wollaston Beach, accompanied by representatives from the media, the parties to the litigation, and interested citizens. Departing from the traditional judicial inquiry process, Haar undertook, with the consent of the parties, ex parte contacts and reviewed documents not strictly introduced as evidence, although it was agreed that the master's findings were to be based solely on information introduced in the record. "The purpose of this process," according to Haar, "was to become as familiar as possible in a short time with an enormously complex and significant problem with many ramifications—environmental, social, political, economic, biological, and hygienic," and then to use that understanding to establish findings of fact and to propose remedies.[30]

Haar focused on the problems associated with Deer and Nut Islands' primary treatment plants and their failure to provide adequate treatment. He did not deal with other pollution problems such as CSOs, toxics, sludge, and the potential upgrade of the Deer Island and Nut Island plants to secondary. Haar made it clear that these issues did not fall withn the "present ambit" of the case.[31] Indeed, while the master was conducting his inquiry, the waiver issue was continuing to evolve. On June 30, 1983, the EPA tentatively denied the MDC's waiver application. Among the findings were that the MDC's proposed discharge would violate Massachusetts' water quality standards for dissolved oxygen and would interfere with the "protection and propagation of a balanced, indigenous population of shellfish, fish and wildlife."[32] During the summer of 1983, the MDC evaluated whether to take advantage of its one-time opportunity to resolve the issues that had led to the tentative denial, and to reapply. In September, after meeting with EPA officials, including EPA Administrator William Ruckelshaus, the MDC decided that the outstanding issues in its initial application could be addressed and began gathering the necessary data to do so. According to James S. Hoyte, secretary of the Massachusetts Executive Office of Environmental Affairs, the EPA officials did not discourage the MDC from reapplying.[33] On June 30, 1984, the MDC submitted its second waiver application.[34] Not until after the state court case had run its course would the EPA decide the fate of this second application.

The special master's 196-page report, presented to the court on August 9, 1983, documented the pollution problems in the harbor and the many ills that beset the MDC's sewage treatment system. The report found that "Due to the age of the plant, insufficient capacity, inadequate maintenance and breakdowns, the Nut Island Wastewater Treatment Plant is unable to treat influent sewage to meet present-day primary standards. Consequently, partially treated sewage is regularly discharged into the surrounding waters, and in wet weather, partially treated sewage flows are pumped out . . . closer to the shore."[35] Similarly, "As a result of equipment breakdowns and staff failures at Deer Island, as well as the inability of the plant to handle wet weather flows, Moon Island periodically discharges enormous volumes of untreated, raw sewage into the waters off Moon Island."[36] The report recounted one of the most frequently told stories about the failures at Deer Island. On Mother's Day 1983, a coupling split on one of the pumps. Two million gallons of raw sewage flooded the building to a height of two stories. Over the next three days, two MDC police scuba divers repeatedly dove into this horrific pool of waste to locate and repair the break. To perform this nauseating task, the divers had to literally feel their way around the building based on the guidance of MDC engineers because visibility was zero. As one of the workers at Deer Island recalled, "We were actually riding around in rowboats in the stuff, trying to get it straightened out."[37] During this incident, 153 million gallons of raw sewage were discharged to Boston Harbor via Moon Island.[38]

One of the main reasons that the plants' peak capacity was often exceeded had to do with infiltration and inflow. Infiltration is "defined as surface or ground water which enters a sewer system through defective pipes, joints, connections, and manhole walls," while inflow is "the quantity of water discharged into a sewer system from roof leaders, foundation and surface drains, streams, catch basins, tidal overflow weirs, etc."—essentially stormwater.[39] The report concluded that infiltration and inflow accounted for 50 to 60 percent of the average influent to Deer Island and 59 percent of the flow to Nut Island.[40] The master also highlighted the chronic staffing problems at the MDC, noting that "as of October, 20, 1982, 441 of the 558 authorized positions were funded to be filled in the MDC's Sewerage Division. On average, however, only 417 were actually filled that year."[41] The discharges from the sewage treatment plants were found to contribute to objectionable odors, color, and turbidity in violation of state water quality standards, as well as bacterial contamination, fin erosion in winter flounder, the closure of beaches and shellfishing areas, and alterations in the natural state of the communities of marine organisms that lived on the harbor's floor.[42] Having laid out the findings of fact, the report turned to the issue of remedies, stating that

> After reviewing the extensive record in this case, the Master is convinced
> . . . that it is both *appropriate* and *necessary* for the court to fashion judicial
> remedies to clean up the Bay and the Harbor. By *appropriate*, it is meant
> that Court is neither overstepping its authority nor improperly imping-
> ing on the prerogatives of our other two branches of government. By
> *necessary*, it is meant that, without judicial intervention, the problem in
> this case will remain with us for the foreseeable future.[43]

Haar first dismissed the plaintiff's request for a sewer moratorium, arguing that new connections to the system were not the "causes or main sources of the environmental degradation problem," and that the growth for which sewer connections were needed was an important element in the continued economic revitalization of the Boston area. "To stop all building," the master stated, "would be to cut the societal nose off to spite the face."[44] The report then went on to recommend a series of twenty-three remedial actions, along with a schedule for their completion. For example, the report recommended that the MDC de-termine acceptable infiltration/inflow rates and design and implement cost-effective infiltration/inflow control projects, and that the MDC initiate the two-for-one influent sewage reduction system that the plaintiff requested. The report also recommended that the MDC: con-tinue ongoing efforts to upgrade Nut Island; devise a plan and time schedule for completing those efforts; submit a plan outlining the im-provements needed at Deer Island to reduce the discharges of raw or partially treated sewage; and present to the court and to the legislature a plan for staffing and a supplemental budget request to cover those staffing needs.

The master argued that what was desperately needed was a long-term financial plan to ensure that the MDC would be able to fund the remedial measures called for in the master's report. To that end, the master recommended that the MDC and the state Division of Water Pollution Control hire an independent financial consultant to prepare the plan. As part of this analysis, the consultant was to evaluate the advisability of adopting a variety of measures designed to enable the MDC to carry out the tasks arrayed before it. These measures included revising the current system of charges to the MDC user communities and changing the way in which the state legislature appropriated funds for sewage treatment. The most far-reaching of those measures was to consider whether "the sewerage division of the MDC [should] be spun off and responsibility placed in an independent, autonomous, self-sustaining financial authority, with the advantages and flexibility of a public authority."[45]

Garrity enthusiastically accepted the master's report. So too did the city of Quincy, the Executive Office of Environmental Affairs, the state attorney general, and the MDC, all of whom agreed that Haar had done an excellent job in establishing findings and remedies. According to the *Boston Globe*, "virtually all experts and citizen's groups concerned with the problem of sewage pollution in Boston harbor have given kudos to the comprehensive report issued . . . [by the] special master."[46] For example, although the MDC's head engineer did not feel that the report's findings were "100 percent correct," they were, he said, "70 or 80 percent correct and that gave . . . [the report] an awful lot credibility; the experts were excellent."[47] The representative from the attorney general's office stated that the findings were "very accurate, very well done. . . . Haar recruited very good people from Harvard and MIT."[48]

As for the proposed remedies, there were equally supportive sentiments, the most important coming from the MDC, which would ultimately have the responsibility for implementing any remedial measures. Reflecting on the remedies, the assistant to the MDC commissioner stated that the agency "intends to implement the recommendations—we think they're realistic."[49] Garrity, with Quincy's support, recommended that the parties enter into a consent decree to implement the master's remedies. But although the state defendants did not challenge the appropriateness of the master's findings of fact or proposed remedies, the state had no interest in entering into a consent decree. As Steven T. Seward noted, the attorney general's office "felt that other consent decrees to which [the state] . . . was a party had led to judicial meddling."[50] This history led to the attorney general's policy of avoiding such decrees. More specifically the attorney general felt that no court order, consent decree or otherwise, was appropriate in this case. According to Assistant Attorney General Michael Sloman, "Our position to date has been that, in view of the willingness of [the] administration as a whole to address the question of pollution in the harbor, why do you also need a court order?"[51] As an alternative, the state proposed that the court retain jurisdiction in the case for six months during which time the court could measure the state defendants' performance against the master's remedies.[52] The state also implied that if the court sought to impose the master's remedies as a court order, it would appeal such a move, arguing, in part, that the extent of the remedies went well beyond what is called for in a preliminary injunction, which is intended to maintain the status quo, not establish a long-term, open-ended, remedial regime.

The state's position put Garrity in a tough spot. He could not get agreement on a consent decree. Although the court traditionally has a great deal of discretion in determining what to include in preliminary injunctions, Garrity himself thought the remedies went beyond what was called for and was concerned that an effort to unilaterally impose the remedies would likely be appealed to and overturned by a higher court.[53] There was, of course, the option of proceeding with a trial, at which time, if the defendants were found liable for the violations, the court would be in a position to order more complete injunctive relief. Both the defendants and Quincy wanted to avoid this option, however, the former because they felt it unnecessary, given their willingness to voluntarily implement the master's remedies, and the latter because of the time and cost involved in litigation.

Garrity's solution was a compromise that satisfied the plaintiffs and the defendants. On September 12, 1983, he issued a procedural order under which the parties made "a voluntary moral commitment to accept and comply with" the remedies and schedule for implementation established by the court, thereby avoiding "further adversarial litigation" and getting on with the "massive . . . effort to clean up Boston Harbor pollution and remove its causes."[54] According to Garrity, the procedural order "was the best I could do," and the plaintiff agreed.[55] As Golden recalled, "The case had the potential to burgeon with appeals and ancillary suits costing millions of dollars, and not one penny would go to clean up Boston Harbor. We wanted to find common ground that would lead to action, and keep the court involved. There's no question that the procedural order was the best we could do."[56]

The remedies in the procedural order were essentially the same ones offered by the master, with one important addition. The master's report did not address the issues of primary versus secondary treatment, CSOs, sludge, and toxics. Thus, even if the master's remedies were implemented, serious harbor pollution problems would remain.[57] Responding to expressed concerns that the scope of the relief was too narrow, Garrity added, with the parties' consent, a requirement that they develop a "supplemental schedule addressing the pollution problems of Boston Harbor at large, including Quincy and Hingham Bays, concerning such matters as combined sewer overflows, sludge management, secondary treatment, and toxic wastes."[58] Haar was appointed to monitor compliance with the procedural order.

The Procedural Order

The parties, along with representatives of the EPA, CLF, and local government, met bi-weekly to discuss progress in complying with the procedural order's list of remedies. Most of the meetings were attended by Haar, who kept Garrity updated on what was happening. By all accounts the procedural order process was frustrating. The parties felt there was little sense of direction. The EPA's general counsel noted that "it was a sort of rolling ad hoc agenda; there was no clear objective or mandate."[59] The representatives from Quincy agreed. One of the problems was that because of the voluntary nature of the order, the court could not apply sanctions if deadlines were missed. This reduced the sense of urgency among the parties to comply. Making matters worse, apparently, was Haar's acerbic style of running the meetings. According to an MDC representative, "no matter what you did and how quickly you did it, he berated you because it took so long."[60] He added, "Every two weeks it was a scolding."[61] Another observer said that "Haar acted like he thought he was running a Roman galley: if he pounded harder and shouted louder he thought the boat would move faster. But the oars weren't lined up and people rowed in seven directions at once."[62] The CLF representative felt that the entire process "was stupid. The notion that a voluntary moral commitment was going to be enough to move metropolitan Boston to do anything that cost money was just flying in the face of fifteen years of real solid history that the legislature was not going to fund the MDC at anywhere near that level that it needed to maintain and operate its facilities."[63] This lack of faith in the ability of the procedural order to produce results moved the CLF to press forward with its lawsuit in district court. On March 27, 1984, however, Judge Mazzone complied with the state's request to stay the proceedings of the CLF's case in order to let the agreement reached in the Quincy case run its course.[64]

The process did achieve some of its goals. Although deadlines were often pushed back, in the year following the signing of the order, a few of the required remedial actions were taken. For example, the MDC analyzed its staffing needs, spent millions on repairs, submitted supplemental budget requests for increased staffing and funding, held a two-day seminar on infiltration and inflow for user communities, and made plans for reducing infiltration and inflow.[65] But these steps barely began to address what needed to be done to improve the MDC's institutional capacity and to significantly reduce pollution discharges. Furthermore, there was virtually no progress in developing a supplemental schedule to address the issues of CSOs, sludge, toxics, and the ultimate level of sewage treatment. It is for these reasons that, at the October 9, 1984, First Year Compliance Hearing on the Procedural Order, Haar could report that although the defendants had complied with some of the order's remedies, the MDC sewage division was still understaffed and underfunded, the plants were still operating poorly, and the harbor was no cleaner.[66] By this time, however, little attention was being paid to the procedural order and to MDC's success or failure in complying with its requirements. All eyes were on the legislature, where bills were being considered that would establish an independent water authority to take over the sewage system from the MDC. The court had advocated the creation of such an authority ever since the signing of the procedural order.

The procedural order required the MDC to hire a consultant to evaluate various options for improving the MDC's financial health and, therefore, its ability to construct, maintain, and operate a sound sewage system. Since the consultant's plan was not due until March 1984, one might assume that the decision on which option to pursue would not be made before then. From the court's perspective, however, the decision was clear. Immediately after concluding the agreement on the procedural order, Garrity told the press that "the ultimate remedy is a separate authority that is pay-as-you-go, with bonding and enforcement authority."[67]

Haar not only agreed; it was his work on the master's report that led to this conclusion. While preparing the report, he consulted with financial experts in New York and Massachusetts. Within two weeks of beginning his job as special master, Haar was convinced that the "MDC couldn't work" and that an authority had to be created.[68] Simply stated, the MDC, as constituted and funded, was incapable of operating and maintaining its existing sewage system, much less taking on future responsibilities relating to sludge, CSOs, and the ultimate outcome of the waiver application. Garrity and Haar had little faith that Massachusetts' politicians would support the institutional modifications—such as much more funding and new hiring rules—needed to make the MDC an effective and efficient organization. The court, however, could not order the creation of an authority, which would require a legislative act.

Instead, Garrity decided to use Haar as the court's representative, informally advocating the authority option both during the procedural order meetings and in his contacts with legislators and the public. In this way, Garrity and Haar hoped they could help develop the political consensus needed to establish an authority.

In deciding to push the authority concept, the court was drawing on a veritable American tradition.[69] Since the creation of the Port Authority of New York and New Jersey in 1921, authorities have proliferated throughout the country to the point that there are now tens of thousands of them, doing everything from building highways and airports to providing water, gas, electric, and solid waste disposal services. Authorities are hybrid entities, having characteristics of both traditional government agencies and private corporations, including: independent sources of funding that are not tied to political processes and legislative control, such as the issuance of tax-exempt bonds that are paid off through the collection of permit or usage fees; the right to set user rates or permit fees; personnel hiring and pay systems that are not determined by civil service requirements, but rather are more closely tied to the methods used by the private sector; a bureaucratic structure with an appointed board of directors at its head and an executive director at the helm; and the right to own property and the right to sue and to be sued.

The theory of public authorities places great stock in the ability of such institutions to be more efficient and effective, and less subject to "political" influences, than traditional line agencies in running government programs, particularly ones involving the implementation of large-scale projects over long periods of time, requiring stable sources of funding.[70] It is the promise of efficiency, effectiveness, and autonomy, characteristics the MDC did not possess, that led Garrity and Haar to view an independent authority as the ultimate remedy.

Other Branches Consider the "Ultimate Remedy"

Political support for an independent authority came quickly. On September 16, 1983, state Senate President William Bulger created a special commission to evaluate ways to improve the MDC's water and sewer services, including the creation of an independent agency.[71] In early January 1984, the commission submitted a bill to create an independent water and sewage authority.[72] At the same time the Senate was considering the options, so too was the Dukakis administration. Dukakis was concerned about the harbor and agreed that something needed to be done to alter the status quo. Upon evaluation, the administration decided that an independent water and sewer authority was the way to go. On January 25, 1984, Hoyte announced the governor's plans to submit a bill that would create such an authority, stating that "We have concluded that the current [MDC] structure just doesn't work. . . . [An authority will mean] we will be able to run the system as a self-sustaining business, not as a bureaucracy."[73]

These political developments were the direct outgrowth of judicial intervention. The Quincy litigation, especially the master's activities, received widespread media coverage and generated significant public and political pressure to improve the area's sewage system and thereby to help clean up the harbor.[74] No longer could these problems be ignored. When politicians began exploring the alternatives for addressing the problems, the authority mechanism was high on the list, in part because Garrity's statement upon signing the procedural order, the pending financial consultant's report, and Haar's behind-the-scenes efforts had placed it there. As Garrity expected, Haar had been able to use his connections at the State House to encourage action on the authority issue. "He [Haar] was really taking the pulse of the legislature," said Garrity. "That's what he likes to do. He's a political junkie. I say that in a very admiring sense. He was trying to figure out what was possible."[75] Indeed, Haar met many times with legislative as well as executive officials and gave advice on the drafting of the bill submitted by the legislative commission.[76]

The decision on the part of the commission and the administration to propose the creation of a combined sewage and water authority was purely pragmatic. Although the Quincy litigation focused on the MDC sewage division and its myriad of operational and institutional problems, the same types of problems clearly affected the water division, though to differing degrees. Much-needed improvements to the water system were going to be expensive and would require long-term investment and excellent management skills. Thus, it made sense to move both the sewage and water divisions into a new authority, so they could both benefit from the improved institutional capacities.

History was another reason the authority mechanism was high on the list of alternative options for addressing the problems highlighted by the court. When Garrity stated that the "ultimate remedy" was a "pay-as-you-go" authority, few were surprised. It wasn't the first time that Massachusetts's politicians had discussed this option. The creation of an independent sewage authority had been considered less seriously, on and off, by government officials as far back as 1972.[77] With the litigation serving as a focusing event, however, the discussion moved from the back burner to the front. The authority concept was now on the political agenda. For an increasing number of politicians, it was an idea whose time had come.[78]

The authority approach received a strong boost on February 8, 1984, when the Bank of Boston came out with the report on financial planning required by the procedural order.[79] To provide high-quality water and sewerage services to the city and towns within the MDC service area, the bank argued, the agency must be able to raise the funds necessary to hire adequate staff, maintain and operate the plants, finance long-term capital programs, and have the ability to develop operating budgets that would be responsive to existing and future needs. Like the Senate commission and the administration, the bank found the MDC's current structure seriously inadequate for achieving these goals, stating, in part, that "the agency lacks the independent control over finances and operations which is essential for managing the enterprise in an efficient and effective manner."[80]

Not only did the report disparage the MDC as an institution and the means by which it was financed, it also argued that the institution was beyond repair—the problems were too widespread and the modifications that would be required too far-reaching to achieve political support.[81] Furthermore, the report cited structural constraints, including legal restrictions that would likely obstruct efforts to modify the MDC. For example, the limitations on increases in public authority assessments created by Proposition 2½ could restrict the MDC's ability to generate the revenue necessary to support needed operation and maintenance costs and capital projects.[82] Instead, the report recommended the creation of an independent water and sewage authority. This approach, it was argued, would result in the long-term system integrity needed to carry out the many extremely expensive and complex sewer and water projects that would have to be implemented in the coming years.[83]

The Administration's Bill and the Senate's Response

The actions of the legislature and the Dukakis administration's plans to submit its own authority bill buoyed both Garrity's and Haar's hopes that the "ultimate remedy" would become a reality. Yet, by the beginning of April little action had been taken on the commission's bill, and the administration had yet to submit its own. Haar publicly expressed his concern about this state of affairs at a Boston Citizens Seminar on April 12. "I feel a lack of progress," Haar said. "Despite the goodwill, the best efforts, the attempt to get out of the usual routine . . . there is no real sense of urgency." In response to Hoyte's statement that the administration would be filing its authority bill soon, Haar responded, with some exasperation, "My question is: where is it?" He added, "I think the plaintiffs will come back to court . . . a year has passed . . . more steps have to be taken."[84]

On April 19, Dukakis officially submitted his water and sewage authority bill to the House of Representatives. Commenting on the need for the bill, Hoyte said, "I'll give you an illustration of how bad a shape the system is in. The Smithsonian Institution in Washington has requested a massive pump in the East Boston pumping station because it may be the last of its kind. It was made in 1895. We can't donate it to them because it is in daily use."[85] The bill was drafted on a pro bono basis by the law firm of Palmer & Dodge, and drew much of its inspiration from the organizational structures of two other authorities, the Massachusetts Port Authority and the Massachusetts Bay Transportation Authority. These two authorities were hardly the only ones the administration could have used as examples; authorities are extremely common in the state. In 1989, for example, one analysis estimated that there were 506 of them.[86] Although various observers have expressed concerns about the sweeping powers of this so-called shadow government or fourth branch of government, the numbers indicate that Massachusetts's government has not been shy about going the authority route.[87]

With the introduction of the administration bill, legislative activity picked up and, as a result, Quincy did not go back to court. Instead, the plaintiffs and the court waited to see what the legislature would do. That spring there were clear signs that the harbor issue had moved higher on the legislative agenda. For example, the Senate Ways and Means Committee's proposed fiscal 1985 budget recommended only a half-year's budget for the MDC's sewer and water divisions, and included $250,000 for the MDC to use as planning and startup costs for a new authority. According to the committee chairman, Chet Atkins, this was a clear indication that the Senate leadership expected to have the new authority in operation by January 1, 1985.[88] On June 19, Dukakis told a packed hearing before the Joint Committee on Urban Affairs, "We are now faced with the reality of a harbor that is outrageously polluted. The sense of urgency is very high. We've got to act soon and we've got to act decisively." Holding aloft a jar of water from the harbor to drive home his message, Dukakis said, "This is not a urine sample, but it comes awfully close."[89] A week later, while touring Deer Island, Dukakis noted that harbor pollution had led to the closing of 2,300 acres of shellfish beds, which, if in use, could have generated $4 million for the local economy. He added that launching a new agency was "long overdue and the present bureaucratic structure simply isn't capable of handling all the demands on it. The new authority would be a far more economical and efficient way of getting the job done."[90]

A few weeks after Dukakis's impassioned speech, consideration of the various bills was put on hold as the legislature went into recess until after the September primaries.[91] While the legislature was out, the Dukakis administration continued to lobby for the creation of a water and sewage authority. Once the legislature reconvened, Bulger submitted his own authority bill, but unlike the Dukakis bill, Bulger's would create a sewage authority, leaving the water division at MDC.[92] Bulger's rationale for splitting off only the sewage division was political. The drinking water for cities and towns serviced by the MDC is piped in from the Quabbin Reservoir in the western part of the state. The area around the Quabbin is used for recreation, and western Massachusetts legislators were concerned about removing it from public control. Those same legislators were also concerned that the new authority might have the power to draw down the Quabbin and divert the Connecticut River.[93] At the same time, legislators in the greater Boston area were concerned about the possibility of water rate increases that might come out of a combined authority. Bulger felt that by leaving the water division where it was, the bill would be more "politically palatable," increasing its chances of passing.[94] He also felt that his streamlined bill might pass more quickly than the other bills being considered. "I desperately want to get this thing started," Bulger said at the time. "Polluted water is denying millions of people full use of the harbor, my constituents among them. We have to get going before the Feds reduce their contribution [of sewage construction grant money] to zero."[95] Bulger's bill passed the Senate on October 4. Commenting on Bulger's sewage-only approach, Haar said, "Either way is good. . . . a combination would be the optimum but isn't essential. . . . sewage is the issue that's concerned the court. . . . If the Bulger bill passes it would be a fine achievement by the Legislature."[96]

The Court Raises the Stakes

Despite a growing number of bills and increased legislative activity, Haar and Garrity were concerned about what they perceived to be the slow rate of movement toward the ultimate remedy. As they saw it, the court had given the politicians a year to build a consensus and to pull the various constituencies together, but the legislature still had yet to pass a bill for the governor to sign. At the October 9 compliance hearing, therefore, Garrity decided to accept Haar's recommendation that the court exert pressure on the legislature to act. Specifically, Garrity stated that if the legislature had failed to pass a sewage authority bill or a combined sewage and water authority bill by November 15, he would consider issuing a moratorium on sewer hookups and placing the MDC in receivership.[97] Clearly, Garrity preferred that the legislature act, but his experience steeled him against letting inaction go on too long. "It's a shame," he said, "that the court has to get involved in situations that are the functions of government. But I probably made a terrible mistake in waiting four years with the Boston Housing Authority before I took it over. We have to make a fresh start, and it has to be made in the next month or so. This case is my highest priority, and I won't leave it."[98]

Ever since the Quincy suit had raised the MDC's and the Harbor's problems to a high place on the public agenda, a political consensus in support of a sewage authority had been building. By the fall of 1984, that consensus was both broad and deep. It included the administration and a majority of legislators on Beacon Hill, along with the head of the MDC urging the diminution of his own agency.[99] Some argued that this desire to create a new authority was a symptom of a larger political disease. It would be just another example of Massachusetts's government failing to face up to its responsibilities and, instead, passing a problem to the "fourth branch of government."[100] As Robert Turner, a *Boston Globe* columnist remarked at the time, "Once again the politicians are trying to give some faceless 'authority' with little accountability a job they should be doing themselves."[101] Despite the argument that the administration and the legislature should have worked harder to modify the MDC rather than create an authority, there were two powerful arguments against modification that, in turn, cemented the political consensus on the need for an authority.

As the Bank of Boston report made clear, the authority mechanism was likely to be an effective and efficient means of overcoming the institutional and financial problems of the MDC and implementing necessary short- and long-term cleanup efforts. Indeed, there were numerous examples in Massachusetts and throughout the country of successful authorities delivering a variety of public services. Thus, the politicians supporting the authority concept could claim, with some conviction, that their solution was not one of shirking responsibility but rather a sound and responsible reaction to a serious problem. It made no difference that the problem was largely of the politicians' making. The issue was "what do we do know?"

However much politicians wanted to paint their support of the authority concept as being based primarily on the institution's virtues, there was a less discussed but more persuasive reason that such support ran high—the politicians did not want to be held directly accountable by the voters for the huge increases in sewer rates that would undoubtedly be necessary to bring the MDC's sewage system into compliance with state and federal law. Everyone knew that the costs of compliance would be enormous, whether the waiver was ultimately denied. For example, at the same time the Dukakis administration announced its plans to create a sewage and water authority, the MDC Sewer Division director, Noel Barrata, stated that necessary improvements to the MDC sewage system would cost between $1.2 and $1.6 billion dollars (1983), and could reach $2 billion accounting for inflation.[102]

Although there were hopes that a significant percentage of the cost would be borne by the federal government, the most recent amendments to the Clean Water Act had slashed the federal share to 55 percent, and there were strong signs that the next round of amendments would see that share go lower or disappear altogether.[103] This meant that much if not all of the costs would have to be paid by local governments and the state, and ultimately would be reflected in higher sewer rates. If the MDC were modified so that it could be properly funded, yet remained under the control of the administration and the legislature, the voters would perceive the politicians as being responsible for rising rates. Given the huge rate hikes that were anticipated, such perceptions might be enough to drive politicians out of office. By creating an authority, the politicians could displace the voters' wrath. After all, it would be the authority, not the politicians, that raised rates. Specious though this argument was, it was likely to be effective.

Politicians, of course, weren't the only supporters of the sewage authority concept by this time. Added to the ranks were the city of Quincy, many environmental and citizens groups, and area media, including the *Boston Globe*. With such widespread support for a sewage authority, why hadn't an authority bill already been passed by the legislature and signed into law by the governor? The reason hinges on the difference between a concept and its implementation. Although by late 1984 virtually no voices argued against the need for an independent sewage authority, there was significant disagreement over how the authority should be structured. Issues that needed resolution before any bill could make it out of the legislature included specifics on the composition of the board of directors and thus the balance of power at the authority, the exact method of funding and how the costs would be allocated among users, management rights, and the extent of police powers. Further complicating the debate was the question of water. Should the authority take over the sewer division's responsibilities or both the sewage and the water divisions? Many of those who supported the creation of an independent sewage authority also wanted to include water; but some didn't, especially western legislators concerned about control over their region's water supply.

The November 15 deadline came and went with no appreciable action. Haar recommended that the court give the legislature five more working days to pass an authority bill, and if the legislators failed to act, receivership proceedings should commence. Haar said, "Judge Garrity cannot afford to wait any longer. The long-promised deadline for action has arrived. . . . The administration and the legislature have had ample time to study the . . . legislation, to air their differences and to negotiate an acceptable compromise. I can assure you that Judge Garrity, however reluctant, is prepared to act."[104] On this point, Haar had no doubt. When Haar made these statements at a citizens seminar, he knew that Garrity would act because Garrity had approved Haar's remarks. Calling the harbor "unsafe, unsanitary, indecent, in violation of the law and a danger to the health and welfare of the people," Garrity issued another ultimatum.[105] The parties to the suit were to report back to him on legislative progress on November 29, at 2 P.M. If the legislature had failed to create a sewage authority or a combined water and sewage authority by that time, or if "there is no hope" of a bill passing, Garrity would begin a receivership trial. While reiterating his reluctance to place the MDC in receivership, adding that receivership is an "inappropriate remedy. . . . [t]he only way is to go through the political branches," Garrity made it clear that he was willing to go this route if no action was forthcoming.[106]

Garrity was not the only one who wanted to avoid receivership. A spokesman for the Dukakis administration stated, "Receivership is something we want to avoid at all costs. . . . [W]e are confident that because of the progress, and the commitment of House Speaker Thomas McGee and Senate President William M. Bulger to take legislative action . . . receivership will not be the ultimate outcome."[107] Similarly, Representative John F. Cusack, an author of one of the pending bills, stated that "We are extremely close to working out a version of the water and sewer bill. It will absolutely not come to [receivership]."[108]

Garrity's deadline did not leave much time. Although the Senate had passed its bill, the House had yet to act, and then there would have to be a House-Senate conference to hammer out the likely differences between the bills. Nevertheless, the House was close, though not "extremely close," to working out a bill of its own.[109] Any thoughts of meeting the November 29 deadline vanished on November 28, however, when the chairman of the House Ways and Means Committee, Representative Michael Creedon, postponed committee action on a new authority, stating that "I have a belief about court orders, I ignore them."[110] In addition to disliking court orders, Creedon decided to postpone action because of his concerns about the authority's potential control over the development in the Quabbin region. Creedon's decision to postpone action, however, was not supported by the majority of representatives, who believed that the House should have already passed a bill. According to Representative Steven Pierce, "we should have the bill out here now. Creedon is way off base on this one." Representative John Flood added, "We have to address this question, regardless of Judge Garrity. It is absolutely of paramount importance that we stop fouling the harbor."[111]

Garrity did not ignore the deadline. He was visibly angered by the legislature's inaction, and on November 29 he issued an injunction imposing a moratorium on all commercial sewer hookups and scheduled the receivership trial to begin the next week.[112] The court's rationale behind halting sewer hookups was that each one would just increase the amount of illegal pollution. Garrity acknowledged that the sewer ban was a "draconian" measure, but he added that it was spurred by his desire to place "people over polluters."[113] Garrity reiterated the court's preference to avoid receivership, stating that he would "back off with pleasure" once the legislature acted. But he warned that if forced to appoint a receiver, he would not relinquish the court's control of the cleanup for several years.[114] Garrity's move mobilized the business community, as he hoped it would.[115] The president of the Greater Boston Chamber of Commerce estimated that the moratorium could affect

$2.3 billion of future construction in Boston alone, and the moratorium had the immediate impact of halting roughly $150 million worth of projects already under way.[116] As Peter Shelley recalled, the developers "swarmed Beacon Hill," generating pressure on the legislature to pass a bill so the judge would lift the moratorium.[117]

Garrity thought the moratorium would do the trick. "The word I got," Garrity said, "was, they caved. They'll adopt the Water Resources Authority."[118] The moratorium, however, was short-lived. The state's attorney general appealed it and, on December 5, Massachusetts Supreme Court Justice Joseph R. Noland overturned it without comment.[119] Garrity fumed, stating later, "He just blew off the moratorium, for no reason at all. I thought, God, we've lost it. If he'd kept it even for two more days, the bill would have passed."[120] Shortly after Noland's decision, the House voted 92 to 52 to postpone a scheduled debate on the authority bill. According to Representative Cusack, the Supreme Court decision "took the pressure off the legislators."[121] But the showdown was far from over. A couple of hours after Noland's decision, the EPA's Region 1 administrator, Michael Deland, announced that in January his agency was going to sue the MDC in U.S. District Court in order to place the harbor cleanup under federal supervision. Deland added that, if the legislature had not acted to create a sewer authority by then, he would ask the district court judge to impose a moratorium on hookups, labeling that "an entirely appropriate remedy."[122] In later years, Deland would state that threatening the moratorium was "one of the moves of which I am most proud . . . [although I had] absolutely no idea on what basis we might do that if indeed we had to."[123]

Garrity was undaunted by the Supreme Court's decision and happy to have the EPA's support. On December 6 Garrity moved forward with the receivership trial and, on December 7 he threatened a new ban on commercial sewer hookups.[124] The next day, Garrity posed for an exceptionally unusual photograph that had him standing in his judicial robes, arms crossed, wearing a serious countenance, with the harbor and the Boston skyline at his back.[125] The photograph first ran in the *Washington Post* on December 9, then was reprinted, with accompanying articles, in the *Boston Globe* later that week.[126] According to Garrity, the photograph was "totally unplanned."

> The reporter from the *Post* called and asked me to pick him up at the airport and I said fine. I used to keep a robe in the trunk. I picked him up and he said let's go take a look at the water from the east Boston side. He said would you mind putting on the robe and I'll take a photograph of you out on one of these piers. He took the photograph. It was in the

paper Monday morning and I almost shit a brick. It just totally happened that way.[127]

It is hard to imagine what Garrity thought the photographer was going to do with the picture if not put it in the paper. Nevertheless, this very public stance reflected a relatively recent change in Garrity's involvement in the case. Ever since he had decided to turn up the heat on the legislature in October, Garrity had been making numerous public statements to the media about his feelings on the legislature's progress or lack thereof. The photograph was just another public statement, albeit pictorial rather than verbal. This change in behavior was a break from Garrity's earlier decision to let Haar be the court's point man outside the courtroom. It was, however, a natural outgrowth of Garrity's judicial philosophy. "It's absolutely essential," he said, "to win the hearts and minds of the local media, both print and electronic, in order to deal effectively with the organizations that are involved in a particular case. A front-page horror story will position a judge in his or her reaction to the parties in that particular case on that particular day."[128] Another time, Garrity added, "It is regrettable in terms of the vitality of democratic institutions that a judge has to kick ass to get the political branch to do what is in the public interest."[129]

The receivership trial, the threatened moratorium, the EPA's response, and the public reaction to Garrity's public statements and actions all combined to place extreme pressure on the legislature. The House resumed debate on December 10, and Garrity stayed the moratorium for "24 to 48" hours to give the legislature time to act; he also asked Haar to stay on Beacon Hill to answer legislators' questions. As would be expected with such a complex and important bill, amendments were being offered left and right—more than fifty in total. At one point, the House minority leader, William G. Robinson, referred to the MDC as a "sick cow" and argued that it should be "beefed up" with the passage of a new authority bill.[130] Viewing the proceedings, Haar commented, "It's time we stopped fighting each other and started fighting pollution."[131] It took two days to debate the proposed changes, and on December 12 the House passed its water and sewer authority bill by a vote of 133 to 12.[132]

As the House was passing its bill, Garrity stepped up his highly visible efforts to generate public support for the authority bills wending their way through the legislative process. On the day of the House vote, he led reporters on a tour of Deer Island, greeting the plant's supervisor with a jocular "Hi, I'm the sludge judge, thanks for laying this on."[133]

That night, Garrity appeared on a local TV news show alongside Representative Creedon to discuss the case. Garrity told the anchor what everybody already knew, that he was planning to leave the bench at the conclusion of the case.

Resolution

The House-Senate conference committee began hammering out a compromise bill immediately after the House action. The biggest point of disagreement centered on whether the authority would have both sewage and water responsibilities. Senate President Bulger, who, in an unusual move, appointed himself to the conference committee, argued for keeping the water division in the MDC. "I agree reluctantly that an authority is necessary but it should be limited to what has to be done right now," Bulger said. "There is no question that water is a serious concern but the question is do we have to do it now?"[134] House members speaking before the committee disagreed, arguing, among other things, that "if we just do sewers" the bill would not pass, that "we are fast approaching the same problems with water as we now have with sewers," and, furthermore, that expanding a sewer authority to include water would be difficult at a later date.[135] Before the conference committee could iron out its differences, the House speaker announced plans to recess for Christmas, leaving the fate of the bill undecided. Garrity immediately responded by upping the ante. If the legislature did not have an authority bill on the governor's desk for signature by December 20, Garrity would place the MDC in receivership. In making this ultimatum, Garrity stated, "I am not frustrated but I am concerned as a citizen that the harbor has become more polluted during these proceedings. The sad part is that the focus has been on what occurs politically and not on the continued pollution of the harbor. I'm not in a confrontation with them [the legislature]. They have to do their legislative thing and I have to do my judicial thing."[136]

Of course, Garrity's distinction was more apparent than real. He was in confrontation with the legislature, using the court's powers, such as threatening sanctions, to prod that branch into action. While the House went into recess, the conference committee continued meeting. In light of Garrity's threat, Bulger said, "We have been working at the task of performing our constitutional function here. The court must do what it must do."[137] On December 17, a compromise was reached that would create a combined water and sewage authority. House arguments in favor of combining sewage and water into a single authority won the day. Dukakis stated, "I'm very pleased with the progress that has been made."[138] Garrity expressed cautious optimism. "Since a bill has not yet passed . . . it would be improper for me to comment on an event that has not yet taken place. I have said all along, though, that if a legislative and political solution is reached by the Legislature, then these proceedings would stop in their tracks."[139]

In the early morning hours of December 18, the negotiations almost broke down. According to Representative Cusak, the primary reason was staff exhaustion. "People have been working around the clock," he said. "They were exhausted and were trying to define language. After a while nobody knew what anybody was talking about."[140] But later that day, the conference committee members met again and hammered out a conceptual agreement on the outlines of the new authority, and left their beleaguered staff to work out the details. Finally, at 1 A.M. on December 19, the conference committee agreed on the working of the compromise bill. Later that day, the House reconvened to vote on the conference committee's bill. Representative Cusak urged his peers to vote yes. "We are putting before the House a fine piece of legislation," he said. "We all know the problems we have had since the 1982 suit by the City of Quincy. It is imperative that Boston Harbor be cleaned up. Even though we have dealt under a crisis situation, we have taken a giant step in deciding how—important our water resources are."[141] The vote was 120 to 11 in favor. The Senate followed suit with a vote of 29 to 1. On witnessing the votes, Garrity said, "It may be a bit injudicious but . . . whoopee!" Calling it "one of the most far-reaching and important pieces of environmental legislation in this state in the last century," Dukakis signed the bill into law on December 19, creating the Massachusetts Water Resources Authority (MWRA). At the same time, he noted that the MWRA was only a "first step, just a beginning in the larger effort to clean up the harbor." Haar observed, "This is no time to coast. Passage of the legislation is a wonderful step, but we should keep in mind that while we speak, the harbor continues to be polluted."[142]

The MWRA was structured like many other authorities. Unlike the MDC, the MWRA had the ability to raise money by issuing tax-exempt municipal bonds, which were paid off through the collection of sewage and water payments from user communities; the right to set rates; personnel hiring and pay systems that were not determined by state civil service requirements; and an organizational structure with a board of directors at the top and an executive director who handled day-to-day operations. The board had eleven members who were intended to represent a broad range of the constituencies that had a stake in the authority's activities. The chairman was the state's secretary of environmental affairs. There were four gubernatorial appointees: one each to represent the Connecticut River and Merrimack River watersheds, and one each from two of the communities that would be most impacted by the MWRA's activities, Quincy and Winthrop. Three members were to be appointed by the mayor of Boston, and three other members were to be appointed by the MWRA advisory board. The MWRA's enabling statute also mandated the composition of the advisory board. It included the chief elected official, or that person's designated representative, from each of the sixty cities and towns serviced by the MWRA, as well as a member from the Metropolitan Area Planning Council and six gubernatorial appointees. The advisory board was to review and comment on the authority budgets and policies, but did not have veto power over those. It also was to serve as a conduit between the authority and the affected communities on issues including the funding and construction of sewerage projects.

Not everyone praised the new law or the way it passed. Representative John McNeil offered the following analysis.

> Many believe the MDC has taken a bum rap. There are some good people there. We have had the judge tell us of impending doom over the harbor. This has not been a glamour issue. It was not a top priority of the Governor who served for six of the last ten years. . . . We're throwing out the baby with the bath water. This could have been done through the MDC. Instead we are creating another giant bureaucracy to suck taxpayer money dry. We know the MDC could have done the job and receivership would have been preferable to this.[143]

Representative Royall Switzer added, "A Superior Court judge forced us into action on a bill which may be a bad idea. . . . We have created something that may come back to haunt us—all because of a publicity-seeking judge."[144]

The Judge Steps Down

Garrity had vowed to stay with case until it was resolved one way or another—by the creation of a new authority or the placing of the MDC in receivership. Now that the ultimate remedy was in place, Garrity stepped down from the bench to enter private practice.[145] At a retire-

ment party for the judge, he and Deland spoke about the legal whirl-
wind that had recently enveloped them. According to Deland, Garrity
said, "Mike, you saved my ass," and Deland responded, "I'm pleased,
but I was trying to save Boston Harbor."[146] Most observers agreed that
Garrity, with key assistance from Haar, was a driving force behind the
creation of the MWRA. The efficacy of the court's actions is reflected
in the comments of various participants in the process. According to
Koff, "There is no question in my mind that without Garrity's involvement and the pressure the court placed on the legislature the authority
would not have been created. It would not have happened voluntarily."[147] A key staff member in the state House of Representatives stated
that "the judge shook a lot of people up. The creation of the authority
might not have happened without the court bringing pressure to
bear."[148] Shelley added that "the MWRA was created at the end of a
gun. It wasn't a free political act. Haar decided that this is what needed
to be done; Garrity cocked the trigger and pulled it a couple of times
and got everyone so gun-shy that they decided to create the authority."[149] And according to an EPA lawyer, Fowley, "Garrity was the right
person, in the right place, at the right time."[150]

Garrity has argued that "the sine qua non for a judge is not to be
political but to be a good politician, and you have to walk that fine line
between blowing your legitimacy as a judge and being political enough
to affect the environment in which the organization exists."[151] In the
Quincy case, at times Garrity clearly stepped over the line. His actions
in the fall and winter of 1984 provide the most significant examples of
judicially unorthodox behavior. Although Garrity stayed in the background during much of the case, letting Haar serve as the court's advocate for institutional change, as soon as the court began applying more
pressure in late 1984, Garrity came out of the courtroom and into the
public eye with increasing frequency. It is during this period that he
posed for a *Washington Post* photographer at the edge of the harbor and
often spoke to the media about the case. These efforts to galvanize
public opinion and to pressure the legislature into taking action violated
the judicial cannon of legitimacy that states that judges are not supposed
to publicly comment on pending cases. Beyond that, such actions also
positioned the court, and specifically the judge, in the role of political
actor as opposed to impartial arbiter of the law.

The questionable nature of Garrity's public actions is confirmed by
the reactions of members of the legal and political communities. Many
area lawyers were "stunned" by the photograph, finding it an inappro-

priate judicial action.[152] House Speaker McGee, reflecting on Garrity's image in the picture, said, "I don't know if he is going to come up here in his robes to tell us what to do, but I think he's a lunatic." After meeting Garrity for the first time, shortly after making that comment, McGee said, "Well, I guess you don't look as though you ought to be locked up."[153] As for Garrity's broader media campaign, one lawyer commented, "I have a problem with a judge who is using publicity to put pressure on the legislature to act. You're not supposed to use publicity to determine what happens in the courtroom."[154] Indeed, even Haar felt that Garrity had "overstepped judicial bounds" in taking the public actions he did.[155]

Most telling, however, are Garrity's own reflections on his behavior.

> My being ready to step down affected my decision to go to the people. I was interviewed a lot on television. I figured, what I'm doing now ultimately the Supreme Judicial Court is going to have my head if I'm still a judge, but I'm not going to be a judge anymore. I planned to get off by the end of the year or as soon as the legislation was adopted. I did a lot of reasonably risky things that I never would have done had I had an interest in staying on the court, because you're not supposed to talk about a pending case with the media if you're a sitting judge, and that was a pending case. Once I left the bench, the Supreme Judicial Court had no interest in going after me, especially because of the results.[156]

Garrity said that, while the case was ongoing, nobody told him he was stepping over the line. "It wouldn't have done any good anyway," he added, "because I was pretty sure I was going to be able to achieve what I wanted to achieve." With respect to the photograph, Garrity said it "was totally fortuitous. If I had it to do over again, I probably would because I think it galvanized a lot of things. [Other lawyers] trashed me and they were probably right."[157] And, although Haar had some misgivings about some of Garrity's public acts, he had no qualms about the broader trajectory of the case and its results. Nearly two decades after Garrity stepped down from the bench, Haar said, "This case shows that when the political system is frozen, you need a judge to step in and move the other branches of government." He added, "It's a rare case of an environmental triumph. Quite often, environmentalists don't have the resources or the legal talent to win. Sometimes they do, but mostly it's a story of big business prevailing."[158]

Although Garrity and Haar deserve much of the credit for their roles in creating the MWRA, it is important to place the role of the court in the proper context. The court's ability to successfully pressure the politicians to act was, in part, due to the way in which the authority concept was received by the administration, the legislature, and the public. Although the court clearly helped to raise consideration of the authority concept on the political agenda, once it was raised both the administration and the majority of legislators embraced it. This occurred prior to the fall of 1984, when the court began seriously pressuring the legislature to act. It was not simply a case of those political actors deciding that they had to support the creation of an authority because the court said they did. Rather, they had evaluated the alternatives, not only because of the court's urging, and found the authority mechanism to be the most attractive one. The politicians were well aware of the costs entailed in upgrading the sewage system, and they had no interest in being held accountable to ratepayers/voters for those rising costs. The authority mechanism provided an alternative with a proven record of performance, in Massachusetts and elsewhere. The antiauthority sentiment that would characterize state politics in later years was not yet in evidence.[159]

The court's ability to pressure the politicians into passing the authority bill also was due, in part, to the nature of the legal violations uncovered and pending litigation. The permit, conditions of which had been violated, had been issued jointly by the state and federal governments in accord with both the Massachusetts Clean Waters Act and the federal Clean Water Act. Therefore, the requirements of the permit could not be erased by state legislative action alone. The politicians had to find a way to comply with the law because the option of changing state law so as to remove the need to resolve the violations was not available. The pending federal court case, lodged by the CLF, combined with the EPA's threat to file suit against the state, only added to the pressure on the politicians to figure out a way to create the institutional means necessary to comply with the law.

In his last act as judge, Garrity ordered court supervision of the MWRA's efforts to address the area's sewage problems and appointed Haar as court monitor.[160] Although this arrangement was to continue for three years, there were already clear indications that the legal wrangling over Boston Harbor was far from over. The CLF was intent on having District Court Judge Mazzone lift the stay on its lawsuit, and the EPA was planning a federal lawsuit of its own. Thus, as Garrity left the bench for the private sector, the next round in the saga of the cleanup of Boston Harbor was about to begin.

7

Enter the Federal Court

The lawsuit that the EPA's Region 1 had promised in December 1984 became a reality on January 31, 1985, when the agency brought a civil action in Massachusetts District Court against the MDC, the MWRA (as a successor agency to the MDC), the Commonwealth of Massachusetts, and the Boston Water and Sewer Commission, requesting "injunctive relief and civil penalties for repeated and continuing violations of the Clean Water Act . . . which have resulted in the unlawful discharge of massive quantities of raw and partially treated sewage and other pollutants into Boston Harbor and its adjacent waters." The agency wanted the court, among other things, to order the MWRA to submit plans and schedules for coming into compliance with the Clean Water Act and for the court, in turn, to approve those plans and schedules and to ensure that they were implemented.[1] This lawsuit was strongly supported by Mike Deland, the regional administrator. Deland had become a lawyer in Region 1 in 1971, and by 1973 was in charge of enforcement, a job he left in 1976 to do private consulting.[2] In 1983 Ronald Reagan appointed William Ruckelshaus as EPA administrator to replace Anne Burford and to repair the damaged agency she had left in her wake. Ruckelshaus, in turn, quickly appointed Deland, a well-respected administrator, to head up Region 1. Ever since taking office as regional administrator on June 30, 1983, Deland had made the cleanup of Boston Harbor one of his top priorities.[3] According to Deland, there were two reasons he felt so strongly about this problem.

> First, it was clear to me that the EPA should have filed a suit about Boston Harbor years ago. I mean, I was embarrassed. When I returned in 1983, I found that the EPA had made little, if any, progress on the harbor since 1976, when I left. I was amazed, to put it mildly. The agency should have long since been the plaintiff in this case. I also recognized

that the EPA itself was in a deplorable state, racked by the scandal of the Burford days. I needed a visible cause to rally people, and Boston Harbor was a natural.[4]

Another motivation for the lawsuit was the belief that the ongoing state case was severely limited in its ability to move the long-delayed cleanup process forward. According to Deland:

[The state proceeding] is an insufficient substitute for enforcement of federal requirements through this federal court action. The Quincy proceeding was instrumental in obtaining the establishment of the new Massachusetts Water Resources Authority (MWRA). The Procedural Orders entered therein, however, have not provided the binding commitments or long-term assurance of compliance sought through this action. In particular, there is no mechanism in the Quincy proceeding for the EPA to obtain resolution on issues about which defendants and it disagree and no way for EPA to seek sanctions or other relief when voluntary orders are violated. . . .

EPA is not satisfied with the slow pace that has characterized the Boston Harbor cleanup. While secondary treatment plants are in operation or under construction in virtually every other major metropolitan area has yet to begin construction of even modern primary treatment plants. Moreover, the MDC continues to discharge unlawfully into Boston Harbor each day the sludge collected by its treatment plants, with no date set as to when this will stop. Such sludge discharges have been stopped in every other major metropolitan area in the country, except Los Angeles, which is under federal court order to cease its sludge discharges. In my opinion, the MDC system currently is the worst violator of the Clean Water Act in New England and one of the worst in the country.[5]

Deland's concerns about the state proceedings were well-founded. Garrity's departure from the bench took away the driving force behind the court's involvement. The case was placed in the hands of Chief Judge Thomas R. Morse Jr., who had neither Garrity's grasp of the issues nor his intense commitment to the case. There were also indications that Morse was beginning to become incapacitated by the illness that would soon end his life.[6]

Of course, Haar was still involved in the case, providing an intellectual and institutional bridge between the past and the present. But the value of such a bridge is predicated on the potential for the voluntary moral commitment among the parties to progress beyond discussing and planning to making the hard decisions and implementing plans. The EPA did not believe that potential was there. The procedural order had faltered during Garrity's tenure, and there were reasons to believe it would continue to do so without his presence, despite the entry of a new and more powerful player, the MWRA. According to Fowley, the lead EPA lawyer on the Boston Harbor case at the time,

> Even with the best of intentions, the MWRA would be subject to a lot of the same political pressure and a lot of the same constraints as the state, and you needed cooperation from lots of other people. We were convinced you needed a combination of the MWRA and the court order to do the trick. The state case worked great in terms of laying the ground-work for creating the MWRA, but it did not work great in terms of actual follow-through and getting things done.[7]

Not only did the EPA look disparagingly on the implementation value of the procedural order, but it also presented federal court involvement as an enforcement tool with a proven track record. For example, Deland noted that:

> Resorting to the federal courts for enforcement of the Clean Water Act has, in EPA's experience, typically been an appropriate and required step to obtain speedy compliance with federal law. Federal lawsuits by EPA have helped speed progress in New York City, Philadelphia, Washington, D.C., and Providence, Rhode Island, among many other examples. The filing of these lawsuits [which led to consent decrees being signed] has not ended cooperation between EPA and the defendants in those actions. Rather, it has helped ensure that cooperative efforts lead to firm decisions and real progress rather than the stalling, indecision, and continuous studies which have characterized the Boston Harbor cleanup effort until now.[8]

The CLF agreed with the EPA on the need for federal court involvement in this case, and the environmental group was pleased to drop the EPA as a defendant in its lawsuit and, in effect, join forces with the agency in its efforts to move the harbor cleanup forward.[9] Fearing that a continuation of the procedural order would go nowhere, the CLF asked District Court Judge Mazzone to lift the stay on its case.

Here, the environmental group ran into opposition. The state argued that the case should remain in the state court system and that the MWRA be given a chance to prove that it was not only willing but also able to move forward, under the auspices of the procedural order in a way that would ensure quick and effective compliance with the Clean Water Act.[10] After all, the reasoning went, because the authority was designed to solve the institutional problems that plagued the MDC, should it not be given a chance? Since it was not until July 1, 1985, that the MWRA would assume "ownership, possession, and control" of the water and sewerage system formerly run by the MDC, should judgment not be postponed to a later date so that the MWRA could be judged on its own merits? As Hoyte had said when the EPA first raised the specter of a federal court case, "I think the new authority ought to have a chance to get up and running first. We've been working well with the EPA and I know Deland is concerned with having a mechanism in place to make sure that what's on paper actually happens but I'd like to avoid court-ordered supervision."[11] The state used the same argument in its request to Mazzone that he place a stay on the EPA's suit.[12]

Mazzone agreed with the EPA that "time was of the essence" and that further delay would result in additional environmental harm. He also believed that the non-enforceable "voluntary agreement" developed through the state process had been relatively unsuccessful in moving the cleanup forward.[13] Part of the problem, as he saw it, was that the EPA, which had an integral role to play in the cleanup, was not an official party. As for the notion of giving the MWRA a chance to succeed on its own, Mazzone felt that although the authority had significant powers it would still face many serious obstacles that could stand in the way of complying with the law. Those obstacles included the need to dramatically raise rates, which could lead to a political backlash, and public opposition to the siting of sewage-related facilities.

Every day that passed, the Clean Water Act was being violated, and Mazzone "couldn't ignore that any longer based only on a promise of good faith."[14] Once liability was determined, the court would be able to more effectively use its powers, such as sanctions, to enforce compliance. As a result, on May 22, 1985, Mazzone lifted the stay on the CLF suit, denied the stay on the EPA suit, consolidated the two suits, and granted Quincy the right to intervene. (On July 10, the town of Winthrop was allowed to intervene.)[15] This joined four parties, along with the commonwealth and the Boston Water and Sewer Commission, in a single action in federal court. Deland was delighted. "Another big step forward in the cleanup of Boston Harbor. We now have an entity which has jurisdiction over all the parties, EPA included."[16]

President Jimmy Carter had appointed Mazzone to the federal bench in 1978.[17] Prior to his appointment he was an associate justice of the Massachusetts Superior Court, an assistant district attorney and an assistant United States attorney, and a partner in a private law firm. Mazzone was a well-liked judge, and many litigants said they enjoyed appearing before him. One lawyer said that "he's a wonderful judge. . . . compassionate, thoughtful, flexible—yet firm . . . a sensible sort of judge you can reason with."[18] Like Garrity, Mazzone was a generalist. His experience in environmental cases was limited to two decisions concerning oil drilling and leasing off George's Bank, and a case on mercury in swordfish.[19] His self-described approach to remedial adjudication was straightforward, pragmatic, and traditional. "In all of these cases, I step in and say: why? And then I judge what should be done."[20] He added, "I make decisions based on the facts and law and nothing else, not personal philosophy or political considerations, except those that flow from the statute being enforced."[21]

The Decision

The court heard oral arguments on the consolidated cases on August 8, 1985.[22] Mazzone handed down his decision on September 5, 1985.[23] He began the document with a description of what the legal fight was all about.

> At the heart of this case lies a fifty square mile expanse of water known as Boston Harbor. It is the largest harbor serving a major city on the East Coast, and is of unique historical, natural, and recreational significance. It was the site of the Boston Tea Party shortly before the birth of this Nation; it was the home for much of the fledgling Nation's merchant marine; it has always been the home port for what is now the oldest ship still commissioned in the United States Navy whose copper fittings were hammered by Paul Revere. Today, it serves millions of citizens who swim, sail, and fish in and around the Harbor. It boasts 15 virtually undeveloped islands; thousands of acres of marshes, tidelands, and fishbeds; and many beaches, rivers, and inlets. The Harbor is used by the largest tankers and container ships as well as the smallest pleasure boats. The importance of this precious natural resource has been recognized by parties on both sides of this lawsuit.[24]

Mazzone determined that the MDC had violated the Clean Water Act by failing to comply with the requirements specified in its permit requiring the Deer Island and Nut Island plants to achieve effluent levels based on secondary treatment. He also found the MDC to be violating permit conditions requiring both plants to cease discharging sludge into marine waters. Finally, Mazzone found the MWRA "liable for the MDC's acts because it is basically a continuation of the MDC." Because of this liability, the MWRA was responsible for remedying the violations to the Clean Water Act that the decision cited. The purpose of the decision was to determine liability, not to establish remedies. Nevertheless, in his concluding statement, Mazzone offered insight into his thoughts about the proper role of the court in formulating remedies and ensuring compliance with them.

> The task the MWRA has been assigned is complex and politically sensitive. It will entail many unpopular decisions. We are all aware that sewage treatment plants are expensive; that they are complicated and time-consuming to construct; and that they will not be welcome neighbors. The MWRA will be in a better position to cope with these problems than the MDC. It is certainly in a better position than any court to make decisions about the myriad of details that will arise during the course of the cleanup effort. . . . The purpose of these proceedings is to ensure that the MWRA fulfills the mission entrusted to it by the state legislature. Delay in this mission only enlarges the problem and means even more expensive and prolonged effort. If the MWRA acts expeditiously, it need not concern itself with interference from this Court. . . . At the same time, this Court was invited into this litigation only when voluntary efforts proved ineffective. The plaintiffs have now proven a violation of a federally protected right, and this Court must protect that right if the entity entrusted by the state to do so should falter in its task. This is not to say that it should be solely a state effort. Despite its present posture as a plaintiff the EPA, as its name indicates, is an environmental protection agency and its duty is to cooperate in and ensure the expeditious design, funding, and construction of the necessary facilities. Fulfillment of this duty will assure that the Harbor will remain a vital economic and esthetic resource.[25]

The Dukakis administration, of course, had the option of appealing Mazzone's decision, but did not. Dukakis strongly believed that it was time to move ahead and to start cleaning up the harbor. As Mazzone recalled, hearing that there would be no appeal was "music" to his ears.[26]

Deferring to the Parties

Mazzone first asked the parties to formulate remedies. Immediately after the September 5 ruling the parties began their negotiations; in early October Mazzone noted the progress being made and decided to give the parties until December 2 to come up with a schedule for both short-term and long-term remedial measures that could be entered as an order of the court.[27] The parties reacted quite favorably to the court's remedial posture. According to Hoyte, "We're heartened that the judge understands that we as the authority are in the best position to get the job of cleaning up the harbor done. He makes it clear that he expects the court to restrain itself from getting directly involved as long as he sees the authority moving ahead." Deland added that "if at any point the cleanup schedule breaks down, there is now a concerned judge who is ready to move and has the legal authority to move." And CLF's Shelley noted that Mazzone was "flashing a strong signal that as long as the authority does its job, it will be given lots of rope. But, once they start to slip, he's going to yank the rope and impose whatever penalties are necessary."[28]

The content and scope of these negotiations was greatly affected by MWRA decisions made shortly before and shortly after Mazzone's September 5 decision. On July 10, 1985, the MWRA board tentatively selected Deer Island as the preferred site for new sewage treatment facilities. In accord with earlier EPA and MDC siting studies, this decision assumed that the sewage flows going to Nut Island would be routed to Deer Island via an under-the-harbor tunnel and, further, that the treated wastewater would be discharged through an outfall tunnel with a terminus in Massachusetts Bay.[29] The board deserved a lot of credit for making this difficult decision, but it got a gentle push from the EPA. Throughout the tenure of the procedural order and even before the state court case began, there had been a history of delayed decisionmaking and missed deadlines for all sorts of reviews and projects. The EPA was concerned that the newly constituted MWRA board might let things slip again and possibly initiate its own sewage treatment plant siting process, rather than build on the years of siting studies already completed. Wanting to avoid this outcome, Deland met with the board and strongly urged its members to make the siting decision by July.

The MWRA board's choice of Deer Island as the preferred alternative still had to go through various environmental impact reviews before the siting decision would be final, and just like all the earlier debates that had swirled around sewage facility siting decisions, the debate surrounding this choice was loud and passionate. The people of Winthrop, the town that abutted Deer Island, were particularly upset with the siting decision, and they made their feelings known. Some expressed concerns that the new sewage treatment facilities would give off odors and would add to the noise in the community. Some worried that the added truck traffic during construction would cause congestion and would ruin roads. Others voiced concern that the new facility would be visually unattractive and would degrade the aesthetics of the area. Still others worried that promises made by the MWRA and other parties regarding mitigation packages for Winthrop, to offset the negative impacts of the new facility, would remain promises and would have no real effect. The MWRA and the EPA took these concerns into account during their deliberations over the siting choice, and stressed that the mitigation measures would not be dismissed or forgotten.[30] In the end, the EPA supported the MWRA's preferred alternative of siting the new facility on Deer Island, and in early 1986 the MWRA board officially chose that alternative.

Picking a site for a new facility was one thing, but knowing what to build was another. On July 10, when the MWRA board had tentatively selected Deer Island as the location for the new sewage treatment facilities, there was still some question as to whether those facilities would include secondary treatment. In late March 1985, the EPA had denied the MDC's second waiver application, but at the time of the July 10 vote the board had yet to decide whether it would exercise its option to appeal the denial.[31] On September 17, the board decided not to appeal, stating that "We take this step to illustrate our profound desire to get on with the business of cleaning up the harbor. Further legal entanglements could well have delayed progress for an additional five years or more. Such a delay is intolerable."[32] According to Phil Shapiro, the authority's director of finance and development and interim executive director at the time, "The reason we pulled the waiver was not because of the scientific evidence, but it was because of the political atmosphere. We could have been on the defensive . . . fighting this thing in court and having the whole thing bogged down, or we could get about the business of designing a plant and being an aggressive environmental agency."[33] Both of these crucial decisions—the siting on Deer Island and the nature of the facility—left the parties with a clearer sense of what they were negotiating about.

The parties continued to meet weekly throughout October and November to hammer out an agreement.[34] On December 2, the MWRA, the EPA, and the CLF each submitted a project schedule. Although there was substantial agreement among the parties as to short-term remedial measures, there was little agreement on long-term measures.[35] Mazzone was thus placed in the position of having to decide how to proceed in the face of conflicting recommendations from the parties.

On December 23, he made his decision and established a "schedule of interim steps to be taken by the MWRA to help achieve and maintain compliance with the requirements of the Act."[36] In so doing, Mazzone found "that there is a need for expedition to resolve the ongoing discharges of sludge and inadequately treated sewage into Boston Harbor and that an interim order is necessary to ensure that initial steps are undertaken expeditiously to address these discharges."

The interim steps focused on the first few years of the project, generally corresponding with the suggestions of the EPA and accelerating some of the deadlines recommended by the MWRA.[37] The judge presented no rationale for choosing the deadlines he did, and none of the parties questioned his choice. Most of the deadlines in the interim schedule required the MWRA to either continue planning efforts that it had inherited from the MDC, or begin developing new plans so that the legally required facilities could be built. For example, the court ordered the MWRA to complete the final facilities plan for the secondary treatment plant by September 1987. It also ordered the authority to develop plans that would ultimately enable it to cease discharging sludge into the harbor. The latter planning effort required the authority to decide, among other things, how to dewater the sludge and what type of land-based facility to build, such as incinerator or landfill, to treat the sludge.

Mazzone decided to give the parties more time to establish a long-term schedule. He ordered the parties to continue their negotiations and set a deadline, February 17, 1986, for them to report back to the court on their progress in reaching agreement on a variety of issues, including commencement and completion dates for the construction of the new primary and secondary treatment plants, the under-the-harbor tunnel, and the outfall tunnel into Massachusetts Bay.

Negotiating the Long-Term Schedule for Secondary Treatment

Throughout January and early February 1986, the parties continued negotiating over the elements of a long-term schedule. One unifying feature of the negotiations was the use of the "critical path method" (CPM) as a means for assessing schedule milestones. The CPM, applied by MWRA's engineering consulting firm, Camp, Dresser & McKee, relied on computer-generated flowcharts to schedule the sequencing of the numerous tasks required to complete the harbor cleanup project in the shortest amount of time. It showed which tasks could be pursued concurrently, those that had to be undertaken sequentially, and in what order. The parties used the CPM as the common referent, or yardstick, in evaluating the schedules they each supported. Although the CPM provided a common analytical tool, the parties differed in their assumptions concerning the sequencing and duration of the required tasks.[38] As a result, on the February 17 deadline set by Mazzone, major areas of disagreement still existed. For example, the CLF proposed a schedule under which the MWRA would complete construction of secondary treatment by 1996.[39] The MWRA urged the adoption of a schedule that would see the secondary plants completed by 2000 and operational by early 2002.[40] The EPA argued that secondary facilities could be completed by early 1998 and promised the court a specific long-term schedule by mid-March.[41] When the EPA submitted its proposed schedule, it called for the secondary plant to be built by the fourth quarter of 1997.[42] The differences among the parties focused not only on the date for constructing the secondary plant, but also on the dates for completion of the new primary plant and the various tunnels associated with the project. For example, the CLF schedule called for the simultaneous construction of the primary and secondary plants; the EPA allowed for some overlap in construction; and the MWRA urged sequenced construction, with the primary plant being built first, followed by secondary.

Mazzone, concerned about the prospects for continued delay, scheduled an evidentiary hearing to resolve the factual issues that the parties had raised. The hearing was postponed at the request of the EPA and the MWRA, which noted that they had reached some agreement on long-term dates and argued that if they were given two more weeks to negotiate, the need for an evidentiary hearing might disappear or, at least, the issues needing resolution at the hearing could be narrowed. In place of the hearing, Mazzone called a conference of the parties at which time they expressed the desire to continue working toward consensus. Mazzone gave them until April 18 to reach agreement and let them know that if no agreement were reached, an evidentiary hearing would be held April 22.[43]

During that two-week period the parties met numerous times and the differences among them were somewhat narrowed. For example, the MWRA and the EPA agreed on the dates for completion of the under-the-harbor tunnel and the commencement of primary treatment construction.[44] And the MWRA, the commonwealth, the Boston Water and Sewer Commission, the city of Quincy, and the town of Winthrop all agreed to support a modification of the earlier MWRA schedule that would have the secondary plant on-line in 1999.[45] Although differences were narrowed, they were far from eliminated, however. The parties had gone as far as they were willing to go to reach agreement, leaving the ultimate decision-making authority with the court.

Mazzone held evidentiary hearings on May 1 and 2, at which time the parties were allowed to present expert testimony and their arguments for and against the adoption of various long-term deadlines. The focus of the hearing was on establishing the start and finish dates for facilities planning, site access, site development, primary plant construction, under-harbor tunnel construction, new outfall construction, and secondary plant construction.[46] Through submissions to the court, including many affidavits by various experts, as well as the testimony presented in court, each party did its best to convince Mazzone why its preferred schedule was the most reasonable and should therefore be adopted. In pushing for the 1996 deadline for the construction of the secondary treatment plant, the CLF argued that its schedule, requiring completely overlapping construction of the primary and secondary plants, was technically feasible.[47] From the CLF's perspective, both the EPA's and, to a greater extent, the MWRA's schedules were too conservative and would allow the degradation of the harbor to continue too long. The EPA also felt that the MWRA schedule was too conservative, but believed that having the primary and secondary plants built entirely at the same time was not wise technically. Instead, the EPA's schedule would allow for some overlap in construction of the two facilities as well as a shortening of the time needed to build the primary plant.[48]

The MWRA argued against both the EPA's and the CLF's schedules. Building the secondary plant before 1999 would be technically unsound, according to the MWRA.[49] Shortening the schedule by overlapping the construction of primary and secondary plants would likely lead to unsafe and congested engineering conditions and added noise pollution and other inconveniences with which Winthrop would have to contend.[50] Furthermore, hasty construction would probably result in a poorly designed and constructed plant that would have a higher likelihood of operational and maintenance difficulties and continuing pollution problems. Saving time at the expense of building right was not worth it.[51]

The MWRA's concern about the shorter schedules went beyond technical to financial feasibility. The authority argued that the shorter schedules would result in significant increases in project costs, which would have to be borne by the ratepayers. And given the likely technical problems associated with shorter schedules, those ratepayers would be in the position of paying more for a less reliable plant. The MWRA's financial advisor contended that the CLF schedule would increase the sewer rate and revenue requirements by roughly $760 million as compared with the costs of the authority's schedule.[52] EPA and CLF experts contested the MWRA's claims about the financial impacts of the various schedules.[53]

The Judge Decides

Mazzone was faced with a difficult task. Having heard all the testimony and read all the submissions, he now had to set the long-term deadlines. As Mazzone stated in his May 8, 1986, Long Term Scheduling Order,

> long term dates are essential to the successful clean up of Boston Harbor. Although my initial scheduling order in this case was entered a mere five months ago, it is already clear that specific dates must be established for each major step of this long and complex construction project. The parties must be held to a clear, understandable, and rational schedule. The Court and the public must be able to hold specific individuals and agencies responsible for accomplishing specific tasks within given time periods. . . . Despite the negotiations between the parties in the last few weeks, and their agreement on certain dates, they have been unable to present to the Court a jointly proposed schedule of specific long term dates for the construction of the new treatment plants and related facilities. This Court has jurisdiction to protect the cleanliness of the Harbor and the safety of the citizens who enjoy and use that Harbor, even in the absence of an agreed schedule. Thus, given that the establishment of long term target dates is essential to the cleanup of the Harbor, I must set such dates at this time.[54]

Mazzone decided to adopt the MWRA's proposed schedule, which included initiating construction of the new primary treatment plant by December 1990; commencing operation of that plant by July 1995; completing construction of outfall by July 1994; initiating construction of secondary during 1995; and completing secondary during 1999. Mazzone's decision turned on his evaluation of the evidence presented by the parties.

On financial matters, Mazzone discounted the validity of the findings of Mark Ferber, the MWRA's expert, and sided with the conclusions of the EPA's expert, John Petersen, which were, in turn, supported by the CLF's expert. Mazzone disputed Ferber's contention that the shorter schedules would result in massive increases in project cost. In support of this view, Mazzone pointed to the Petersen affidavit that clearly showed, based on the MWRA's own data, that more than 50 percent of increased costs were "attributable to operation and maintenance costs arising from earlier completion of the project. Earlier completion means earlier compliance."[55] The claim that costs necessary to comply with the law should be used as an argument against early compliance simply fell of its own weight.

As for the MWRA's claims that adoption of the EPA's schedule would result in a 20 percent reduction of federal funding, Mazzone agreed with Petersen, who noted that the amount of federal dollars potentially available under any of the schedules was too uncertain to support the MWRA's contention. Finally, Mazzone used the Petersen affidavit as well as the one submitted by the CLF's financial expert to refute the MWRA's claim that the authority would find it more difficult to float the bonds necessary for construction under the EPA's or the CLF's scheduling scenario. Although Mazzone questioned Petersen's assumption that there would be no difference in capital costs between the three proposed schedules, he was not "presented with sufficient evidence to the contrary to disbelieve him." Given the available information, Mazzone dismissed the determinacy of the financial issue, stating that "the differences in cost associated with the different target completion dates are insufficient to affect my decision as to the appropriate long term construction dates."[56]

On the issues pertaining to construction timelines, Mazzone reviewed the backgrounds and findings of the EPA's, the CLF's, and the MWRA's construction and engineering experts. Mazzone was clearly most impressed by the MWRA's expert, Richard D. Fox. According to Mazzone,

> [Fox] was clearly a qualified expert. Mr. Fox has had extensive, direct contact with many large wastewater treatment plants. . . . Mr. Fox was clearly better qualified and more familiar with the intricacies of the existing construction schedule than any other expert at the hearing. He explained satisfactorily to the Court why the dangers of accelerated construction could outweigh the benefits to be gained by the advancement of two years over the EPA's schedule, and several years over the schedule of the CLF. Further, while I am somewhat curious about the recent advancement in the MWRA's proposed target dates, I nonetheless find

that the MWRA has made very substantial efforts to show that it intends to complete the project at hand in as expeditious a manner as it believes consistent with good engineering practice. . . .

Mr. Fox persuasively pointed out the flaws in . . . [EPA's schedule], and I am forced to accept his opinion. I must also agree with Mr. Fox that the schedule proposed by CLF must be rejected. . . . I agree with Mr. Fox that an overly compressed construction schedule will result in the long run in a plant that is less reliable and, consequently, expensive to maintain. This community has long suffered the effects of living with an unreliable sewage treatment system. Despite my inclination to expedite the process, I cannot avoid the more convincing evidence and impose a schedule that may haunt the citizens of the Commonwealth for the next fifty years or more.[57]

In adopting the MWRA's schedule, Mazzone noted that its deadlines were target dates that could and, most likely, would be altered as planning progressed to take into account changing circumstances and opportunities.

The complexities of the construction project before the Court are vast in scope. There will, of course, be instances in which various specific deadlines will have to be altered due to circumstances unforeseeable at the moment. There will also be occasions on which specific tasks can be completed more quickly than currently anticipated. Therefore, these target dates will be subject to review at the end of facilities planning. Nonetheless, target deadlines create a framework within which the parties may work together to accomplish the common goal. I also do not underestimate the importance of giving the citizens of this commonwealth a public assurance that Boston Harbor will be cleaned up within a defined period of time.[58]

Although Mazzone's long-term scheduling decision was based primarily on his evaluation of the weight of evidence presented, he was also fully aware of, and partially influenced by, the implementation benefits associated with giving the MWRA the schedule it requested. The authority now could not blame the court for forcing it into doing something it felt was unreasonable. The defense that "it's not our plan" would be unavailable and, therefore, the authority would have a greater incentive to comply. As Mazzone saw it, "They have only themselves to blame if they can't comply."[59]

8

"A World-Class Project"

All of the various projects outlined in the court's long-term scheduling order became known simply as the Boston Harbor Project (BHP). Over the next fourteen years, under the watchful eye of the court, the project moved from concept to reality. The official groundbreaking for the BHP took place on August 10, 1988, when those gathered at Deer Island watched enormous cranes bite into the earth and lift large mounds of dirt skyward. "This is a glorious day for Boston Harbor," said the MWRA's executive director, Paul Levy. "For the first time in 150 years, actions are being taken to clean rather than dirty this valued body of water." Boston's mayor, Ray Flynn, looked down the road, arguing that the cleanup would "mean new recreational opportunities for the young and poor and the needy . . . for kids who don't have the money to go to Kennebunkport or Cape Cod." Governor Dukakis added, "If ever there was a day to be on Boston Harbor, this is it. We are making one of our most important investments in the future of the harbor, of metropolitan Boston and the future, really, of New England."[1]

Given the turbulent history surrounding the harbor, it was only fitting that at this moment of intense optimism, a political storm was brewing. At the time, Dukakis was the Democratic nominee for the presidency, and his opponent was Vice President George H. W. Bush. Dukakis touted his environmental record, and Bush used Boston Harbor as a battering ram to demolish Dukakis's claims to the pro-environmental mantle. On the day of the groundbreaking, Bush's campaign manager, Lee Atwater, said, "If it takes the governor of Massachusetts 11 years to clean up his own harbor, Americans must question his commitment to the even-larger environmental questions which face our nation."[2] Less than a month later, Bush went on the attack during a boat tour his campaign staged in the harbor. Speaking to the assembled reporters and observers, Bush stated, "My opponent has said he will do for America what he has done for Massachusetts. That's why I fear for my country." Later, Bush referred to a meter at the New England Aquarium that measured discharges to the harbor. "That sewage meter," Bush argued, "is a measure of the cost of my opponent's neglect of the environment. While Michael Dukakis delayed, the harbor got dirtier and dirtier."[3]

As is too often the case in political campaigns, the truth was a casualty. Of course, Dukakis, as governor of Massachusetts during some of the years when the MDC and the harbor were in their worst shape, could have done more to turn the situation around. But his actions or lack thereof were certainly not the only or even the main reasons that the harbor had descended to its pitiful state. There was plenty of blame to go around, and that extended to other governors, state politicians, state agencies, including the MDC and the Executive Office of Environmental Affairs, the EPA, environmental organizations, and the public. Furthermore, once the court cases got going, the Dukakis administration worked hard to establish the MWRA and to ensure that the cleanup project got off to a good start.[4]

The arguments over who was to blame for the state of Boston Harbor died down once Dukakis lost his bid for the presidency; however, the cleanup of the harbor had only just begun. The BHP's official end came on September 6, 2000, a bright and glorious late summer's day. At 11:45, with hundreds of dignitaries, special guests, and workers looking on, the gates that fed sewage to the old Deer Island outfall pipe were shut. At that instant, for the first time since the early years of Boston's existence, the bulk of the city's sewage ceased being discharged directly into the harbor. Within twenty minutes, treated wastewater was flowing into the new outfall pipe that would take it nine and a half miles out into Massachusetts Bay. Richard Kotelly, former deputy director at the EPA's Region 1, marveled at the accomplishment. "It's amazing to say there is no more discharge [of sewage] into Boston Harbor," he said. "It's been five years since I retired, but this is one day I couldn't miss." Deland summed up the general feeling of all those on hand, stating, "This is a wonderful, momentous day for Boston, for the Commonwealth, and for the country."[5] A few days later, the *Boston Globe* reflected on this achievement. "The region now has a multidimensional asset of enormous practical, scientific, and aesthetic value that will benefit generations to come. Its worth cannot be overestimated."[6] The success of the BHP is a fascinating story from numerous perspectives.

Building the Plant and Treating the Sewage

The BHP is an engineering marvel. Every day, an average of 390 million gallons of raw sewage from over 2 million people, in 43 communities, as well as from 5,550 businesses and industrial sites travels through 5,400 miles of local sewers, 228 miles of MWRA interceptor sewers, and four large tunnels on its way to the secondary sewage treatment plant at Deer Island, which has a maximum capacity of 1.27 billion gallons per day, making it the second largest sewage treatment plant in the United States, after Detroit's.[7] The sewage from the 21 communities in the southern sewer system first arrives at the Nut Island headworks, where it receives preliminary treatment as it passes through screens and grit chambers to remove large objects, gravel, and sand. The old Nut Island sewage treatment plant is gone, a beautiful park that the residents of Quincy and beyond can enjoy has replaced it. After receiving preliminary treatment at the Nut Island headworks, the sewage from the southern system is transported through a 260-foot-deep shaft to a 4.8-mile-long, 11.5-foot-wide inter-island tunnel that connects the Nut Island headworks to the Deer Island sewage treatment plant. It took millions of dollars of geotechnical studies, including over 26 unique test drills, to determine the tunnel's path. The findings of these studies were not encouraging. The tunnel would have to go through considerable areas of fractured rock where significant inflow of water could be expected. In order to avoid one particularly troublesome geological pocket, the tunnel's design included a slight dogleg.[8]

The tunneling began at Deer Island, where a 292-foot shaft was dug straight down. The reason that this shaft was deeper than the 260-foot one it would connect to at Nut Island had to do with grade. Underground tunnels are bored on an uphill grade so that any water that seeps in will flow to the lowest point, away from the area of active tunneling, where it can be removed by large sump pumps.[9] If you tipped the tunnel in the other direction, the workers might need scuba gear to do their job. Tunneling is hard and dangerous work that relies on a combination of blasting, rock excavation using picks, shovels, and hand drills that can weight 135 pounds each, and, most important, the brute power of a tunnel boring machine (TBM). The TBM used on the inter-island

tunnel measured 13.8 feet in diameter. Its blunt, rotating, cutting face
was dotted with sharp-edged, nickel-alloy disks that could bore into
solid rocks at a pace of up to 15 feet per hour.[10] The workers who lead
such tunneling effort are affectionately called sandhogs, or hogs for
short, a name that dates back to the late nineteenth century, when it
was used to identify tunnelers in New York City who, by virtue of the
local geology, spent a lot of their time and effort tunneling through
sand. Sandhogs are a unique breed, and they take great pride in their
work. As one of the sandhogs working on the BHP commented, "We're
the guys that slay the dragon."[11]

The sandhogs worked around the clock, cycling through three eight-
hour shifts. Unfortunately, they encountered problems near the dogleg.
About 300 feet below the harbor's floor and 3.5 miles from the shaft on
Deer Island, the TBM hit a patch of soft ground that collapsed, immo-
bilizing the machine. The sandhogs and the engineers were able to get
the TBM through this 600-foot-long patch of unstable ground, but it
took eight months and cost in excess of $20 million.[12] And that wasn't
the end of the problems. Water, a particularly unwelcome intruder,
especially with so much electrical equipment in use, constantly leaked
into the tunnel, at one point reaching the torrential rate of 5,700 gallons
per minute. Then, on June 15, 1994, a massive fire broke out in the
tunnel, forcing the emergency evacuation of 40 workers through a 42-
inch ventilation shaft on Long Island. That nobody was killed or seriously injured during the accident was a testament to the quick thinking
of those who responded and the skills they had learned while rehearsing
emergency drills. The fire halted construction for 84 days, but once the
sandhogs got back in they kept on digging. The excavation was completed on November 4, 1995, when the TBM punched a hole through
the final section of rock at the Nut Island end of the tunnel. "It was,"
said one of the sandhogs, "like winning the pennant."[13] The tunnel was
then lined and opened for service in 1998.

While the sewage from the 21 communities to the south makes it
way through the inter-island tunnel, the sewage from the 22 communities of the northern sewer system gets to the Deer Island plant
through three other large underground tunnels. The next step is getting
all of the influent sewage, from the north and the south, up to the Deer
Island plant, a feat that is accomplished by 24 massive pumps that raise
the sewage roughly 150 feet. After pumping, the sewage moves through
grit chambers that remove sand and gravel that is, in turn, disposed of
at an off-island landfill. Then the sewage goes on to the new primary

treatment facility, which bears no resemblance to the dilapidated primary plant it replaced. The primary facility is state-of-the-art, as are all of the other parts of the new sewage treatment facility, and contains 48 concrete settling tanks called clarifiers, which use the force of gravity to separate out sludge and scum. Each of these clarifiers is 186 feet long, 41 feet wide, and 40 feet deep. The size of the clarifiers posed an engineering problem—namely, how they could be built so that they conserved one of the most critical resources on Deer Island, space. The answer was to stack them, two deep. This technique originated in land-poor Japan, and the Deer Island plant is only the second facility in the United States to use it.[14] The stacked clarifiers take up 30 acres, whereas a more conventional, side-by-side design would have needed 70.[15] Despite its relatively compact size, Deer Island's installation of stacked clarifiers is the largest in the world. The construction of the primary facility was an all the more impressive accomplishment because it had to be built next to the old primary plant that operated up until the moment that the new plant could take over, at which point the old plant was demolished.

By the time the sewage exits the new primary facility, roughly 50 to 60 percent of the total suspended solids and 50 percent of the toxic contaminants have been removed.[16] The next stop for the sewage is the secondary treatment facility, which is composed of three batteries that mix, react, and clarify the waste. Here, a pure-oxygen-activated sludge system relies on the work of microorganisms to further purify the wastewater through the consumption of organic matter. To supply the secondary plant with a continuous supply of pure oxygen, at a rate of 100 tons per day, the MWRA built a cryogenic facility on-site that manufactures the gas. The large amounts of sludge and scum produced by the secondary plant are collected and sent to massive centrifuges to be thickened, a process that is made more efficient by the addition of polymers. Once the thickening process is complete, the secondary sludge meets up with the sludge and scum generated by the primary plant, which has also been thickened by centrifuges. Then, the sewage moves along to the "eggs."

The twelve enormous anaerobic egg-shaped digesters, each 130 feet tall, 90 feet wide, and weighing in at 720 tons, are the most distinctive features on Deer Island. Whether seen from an airplane flying into or out of Boston's Logan International Airport, or from the land or water, the eggs command attention. They are so unusual and alien in shape and size that it does not take much imagination to view them as the spawn of enormous extraterrestrial life forms or, perhaps, discarded landing pods from outer space. Despite being visually arresting, the eggs perform rather mundane, yet essential, service. They act like your digestive system, but instead of breaking down food they break down sludge and scum into carbon dioxide, methane gas, water, and solid organic byproducts. Over the course of fifteen to twenty days, the eggs, which are heated to 95 degrees Fahrenheit, continually mix the sludge, killing bacteria, and reducing the sludge's volume by as much as 50 percent. Although only a few U.S. cities use eggs, they are fairly common in Europe and Japan. They are more energy efficient and require less maintenance than traditional "pancake" digester tanks, and perhaps most important, they take up only half the space of traditional designs.[17] Getting the massive eggs into place was a Herculean task, ably assisted by the services of a 300-foot-tall Lampson crane that is capable of lifting a staggering 1,200 tons.

The methane produced by the eggs goes to an on-site power generating facility, thereby reducing the need to purchase electricity from off-site and saving $900,000 per year. Sludge is the largest byproduct of the egg digesters and it is transported by barge, five times a week, with 700,000 gallons per transit, from Deer Island to the sludge processing facility at Fore River Shipyard in Quincy. (One day the sludge will be sent through pipes in the inter-island tunnel.) The centrifuges are the first stop at the facility, and they turn the soupy sludge, which is 95 percent water, into a cake that is 70 to 75 percent water. The cake moves on conveyor belts into the rotating, high-temperature dryers that transform it into small pellets that are roughly 60 percent organic matter.

The New England Fertilizer Company, under contract with the MWRA, operates the sludge processing facility. Fertilizer production has grown considerably over the years. In 1993, nearly 9,000 dry tons of pellets were produced; in 2001, the number topped 34,000. The disposition of the pellets has also varied over time. In the early years, because of various problems, including pellet quality concerns, and construction, maintenance, and operations shutdowns, significant quantities of fertilizer had to be shipped to a landfill in Utah at prices approaching $100 per ton. Today, none of the fertilizer goes to a landfill. Two to 4 percent of the annual production of pellets is distributed by the MWRA as Bay State Fertilizer. In 1994, when Bay State Fertilizer was first produced, all of it was given away to MWRA communities as a means of introducing the product. In 2001, roughly 60 percent of the

Bay State Fertilizer was given away, for use on public lands, including ball fields, golf courses, and parks, the balance was sold to customers such as garden centers and landscapers. As for the rest of the pellets, New England Fertilizer Company is contractually obligated to get rid of them, and it does so by selling them to fertilizer blenders as far away as Virginia, Florida, and Colorado, which, in turn, sell their product to farmers.

In the late 1800s, when Boston built the main drainage, the engineers for the project had briefly considered making money from using sewage as a fertilizer, but quickly determined that such an operation would lose rather than make money. That is still the case today. According to Richard Mills, director of residuals management at the MWRA, "production of pelletized product has never been, and will never be, a profit generating undertaking. It is produced as a means to recycle material and reduce disposal costs."[18] Indeed, the cost of pelletizing and marketing the fertilizer is significantly less than the cost of shipping it to a landfill. And the value of not having sludge going into Boston Harbor is immeasurable. The production of fertilizer from MWRA sludge, however, has not been without controversy. Although the pellets meet all federal standards for unrestricted use as a fertilizer, and have only occasionally exceeded state standards for the heavy metal molybdenum, some environmental and community groups continue to raise concerns about the use of the fertilizer in public areas and on agricultural lands.[19] A July 2002 report by the National Research Council raised questions about the adequacy of the EPA's standards governing the use of treated sewage sludge as a fertilizer, and urged the agency to update those standards and to further study the possible link between treated sewage sludge and human health.[20]

While the sludge is being digested and pelletized, the watery secondary effluent follows a different path. First the wastewater flows into two 500-foot-long disinfection basins, each of which can hold up to 4 million gallons, where sodium hypochlorite is added to kill the bacteria. Then sodium bisulfite is added for dechlorination, an essential step because if chlorine levels are too high the effluent can harm marine life in and around the point of discharge. The effluent's long journey begins with a 400-foot drop to the base of the outfall tunnel, and then it travels through the tunnel for 9.5 miles into Massachusetts Bay. The tunnel is largest single entry and exit tunnel in the world, most of it was drilled by a gargantuan TBM that is 27 feet in diameter and weighs 720 tons. The TBM had to be lowered down the 400-foot shaft piece by piece and assembled in place. The tunnel is composed of two parts. The outfall tunnel proper runs for 43,000 feet, at which point it connects to the diffuser portion of the tunnel, which runs 6,600 feet farther. Aligned along the path of the diffuser tunnel at 125-foot intervals are 55 30-inch-diameter discharge riser pipes, each one of which extends 250 feet from the tunnel to the floor of the bay, roughly 100 feet below sea level. Perched atop each riser pipe is a 60-ton, conical, concrete and fiberglass diffuser cap with eight exit ports.[21] The treated effluent from Deer Island flows from the tunnel to the riser pipes and into the bay through these multiple diffusers and ports in an effort to maximize dilution and to minimize the impact on the ecosystem.

Installing the riser pipes for the diffuser system required eighteen months and the assistance of a four-legged, 3,500-ton, jack-up barge that resembled an offshore drilling platform. The work went on twenty-four hours a day, six days a week. Each forty-person shift was transported to the site on a five-passenger helicopter that took off from a parking lot on Long Island and spent five minutes in the air.[22] Getting the riser pipes in place was a huge task but only part of the job. The risers still had to be connected to the tunnel. Using sophisticated surveying and positioning instruments, the tunnelers had to locate the bottom ends of each of the riser pipes, and in between the outer edge of the tunnel and the pipes lay 24 feet of solid rock. To help the tunnelers figure out when they hit the spot, each of the riser pipes was filled with 8,000 gallons of water colored with green fluorescein dye. In January 1995, the tunnelers knew they had successfully connected to the first riser pipe when a green fountain erupted from the exploratory hole, a scene that was repeated fifty-four more times.[23]

Although the construction of the outfall tunnel was a stunning success, it was tinged with great sadness. Three workers lost their lives as the result of accidents. In 1992, a tunnel worker was crushed to death when a concrete manhole fell from a crane. The two other deaths occurred just as the tunnel was nearing the completion in the summer of 1999. After the tunnel and the risers were connected, safety plugs were bolted in place as a precaution against flooding should an anchor or some other disturbance damage the diffuser caps. Once the tunnel was ready for operation, the final construction task was to remove the safety plugs so that the treated effluent could flow up the risers and out the diffuser caps into Massachusetts Bay. Because the ventilation system had been removed, the specially trained five-man team tasked with taking off the safety plugs had to do so using a supplied-air breathing system that was transported to the worksite by a Humvee. While three team members worked on the plugs, the two others, whose job was to monitor the air supplies, remained with the vehicle. The first three plugs came off with no problem, but while work was progressing on the fourth plug the breathing system supplying the two men in the Humvee failed. When the workers outside the tunnel could not reach those two on the radio, they got concerned and asked the other three to check on the situation. The three rushed back to the truck and found that their coworkers had lost consciousness and could not be revived. It took two hours to drive through knee-deep water back to the base of the 400-foot shaft on Deer Island, where emergency crews were waiting with a cage to transport the stricken workers out of the tunnel to helicopters and on to local hospitals. One of the emergency personnel on the scene said, "We've had missions in that hole before, but nothing like this. This is not a call we get every day. It's hard to describe, but while you're in the middle of it, you do everything you can to save someone." This time, unfortunately, everything was not enough. The two workers were already in cardiac arrest when they were pulled from the shaft and were pronounced dead on arrival at the hospitals. After the accident, the MWRA's executive director, Douglas B. MacDonald, said, "We're all in a state of shock here. It is really devastating for everyone connected with this project. We have lost two workers today, and we still have a challenge of finishing this project. But people do fly in airplanes again, and we will fly again, too."[24]

This tragic accident halted work on the tunnel for a year, while the construction team figured out how best to proceed. The key obstacle was getting breathable air into the tunnel. The solution was very creative and used the services of the same jack-up barge that had originally placed the risers in the seabed. The barge was positioned over one the risers from which a safety plug had been removed, and then a 84-inch-wide cofferdam was extended from the deck of the barge to the diffuser cap and attached to the cap with special seals. After water was pumped out of the cofferdam and the diffuser cap was opened, a ventilation pipe was connected to the cap. With the help of a large fan, fresh air was sucked down the 400-foot Deer Island shaft and throughout the entire length of the tunnel, finally exiting out the end of the ventilation pipe on the jack-up barge. Soon thereafter, workers went back into the tunnel and completed the removal of the safety plugs in a couple of days.[25] With that, the last major element of the Boston Harbor Project became operational.

Considering the facility's many massive and complicated working parts, one might assume that an army of workers would be needed to keep the Deer Island facility working properly. But instead of an army, only about 350 people work on the island at any one time. Walking through the facility can be a little like entering a ghost town. In building after building, through long corridors and cavernous halls one's only company might be the whirring engines and pumps, and pipes and containers of various sizes. Outside the buildings, too, near the disinfection basins and the entrance to the outfall tunnel, people are scarce and the only noises are the hum of machines, the gurgling and rushing of water, and the plaintive cry of hovering seagulls. The scarcity of people is a tribute to the sophistication of the facilities. A state-of-the-art computer system monitors and controls the operations and maintenance of the sewage treatment plant. Standing before one of the central Process Information and Control System's fifty-eight computers, workers have access to critical operational information that is continually streaming in from 25,000 control points.[26] As is often said, you cannot manage what you cannot measure, and at this facility they measure almost everything. For example, the press of a button reveals a real-time flow-meter that tracks the number of gallons of wastewater entering Deer Island. Thus, a worker sitting in front of the computer screen, within a building, can see how the amount of sewage in the MWRA service area fluctuates in dry and wet weather, throughout the days and nights of the months and seasons of the year. Those numbers offer the ultimate sanitary profile of the region. As an MWRA supervisor, Joe Duplin, said, "It's like going in the Starship Enterprise compared to what we were doing."[27]

The engineering feats of the Boston Harbor Project are reflected not only in the structures that compose the new sewage treatment and related facilities, but also in the work that preceded construction. Years of planning and the work of over one thousand engineers from over one hundred firms, along with the engineers from the MWRA, went into the design of the new facilities.[28] Massive new piers were constructed on Deer and Nut Islands, and at Squantum Point and the Fore River Staging Area in Quincy, to transport workers as well as construction materials and vehicles to and from worksites. Parts of Deer Island had to be removed or rearranged to make way for the new facilities. In December 1991, the Suffolk County House of Correction, which until then had housed 350 inmates, was razed and relocated to South Boston to make way for the new primary and secondary plants. This demolition meant that for the first time in over one hundred years, Deer Island no longer had a prison, thereby ending the island's distinction as being the site of "one of the oldest continuously-operated penal institutions in the western hemisphere."[29] A glacial drumlin (a large hill) in the center of the island was moved to make way for the new facilities. Nearly 700,000 cubic yards of the glacial till was taken to the edge of the island nearest the town of Winthrop to form a visual and sound barrier between the plant site and the townspeople. The remaining 800,000 cubic yards of till was shipped off the island.[30] World War II–era bunkers also had to be demolished for construction purposes.[31] This posed a problem because the bunkers, which had been built to take the pummeling of enemy shelling, had concrete reinforced walls and ceilings that were up to seventeen feet thick. When the MWRA's contractors contacted the military for guidance, they were told that they would "never be able to take those bunkers down."[32] Although the bunkers could withstand enemy bombardment, they were no match for seismic tests and a series of strategically positioned drill holes, loaded with modern explosives. The bunkers came down and the project proceeded.

During the pre-construction and construction phases of the project there were so many people and machines on Deer Island that it resembled a "human ant colony."[33] The relatively small area on which they were working complicated the logistics of the work. Deer Island is only 210 acres. Although that might seem like a fair piece of real estate, it becomes very small when the aim is to build a sewage treatment facility of colossal proportions, especially when the time frame is short. To keep to the schedule, the construction management team did not have the luxury of building one part of the facility first, then another, and then another. Most of the time, multiple projects moved ahead simultaneously. As one of the workers on the island said, "You turn your head for a minute and you risk being hit by an earthmover."[34] The construction moved at a feverish pace.

Huge Numbers

The dimensions of the Boston Harbor Project are staggering. The construction used 4 million bricks, 1,500 miles of electric cable, 470,000 tons of gravel, 1 million cubic yards of concrete, and 813,000 square feet of concrete block, enough to cover 100 baseball diamonds. An army of 16,000 union workers representing 22 trades built the new facilities.[35] Peak employment on the BHP reached 2,200, and all told, the workers on the project logged more than 30 million craft hours, which is roughly equivalent to 15,000 worker years.[36] The project's water and bus transportation system racked up more than 3.5 million construction worker trips to and from Deer Island. More than 200,000 vehicles traveled to Deer Island on barges. Before the work could be done, over 400 environmental licenses, permits, and approvals had to be obtained. And, amazingly, but for the tragic accident in the outfall tunnel, which shut down operations for a year, the entire BHP would have finished on time and in accord with the ambitious schedule set out by the court. To understand the magnitude of this accomplishment, one need not look far. Virtually next door to the new Deer Island facility is the infamous Central Artery/Third Harbor Tunnel Project, also known as the Big Dig, which is designed to improve traffic in downtown Boston using a range of transportation projects, including a massive underground tunnel and highway. This project is already many years and many billions of dollars over budget, and the end is just now coming into view. If this comparison will not do, consider Chicago's sewage treatment plant, which is on a par with Boston's. Although Chicago took nearly fifty years to complete its works, the BHP took only twelve.[37] The BHP has won numerous kudos and dozens of awards for its engineering brilliance. In 1998, for example, the American Academy of Environmental Engineers gave an Annual Excellence Award for the secondary treatment plant facilities. A year later, the *Engineering News Record* placed the BHP on the list of the 125 greatest projects of the last 125 years.[38] And in 2002, the American Public Works Association named the BHP as the Public Works Project of the Year (for projects worth over $10 million).

The most staggering number of all is $3.8 billion, for that is what the BHP cost. That number could have been much higher, considering that initial estimates of the project's cost were over $6 billion.[39] Not all of those costs are being borne by the MWRA ratepayers. Through the work of the Massachusetts delegation, in particular Senators Edward Kennedy and John Kerry, as well as Congressmen Barney Frank and Edward Markey and former Congressmen Joe Moakley and Tip O'Neill, the BHP has received more than $800 million in state and federal grants.[40] This number takes on added significance in light of the history of the waiver applications. In the late 1980s, Deland referred to those applications and the delay they caused as "the most expensive public policy mistake in the history of New England."[41] There is some merit to this characterization. Every year that the project was put off, the price tag grew as a result of inflation and a rise in construction costs. But Deland's comment implied an assumption that many people made: that had the cleanup moved ahead earlier, the Boston area would have been eligible for large amounts of federal grant money through the construction grants program under the Clean Water Act. But, the argument continues, because of the delay, by the time the MWRA was in a position to apply for such money the construction grants program had been discontinued, leaving the Boston area high and dry. This argument is probably wrong however, or at least exaggerated. Construction grant program money was given to each state based on a national formula. Each state, in turn, distributed it to cities and towns based on need. While the grant program was flush, Massachusetts always got its entire allotment, which was distributed throughout the state to many other projects. Had the waivers never been submitted and had the MDC applied for federal construction grant money, it might have gotten some, perhaps even a considerable amount, but that would have meant that other equally deserving sewage projects in Massachusetts would have received less money. And there is no way of knowing, in hindsight, how the funding scenario would have played out had Boston waived its option to apply for a waiver. Nevertheless, it is clear that the state's congressional delegation has managed to get the MWRA a considerable amount of grant money, notwithstanding the demise of the construction grants program. For its part, the state has come up with over $300 million in debt service assistance. Although only about $65 million of this is in the form of outright grants, which need not be repaid, all of this assistance helps to pay the bills.

Despite the federal and state assistance, the MWRA ratepayers are shouldering a heavy load. They have seen their water and sewer bills rise rapidly. In 1986, the average annual water and sewer bill for a family of four within the MWRA service area was $113, based on the MWRA's calculations and typical usage rates reported to the Massachusetts Department of Environmental Protection. Since then the MWRA has raised rates year after year, in large part because of increasing sewage related costs. For example, in 1995 the MWRA estimated that the average annual water and sewer bill was $419, in 2000 it was $477, and in 2002 it was $511. The MWRA advisory board uses different assumptions from the MWRA's in calculating average annual rates, including higher usage rates, and the board's numbers are different from the authority's. In 2000, for example, the board pegged the average annual water and sewer bill for the MWRA service area at $724. Comparing

MWRA rates with those paid by homeowners in other parts of the country is tricky because of differences in billing practices, consumption and usage rates, the definition of a "typical" household, as well as other regional and local factors. Even within the MWRA service area, charges vary dramatically, in some cases by more than a factor of five. Nevertheless, there is no arguing that water and sewer rates paid by those living within the MWRA service area, whether calculated by the MWRA or its advisory board, are among the highest in the country and are likely to remain so for years. Current MWRA projections estimate that annual rates will rise to roughly $610 in 2005 and $792 in 2010.[42]

Few if any of the ratepayers are happy about the rising rates. There have been sporadic protests, such as the one that occurred in Chelsea in 1993, when more than three hundred residents gathered to burn copies of their MWRA bills outside City Hall, whereupon they marched to nearby Revere and were joined by similar-sized group of outraged citizens.[43] At the same time, none of the MWRA communities have failed to pay their assessments to the authority, and many of the ratepayers realize that the numbers could have been much worse. When the BHP started, widely reported and supported analyses projected average rates to rise to well over $1,000 by 2000.[44] The combination of grants as well as a variety of other factors discussed later kept such rates from materializing. The double-digit rate increases in the early years of the project have given way to much more moderate increases that have often been below the rate of inflation. But those days may be over. Indeed, in January 2003, Massachusetts Governor Jane M. Swift cut the entire $48 million dollars that was slated to go to the MWRA for rate relief. The MWRA responded with a three-pronged approach to deal with the sudden deficit created by this action. First, the authority reduced operating expenses through layoffs and debt refinancing, thereby saving $16 million. Second, a portion of the authority's reserve funds were used to cover some of the shortfall, and finally, the board approved a first-ever midyear rate increase, of 3.9 percent. With this increase added to the 2.9 percent increase the board had already approved at the outset of the fiscal year, the MWRA ratepayers were subject to a 2003 rate hike of nearly 7 percent,[45] which was considerably higher than the rate of inflation. Whether such large increases will become the norm is too early to tell.

A Harbor Reborn

The real measure of the BHP's success is found in the harbor. After all, the primary impetus behind the BHP was the need to comply with the Clean Water Act and to improve the environmental quality of the waters into which the Boston area's sewage flowed. Has the BHP succeeded by this measure? The answer is yes. The harbor is much cleaner. With each step in the progression of the BHP, the pollution loads entering the harbor have decreased. Perhaps the most important and dramatic shift occurred on Christmas Eve 1991, when the pelletizing facility began operations and direct sludge discharges to the harbor ceased. Mazzone, on hand as the facility went on line, called it a "major event. We've been dumping for generations, and now it is going to stop. On time and under budget."[46] Next came the opening of the inter-island tunnel and the closing of the Nut Island facility, improvements in the level of treatment from upgraded primary to the addition of secondary, and, finally, the opening of the outfall tunnel.

The MWRA realized early on that accurately monitoring and measuring the impact of the BHP was essential, and it established a highly professional and competent Department of Environmental Quality. The research performed and sponsored by this office provides evidence of improvements to the harbor. The sediments in the harbor, which used to be almost devoid of life and were referred to as "black mayonnaise," now contain thriving bottom-dwelling communities, in which biodiversity is much higher than the levels recorded in the late 1980s. The concentrations of lead and other heavy metals in the sediment are roughly half what they were twenty years ago. Populations of *Ampelisca*, a tiny, shrimplike crustacean that serves as an indicator of the environmental health of sediments, are on the rise. Water quality in the harbor has improved to the point that the vast majority of the harbor meets federal and state water quality standards. Harbor waters are much clearer than in years past because of a major reduction in suspended solids. Nutrient concentrations, which in the past have overstimulated the growth of algae and seaweed, are now at healthier levels. During the early 1980s it was not uncommon to catch flounder that had liver tumors and fin rot caused by environmental contamination. Today, liver tumors are rare and the concentrations of PCBs and pesticides in flounder meat are within Food and Drug Administration guidelines. The lobsters hauled out of the harbor are also much cleaner than those caught before the BHP. And the levels of polycyclicaromatic hydrocarbons in mussels have also decreased roughly 50 percent in the last decade. Much of the credit for this success goes to the MWRA's aggressive Toxic Reduction and Control Program, which works with more than 1,200 area businesses and industries to reduce the contaminant levels in their discharges to the sewer system.[47]

With the bulk of the Boston area's sewage flowing into Massachusetts Bay instead of into the harbor, a logical question is whether the BHP hasn't simply shifted the pollution problem offshore. At the end of the nineteenth century, the best engineers and sanitarians of the day agreed that the solution to pollution was dilution and that discharging sewage into the harbor would do no harm. They were wrong. But before judging the outfall tunnel in the same way that we assess the former system, it is important to understand why they were wrong. At least in part, the solution to pollution is dilution. Indeed, many of our modern environmental laws are based on that premise. If the concentrations of pollutants in a body of water or in the air are low enough, they are acceptable for the purposes of protecting human health and the environment. Where the engineers and sanitarians of the late 1800s erred is in assuming that the relatively shallow and unevenly flushed waters of the harbor would provide enough dilution to minimize the harmful impact of all that sewage. Fortunately, there is ample reason to believe that, this time, the sanitarians, engineers, biologists, and others involved in the siting decision got it right. Of course, they were given an able assist by the treatment afforded by the new plant on Deer Island. The effluent flowing into the harbor around the turn of the nineteenth century was raw sewage. The effluent coming from the new plant on Deer Island is, in comparison, incredibly clean. Thus, the benefits of dilution are amplified by the benefits afforded by properly treated sewage.

The placement of the outfall tunnel and its design was based on exhaustive studies. The scrutiny given the siting decision was heightened by the public opposition to the tunnel that manifested itself in the early 1990s, when Cape Cod groups sued the EPA. The groups were concerned that the effluent coming out of the new outfall would increase nutrient levels in Massachusetts Bay and would lead to phytoplankton blooms that could negatively affect endangered North Atlantic right whales and humpback whales. The lawsuit alleged, in part, that in conducting the environmental impact study on the outfall tunnel the agency had inadequately studied its impact on such species.[48] This suit, which ultimately failed, and the broader public outcry about the tunnel led to additional studies and evaluations of how the tunnel might affect the ecology of the bay.[49] The consensus of all this work was that the depth and currents combined with the multiple diffuser ports spread out over more than a mile would satisfactorily disperse the treated effluent. To make sure that this was the case, one of the conditions of the MWRA's discharge permit, jointly issued by the EPA and the state, was that the authority sponsor a $3 million annual monitoring and evaluation program on the water of the bay. An independent Outfall Science Monitoring Advisory Panel composed of nine scientists reviews the monitoring data and provides guidance to the EPA and the state Department of Environmental Protection on scientific issues relating to the outfall and discharge permit. To date, the monitoring program, which is one of the most extensive in the nation, has shown that optimistic predictions about the impact of the outfall have been borne out. The effluent becomes diluted rapidly as it moves away from the diffuser ports, and no significant effluent-related impacts on the local ecosystem have been observed. It is still early in the monitoring program, however, and there is still the possibility that problems will arise. In light of this, the MWRA's permit requires the authority to establish "caution" and "warning" levels for a variety of environmental indicators, such as the occurrence of an algal bloom or an increase in the level of toxic contaminants in fish. If any of those indicators reach a triggering level, the MWRA must evaluate the problem and, if necessary, develop a plan to resolve it. One of the by-products of the monitoring and evaluation program is improved science. According to Dr. Andrea Rex, the director of the authority's Department of Environmental Quality, "the science program prompted by the outfall has created unique research opportunities and led to important scientific and public policy results. Massachusetts Bay and Boston Harbor have become one of the best-studied and best-understood marine environments in the world."[50]

The improvements in the harbor have not been lost on the people in Boston and beyond, and the beaches are one of the best indicators of this. The MDC, which operates many of the public beaches along the harbor's edge, has seen the change. "The crowds are coming back," according to John Ciccone, director of waterfront operations for the MDC. During the summer of 2002, the MDC hired 350 lifeguards; seven years ago, only 180 were needed.[51] Still, many people who might otherwise visit the beaches are shying away, perhaps because of doubts about water quality and memories of Boston Harbor's dirty past. To lure more people to the beaches, Save the Harbor/Save the Bay, a Boston-based non-profit that has worked for years on behalf of cleaning up the harbor, sponsored a television advertising campaign during the summer of 2002, with the message "Come back to Boston's beaches. They're better."[52]

Fishers and pleasure boaters, too, are coming back in increasing numbers. Not only is the harbor's water drawing people back, but so too are its islands. For decades the harbor's islands were not really part of the regional fabric of life. Many people saw the islands from the land, sea, or air, but few experienced them, or even had the opportunity to do so. That changed on November 12, 1996, when the National Park Service designated the Boston Harbor Islands National Recreation Area, which is commonly referred to as Boston Harbor Islands, a national park area. Now, the harbor's thirty-four islands, covering roughly 1,600 acres, are managed by a unique partnership of organizations, for the public's benefit and enjoyment.[53]

Both Deer and Nut Islands are part of the park. Although at first it might seem odd to include in a national park area an island that houses a massive sewage treatment facility, it is an excellent addition, made more so by the extensive work that the MWRA has performed to transform the perimeter of the island into the multifaceted Deer Island Public Access Area. From sunrise to sunset, year-round, visitors can access the sixty-acre area and its five miles of trails to walk, ride, jog, picnic, sightsee, fish, or, perhaps, check on how the treatment facility is operating. In addition to recreation, Deer Island will someday offer visitors an opportunity to reflect on two important episodes in Boston's history. During King Philip's War (1675–1676), about five hundred Native Americans from the Nipmuc tribe were kept prisoner on Deer Island, despite the fact that they had been friendly to the colonists. They were poorly fed and were often exposed to the elements; many of them died on the island and were laid to rest in unmarked graves. Nearly two centuries later, another sad passage in Deer Island's history was written. During the 1840s, many Irish immigrants came to Boston to escape famine in their native land. In 1847, the influx from Ireland rose to twenty-five thousand. Unfortunately, many of them were ill on arrival. "As a precautionary measure to ward off pestilence that would have been ruinous to the public health and business of the city," the state legislature established a quarantine hospital on Deer Island. Many who were taken there died and were buried in a cemetery on the island.[54] The MWRA is working with local community and historic organizations to determine how best to interpret these events and to create permanent memorials so that visitors to the island will know what happened there.

Despite the success and the much-deserved praise that the Boston Harbor project has received, there is still a long way to go until Boston Harbor is truly cleaned up, and as is usually the case with environmental protection, the task will never truly be finished. The combined sewer overflow (CSO) problem, which has plagued the waters of the harbor ever since the first combined sewers were built in Boston during the 1800s, still exists. Shortly after Mazzone established the long-term schedule for the BHP, he and the parties hammered out a long-term schedule to address CSOs. Years of debate then addressed how best to deal with the CSO problem, and the MWRA is now in the midst of a twelve-year, highly ambitious CSO program, overseen by the court. The program includes numerous projects with multiple goals, including closing CSOs, separating stormwater and sewage flows, treating CSO discharges, and constructing storage facilities so that some CSO discharges can be held until dry weather, when they can be routed to the Deer Island facility for treatment.

In addition to CSO discharges, a large amount of pollution makes its way into the harbor via the area's three major rivers, the Mystic, Neponset, and Charles. Each of these rivers travels through heavily populated areas and washes all sorts of contaminants into the harbor. These contaminants come from the discharge pipes of upriver CSOs and CSO treatment facilities, as well as from the stormwater runoff from dirty city streets, which is a problem in Boston proper as well. Other assaults on the harbor come from above and below. Airborne contaminants settle on the harbor's surface through precipitation. And although the harbor's sediments are much cleaner than they were, there is still plenty of contamination to be found. As worms and other marine organisms move through the sediments, they invariably bring past environmental insults to the surface and into contact with themselves and the water.

Because of these continuing pollution problems, complaints about the state of the harbor continue. For example, even though the beaches are much cleaner, on some days some of them must be closed because of high levels of bacteria.[55] After heavy rainfalls, in particular, when the CSOs and storm drains are called into duty, the levels of pollution entering the harbor can be quite high. But the connection between sewage sources and water quality is not always clear. Carson Beach in

South Boston, for example, is one of the cleanest in the harbor, yet it is in close proximity to seven CSO outfalls and storm drains.[56] Whether there will ever come a time when beaches are never closed for health reason and all of the harbor meets state and federal water quality standards all of the time is an open question. Yet the admission of continuing and very real problems is in no way a negative reflection on the great successes that have been achieved. The Boston Harbor of today is a far cry from the body of water that Vice President Bush called the "filthiest harbor in the country," during his run for the presidency in 1988. Indeed, Boston's is now one of the cleanest harbors in the country. According to Ken Kirk, executive director of the Association of Metropolitan Sewerage Agencies, the BHP "will go down in the annals of water-quality history as a very significant project. Boston is a model for other cities around the country." Ken Moraff, the chief of enforcement at the EPA's Region 1, notes that the harbor "was in very, very bad shape. Now, it's very, very good." Bruce Berman, communications and BayWatch director for Save the Harbor/Save the Bay, contends, "It's fair to say that this is the most dramatic [water-related] success in environmental history."[57] And John Devillars, former administrator of EPA Region 1, calls the cleanup of Boston Harbor "without question . . . one of America's greatest environmental success stories."[58]

There are many reasons for the success of the BHP, including effective management, the financial capability of the authority, labor practices, and the power of the court.

Management

One of the theoretical virtues of an independent authority is that it allows for the hiring and retention of highly qualified managers who can run the authority more like an efficient business than a weighted-down, ossified bureaucracy. The MWRA has certainly fulfilled this goal, but there were some bumpy times in the early years. On July 1, 1985, the MWRA officially assumed ownership, possession, and control of the MDC's sewage and water systems. During the first four months of the authority's existence, Phil Shapiro, its director of finance and development, acted as interim executive director of the authority. Shapiro and the first board of directors did an excellent job confronting a number of crucial decisions facing the authority. For example, during Shapiro's tenure the authority selected Deer Island as the site for the new sewage treatment plant and decided not to pursue legal actions to appeal the second tentative denial of the MDC's waiver application.

While Shapiro and the board were laboring to make sure that the MWRA hit the ground running, a national search for a permanent director was under way. There were essentially two schools of thought on what type of person the new director should be. To Governor Dukakis, given the high profile of the MWRA and the fact that it would have to deal with an often questioning and angry public, the executive director needed to be a good manager as well as someone with the political acumen needed to address community fears and concerns. Although knowing about the engineering aspects of the project would be a plus, that was clearly secondary in the governor's mind.[59] The majority of the board at the MWRA, however, felt that the executive director's engineering qualifications trumped all others. In the end, the board, who had to vote on the appointment, held sway and chose Michael Gritzuk, an accomplished engineer who had earned respect for his work with sewage treatment facilities in New Jersey and Florida. According to James Hoyte, the chairman of the MWRA's board of directors and the state's secretary of environmental affairs, when he told Dukakis of the appointment, the governor said, "My gosh, Jamie, what's wrong with you folks? I told you, you need to have a strong public manager, I don't care what kind of engineer he might be, that's not the issue. When it's time to deal with the cities and towns, time to deal on rate questions, and time to deal with the legislature, and mobilize support, that is not going to be critical."[60]

Gritzuk said he pursued his new job, "with a heart of an engineer." As he saw it, his responsibility was to build a great sewage treatment plant that used all the latest designs and technology. The political aspects of the job were of much less interest, in part because of Gritzuk's own abilities. As he once noted, "I never professed having political skills."[61] During Gritzuk's eighteen-month tenure, the authority experienced a number of public relations disasters. For example, when the MWRA needed to furnish its offices, the authority's leadership, perhaps thinking a bit too much how authorities are like private businesses and too little about the importance of public perception and trust, ordered "$1,200 leather chairs, custom-made solid oak tables and desks, $200 chromeplated desktop In-Out baskets, marble ashtrays, and designer lamps."[62] When the Boston media, not famous for their restraint, got hold of this information, they had a field day. The marble ashtrays seemed to elicit the most indignation and became a virtual symbol of the supposed recklessness of the authority. For a while, all discussions of the cleanup of the harbor were clouded by the figurative weight of those ashtrays. How, many MWRA ratepayers wondered, could the authority be so insensitive about costs when it was about to launch a massive project that would force many of them to dig deep in their pockets to cover their skyrocketing water and sewer bills?

During Gritzuk's tenure, the authority was not only losing the public relations battle; it was losing the organizational battle as well. Morale at the authority plummeted, not only because the agency was being tarred by the scandalous marble ashtrays, but also as a result of Gritzuk's management style. Although Gritzuk was a very competent engineer, he was not as strong as a manager. Doug Foy, the executive director of the CLF, captured the widely held perception of the authority during the latter part of Gritzuk's tenure. "I don't think the MWRA knew what it needed and what it wanted," he said. "There was a lack of leadership at the top. They had a terrible case of institutional blues. There was a paranoia about the public's view of the authority. They needed somebody to step in and say, 'this is bullshit. We're going to meet that schedule and have some success.'"[63] To Arleen O'Donnell, of the Massachusetts Audubon Society, the authority was, at the time, "a horse without a rider."[64] Koff, one of the lawyers who had set the ball in motion with the Quincy court case, was disappointed with the authority's rocky start. "We saw a more active, aggressive agency coming out of the legislation—one that would create more of a vision and a public presence." He added that the MWRA "hasn't justified the fight to create it."[65]

Although the board had brought Gritzuk on and had a vested interest in seeing him succeed, its members were also wise enough to admit their mistake and to realize that for the authority's mission to be accomplished, the authority would need a new executive director. Even the board's most ardent early advocate for Gritzuk knew that the time had come for a change, and told Hoyte one day, "Jamie, we've got to get rid of this guy, he's just doing a terrible job."[66] As another board member, Lorraine Downey, later said, Gritzuk's appointment "was totally our fault. We were so focused on building the treatment plant that we only thought about an engineer."[67] In April 1987, the board voted to remove Gritzuk and to look for another executive director. Commenting on Gritzuk's tenure, Hoyte later said that he "went down in flames." Shapiro again stepped in as interim director, while the board considered its options. Then, on August 10, 1987, Paul F. Levy took the helm.

Levy was no stranger to state-level management and politics. His past positions included stints as chairman of the Massachusetts Department of Public Utilities, under Dukakis, and director of the Arkansas Department of Energy, under then-Governor Bill Clinton. Levy had a reputation of being intellectually nimble, politically shrewd, decisive, and a natural leader. By virtue of his work in the Dukakis administration, he was well connected on Beacon Hill. He knew whom to contact to get things done.[68] If there was any doubt that Levy would be a different type of executive director from Gritzuk, it was erased almost immediately. Prior to Levy's appointment, the MWRA had been in lengthy negotiations with General Dynamics over the purchase of the Fore River Shipyard in Quincy, the plot of land that the authority wanted to use for a staging area to get construction supplies and people over to Deer Island. No sooner had Levy gotten into his new office than he called General Dynamics and asked to meet. Within two days, Levy had inked a deal with the company and submitted it to the board, which quickly approved it.[69] Levy knew that if this project were to have any chance of succeeding and meeting the court-ordered schedule, many key decisions would have to be made quickly. The decisions also would have to be sound, for wasting money on bad projects was not an option.

Shortly after arriving, Levy proposed to the board that it establish a Project Management Division to oversee the construction projects. Levy argued that this was critical to creating "accountability in the MWRA for the timely completion of the project" and to creating a "strong 'owner's representative' in dealings" with the numerous engineering and design firms that would work on the project.[70] Levy also knew that a key to the BHP would be having the best people working on it. Many highly qualified and talented engineers and planners already worked at the MWRA, and Levy added more. The most important appointment, of course, was the person who would oversee the project, and Levy tapped Richard Fox to take that position. Fox was a lawyer and an engineer who had directed many sewage treatment projects, including ones in Concord, New Hampshire, and Louisville, Kentucky. He was senior vice president at the consulting firm of Camp, Dresser & McKee, which had done much of the previous planning for the BHP. He knew the project inside and out and was widely hailed as a highly competent manager. In order to lure Fox away from the private sector, Levy offered him an annual salary of $125,000. That was not much, considering his background, but it made Fox the highest paid government employee in Massachusetts. By comparison, the governor earned a meager $85,000.[71] Some feared that this would rekindle the acrimony that surrounded the purchase of marble ashtrays, but the forthright way in which Levy handled the appointment and presented it to the press precluded that. "You don't skimp when you are looking for a project manager on a $3 billion project," he said. "We found one of the best people in the country."[72] Levy was correct. Every delay in the project meant that more money would have to be spent. By keeping the project on track, a strong manager like Fox could pay back his salary to the ratepayers a hundredfold easily. Later, when Fox left his position, another extremely capable manager, Walter G. Armstrong, who had been Fox's deputy, replaced him.

The Project Management Division quickly proved its worth. During the late 1980s, when the state's economy was crumbling and area construction firms were desperately seeking work, the authority knew that it would have an edge at the bargaining table when it came to hammering out financial terms of contracts. To take advantage of the situation, the authority sped up the negotiation and issuance of construction contracts and was able to lock in significant amounts of work at up to 18 percent below what the authority's engineers had originally estimated it would cost—good news to MWRA ratepayers.[73]

Another innovative approach initiated during Levy's tenure, and which was continued and expanded after he left, was the use of financial mitigation packages. The idea was simple and powerful. The new sewage treatment facilities would benefit everyone in the MWRA service area. Similarly, the costs of the new facilities would be shared broadly, but some cities and towns would shoulder a greater burden by virtue of either hosting MWRA facilities or being adversely affected by them. The mitigation packages were designed to make such burdens more palatable and easier to bear. For example, Winthrop not only abuts Deer Island, which is owned by Boston, but it also had to cope with years of construction and the increased heavy truck traffic that entailed. Winthrop's mitigation package has provided tens of millions of dollars over many years to pay for road repairs, improved firefighting services, and the soundproofing of homes nearest to the island. Quincy and other MWRA communities also have received significant mitigation packages. Although some argue that such mitigation is a crass payoff, that is not the way the MWRA views it. A former MWRA board member, Robert Ciolek, saw the mitigation agreements "as a pacesetter, a trend-setter. Yes, from one point of view there's the theory that you pay the barbarians not to attack, but that's not the theory here. We admit that we'll have effects on neighborhoods and that it'll be expensive, and here's a way of alleviating those effects."[74] To Levy, mitigation just made sense because the "alternative to [offering mitigation packages] . . . would be court fights every step of the way from local opposition," an expensive proposition when each week that was lost on the BHP increased costs by $2 million. Levy's experience in the electric utility field added to his confidence that mitigation packages were a good idea. "Power companies have known for years," he said, "that if you pay mitigation costs to a community, a lot of local resistance to siting big projects disappears."[75]

Unlike Gritzuk, who remained largely out of the public's eye, Levy ventured forth every chance he got to explain to the people what the MWRA was doing and why. This was not a job for the faint of heart. During these early years, Levy had to make many tough and controversial decisions, such as siting the pelletizing facility in Quincy. Being the most visible symbol of the MWRA, Levy became a lightning rod for attacks on the authority. Ratepayers complained about rising rates and for good reason. In the twenty years before the MWRA was established, the MDC had spent an average of $11 million annually on improvements to the water and sewer system. At that rate, it would have taken two hundred years to upgrade the systems and to replace them with modern equipment.[76] Now, even though the BHP was still in its early stages, the rates were jumping by double digits every year, creating a violent case of sticker shock. Although much of the public anger directed at the MWRA was impersonal, a good bit of it was aimed squarely at Levy. He was referred to as the sludge king and the sludge monster, and, for a time, one could find telephone poles in Quincy with wanted posters featuring Levy's photograph.[77] Reflecting on how he handled these turbulent times, Levy said, "I learned to take a deep breath, keep my blood pressure down, and focus on my goal."[78]

Through all the controversy, Levy persevered and kept the BHP on track. In the process, he restored morale to the authority and made it an exciting place to work.[79] The employees could now see that they were part of a dynamic project that was succeeding. By early 1992, Levy felt that it was time for him to step down. "I have accumulated so much baggage with the decisions I've had to make," Levy said, "it's a good time for another person."[80] Douglas MacDonald succeeded Levy on January 29, 1992. On Levy's last day as executive director he offered MacDonald a piece of advice. "When you get into trouble," he said, "blame your predecessor."[81]

MacDonald was an excellent choice to follow Levy. While a lawyer at the Boston firm of Palmer & Dodge, specializing in environmental law, he had taken the lead in drafting the legislation that would create the MWRA, and for a time at the beginning served as the authority's general counsel. He not only knew about the authority and the BHP, but he was also very familiar with the local political scene. Upon taking over the mantle of executive director he said that the biggest challenge facing the MWRA would be to "convince our ratepayers that every dollar spent here is spent well. . . . If we can show people that the rates are not being wasted, I think they will accept the rates." MacDonald also set a course that would deepen and strengthen the authority's connection to the communities it served.[82]

MacDonald was an intense and tireless worker on behalf of the authority, often working late into the night and on weekends. One of the people who knew MacDonald well referred to him as "very proactive" and said "he makes things happen."[83] He focused his energies and keen intellect not only on keeping the BHP and other projects on track, but also on following through on his commitment to keep the ratepayers and their communities informed and engaged. At the Boston Harbor Project Symposium, on May 16, 2001, James Sheets, the mayor of Quincy from 1989 to 2001, commented on the nature of the relationship that he and MacDonald had created. Sheets noted that it was "essential to develop some sort of progressive public policy for bringing the people of my city together with the MWRA on common ground." The way in which that was accomplished, according to Sheets, was through the "creation of a process that was open," in which a "relationship of honesty, integrity, and trust" could be established. Sheets told of how he and MacDonald had decided early on that they would be "open with each other, honest with each other, and . . . [they] would tell all the facts and we would not keep anything related to the Fore River Shipyard secret from each other. That relationship was tested" many times. "The phone would ring," Sheets recalled, and "Doug . . . [would say], 'Mayor, we've got a problem at the pelletizing plant,' and we would go to the pelletizing plant, and the next two or three or four days we would work on determining the source of that problem. And over and over again that occurred." After a fire in the pelletizing plant, for example, instead of getting up on a soapbox and complaining about the authority, Sheets joined forces with the authority to solve the problem. According to Sheets, his phone would ring probably once a week, and on the other end would be MacDonald, saying, "Sheets, you need to be involved in this."[84]

MacDonald shepherded the MWRA for a little over nine years, through early 2001. During that time he kept the authority on track as it transitioned from the construction mode to the operations mode, as, he said, "the Deer Island facility came on line and the maintenance/operations issues became paramount to the long-term sustainability" of the environmental success of the BHP. MacDonald also played a key role in fending off efforts to privatize the MWRA that were supported by those who believed that such a change would result in leaner and less costly operations and would therefore ultimately benefit the ratepayers. MacDonald argued that privatization "would have been financially unsatisfactory, and, over the long run, a huge threat to the 'ownership' which the entire community must take in the MWRA system if the environmental gains of the program are to be sustained and enhanced into the longer term future." Of all the successes that MacDonald enjoyed during his long involvement with the MWRA, he singled out two that were the most personally satisfying. One was the time he spent drafting the authority's enabling act and then working with the fledgling organization to get it up and running. The other was effectively "surmounting the outfall crisis" that ensued after the tragic deaths of the two tunnel workers in 1999.[85]

When he stepped down as executive director in April 2001, the *Boston Globe* printed an editorial lauding his accomplishments. "He will leave a strong record as the manager of the region's second largest public works project," the paper said. "His legacy is a model for his successors: high standards for performance and dedication to the principle of civic administration governing public projects."[86] Fred Salvucci, the former Massachusetts transportation secretary who was responsible for initiating the infamous Big Dig, bestowed one of the highest compliments paid to both MacDonald and Levy. Musing about why the BHP had been so much more successful in achieving its goals than the Big Dig, Salvucci said, "They have had extremely good managers."[87]

The MWRA's current executive director, Frederick A. Laskey, assumed the position on May 9, 2001. He is a familiar figure in Massachusetts politics, having been the commissioner of revenue for the state since 1998 and before that holding other state finance positions stretching back to 1980.[88] Laskey's legacy remains to be seen, but at the outset of his tenure he indicated that his "commitment will be to the rate-payers and member communities—to provide high quality water and wastewater services at an affordable price." Laskey has continued and furthered the cost-cutting measures put into place by MacDonald. As a result, the authority is spending less on operations now than it was in 1999, which is a trend that, Laskey said, "may be unprecedented in a government entity."[89]

Although the executive director is the most visible part of the MWRA's management team, he is not the most important. Ultimately, it is up to the board of directors to approve the authority's projects and budgets. Over the years, each executive director, with the exception of Gritzuk, has worked extremely well with the board. Together they have focused on achieving the authority's mission and doing so as a team. Of course, disagreements have occurred over the direction of the authority, but those disagreements have been almost uniformly acknowledged and resolved without acrimony in a fair and, for the most part, consensual manner. According to Ciolek, even when there were split votes on the board, "losers never felt quite vanquished, [and] winners were never permitted to chortle." The nature of the board has helped it address the concerns of the cities and towns served by the MWRA. In Ciolek's estimation, because the board is made up primarily of representatives of the affected communities, it has a "local orientation" that "has re-sulted in an agency culture that is responsive to the ratepayers and mostly sensitive to legitimate community needs."[90] According to MacDonald, the board played a critical role in the success of the BHP, by "providing extraordinarily committed, non-parochial, sustained leadership."[91]

The MWRA Advisory Board also deserves much of the credit for the MWRA's success. It has been an active and effective advocate for rate-payers. One of the advisory board's greatest successes was getting the authority to reconsider the scope of its plan for secondary treatment. In the early 1990s the board began pushing the MWRA to seek ways to reduce the cost of the BHP. The MWRA took up the challenge, and, after two years of study, concluded that the secondary plant, as origi-nally envisioned, was larger than it had to be to effectively treat all the waste it would have to handle. Instead of needing four batteries of sec-ondary, the MWRA argued that three would suffice. In October 1995, Judge Mazzone approved the MWRA's plan to scrap battery D, thereby shaving $165 million off the overall cost of the BHP. In agreeing to the change in the schedule, Mazzone stated, "This is a significant savings, and it is a demonstration of the care and efficiency of the authority in managing the project." MacDonald said that the authority had "responded positively to the challenges put before it by the MWRA Advisory Board and the ratepayers. We are thrilled by today's court ruling." For Joseph Favaloro, the executive director of the advisory board, the judge's ruling was "environmentally sound and ratepayer equitable."[92] The advisory board has also been instrumental in getting federal and state grants for the BHP.

Financial Capability of the Authority

The main reason the MWRA was created was that virtually everyone thought that it would be able to raise the huge sums of money necessary to see the BHP through to completion. Virtually everyone was right. Through the issuance of bonds, the MWRA has raised billions of dollars. In the beginning, however, how MWRA bonds would fare on the open market was not clear. The purchaser of a bond is essentially placing confidence in the issuer that the latter will be able to repay the bond at its maturity, with interest. Generally speaking, municipal bonds are good at instilling investor confidence. According to Shapiro, municipal bonds are viewed favorably because "communities and providers of essential public services don't go bankrupt. Relative to other options, such as the stock market, municipal bonds are safe. Moreover, bonds are not subject to state and federal taxes."[93] Still, the MWRA had significant hurdles to overcome. One potential obstacle to the MWRA's earning investor confidence was the authority's source of income—rates. Investors would shy away from investing in the authority if they believed that the ratepayers would either be unable to pay the rates or stage a revolt and refuse to pay. Another potential obstacle was the collapse of the so-called Massachusetts Miracle in the late 1980s, when the state's economy, which had been riding high for years, took a precipitous nosedive. How would potential investors react, wondered MWRA management, when they saw Massachusetts on the name of their bonds? Would it be a case of guilt by association?[94]

Through some very creative financing mechanisms, the MWRA was able to calm fears about investing in the authority's bonds. For example, the authority's enabling statute included a mechanism called a local aid interceptor, which essentially allowed the MWRA to intercept a city's or town's local aid payments from the state should the city or town fail to pay its assessment to the authority. But, because such local aid was contingent on the financial health of the state, which at the time was quite shaky, the MWRA developed other credit mechanisms designed to show its financial viability, regardless of what happened at the state level. One of those was the Community Obligation and Revenue Enhancement Fund, which basically put aside extra cash to serve as a rainy-day fund should one or more of the MWRA's service communities default on their assessments.[95] Other factors also worked to the MWRA's advantage in presenting itself to the bond market. One was the quality of the management team the MWRA had created and its dedication to doing an excellent job at the minimum cost. The presence of the court, too, added considerable weight to the argument that, come what may, the authority and its mission would continue.

All of these features of the MWRA worked to its benefit in 1989, as it prepared to enter the bond market. The two ratings services, Moody's and Standard & Poor's, gave the authority a very good, combined A/A− rating. Such high ratings were of critical importance to the MWRA's ratepayers, for the higher the rating, the lower the cost of borrowing, and the lower the cost of borrowing the lower the rates. A rise of as little as a quarter percent in the interest rate charged to the MWRA would cost its ratepayers hundreds of millions of dollars. To help generate excitement about its bonds, the MWRA staged a road show in major cities throughout the country to tout the quality of its upcoming offering. Then, on January 23, 1990, the MWRA issued $824 million in bonds, one of the largest bond offerings in history. If there were any doubts about the bond's viability, they were erased within five hours, the amount of time it took for the bonds to sell out.[96] The benefits of being independent from the state of Massachusetts were revealed in the numbers. Had the state, with its BBB bond rating, issued the bonds, they would have had to pay an additional $57 million in interest, a cost that would have been passed on to the ratepayers.

Since that auspicious start, the MWRA has successfully floated billions of dollars of bonds. The authority's structure, operations, and track record have continued to inspire confidence on Wall Street, and, as a result the bond ratings have stayed high. According to Fitch Investor Service, writing in 1998, the MWRA's success was a major part of Fitch's reason for improving the authority's rating from A to A+. "The upgrade reflects the authority's accomplishments since it was organized. Construction of the Deer Island Harbor Project . . . is substantially complete . . . actual rate increases have been below forecasts. . . . The authority's sound management team has provided leadership for the organization through a significant part of its complex construction program, balancing its mandate to meet environmental requirements with customer concerns about costs and neighborhood disruption." The same year, Standard & Poor's similarly revised the authority's rating, noting that "strong management . . . has generated strong reserves and solid liquidity."[97] Two years after these words were penned, the authority's ratings from these two organizations rose again.[98]

Labor Practices

The bigger the construction project, the more labor that is involved, and the more labor that is involved, the greater the likelihood that there will be labor disputes with management that can slow progress. With a project as massive as the BHP, spanning twelve years, involving more than thirty union locals and thousands of union members working with scores of companies, having no major work stoppages due to strikes or lockouts would have been almost impossible. But that is exactly what happened. In fact, no minor work stoppages occurred either. The reason for this amazing record was the Project Labor Agreement hammered out by the MWRA, the unions, and the construction manager for the BHP, ICF Kaiser Engineers of Massachusetts.

The agreement, which was challenged on legal grounds and ultimately upheld by the U.S. Supreme Court, calls for the use of dispute resolution mechanisms to resolve labor disputes fairly, quickly, and amicably. Hundreds of disputes have gone through the multistep grievance procedure, with only a few making it to the final stage of arbitration.[99] According to Joseph Nigro, the general agent secretary treasurer for the Metropolitan Building and Construction Trades Council, the Project Labor Agreement "benefited everyone" because "the workers can go to work and have any grievances and disputes settled in a timely manner. That saves construction time for MWRA and time saved is money in the pockets of ratepayers."[100] While on the job at Deer Island, Vito Cucchiara, a member of Laborers International Union, Local 22, and a union shop steward, credited the labor agreement with having a positive influence. "There is a sense of respect between the unions and the contractors. Both sides know that in order for the job to be completed on-time and on-budget, there has to be give and take by the unions and management."[101] As Ken Willis, the project director for ICF Kaiser, noted in the mid-1990s, after the BHP had amassed thirteen million worker hours with no strikes or lockouts, "We've been blessed with labor harmony that's a record for a project of this size and complexity."[102] And that success continued through the end of the project. Indeed, the BHP's trailblazing Project Labor Agreement has served as a model for 1,600 other construction jobs throughout the country, including Boston's very own Big Dig.

Another part of the labor equation is much harder to quantify. When people feel good about their work, they tend to work harder and to work better. The BHP greatly benefited from this truism. Throughout the BHP an almost palpable air of excitement and pride existed among not only the laborers working on the project, but also the other workers and managers employed by the MWRA and its contractors. As Fox remarked early on, referring to the BHP, "This isn't just the major leagues. We're jumping into the Super Bowl. It's a world-class project."[103] And it was not only the magnitude of the project that generated strong positive feelings, but also the end toward which the BHP was directed. All of those associated with the project felt that they were doing something important by helping to clean up the harbor and were thereby benefiting themselves and generations to come.

The Power of the Court

Of all the reasons for the MWRA's success in completing the BHP, none is more important than the role of Judge Mazzone. In countless ways, Mazzone used the court's power to shape and to guide the BHP and ensured that it stayed on track. What he did was not easy. Through court orders, many judges have overseen the operation of large public institutions and have done so with far less success. The history of remedial adjudication in the areas of integration, prison reform, and mental health institution reform offers numerous examples of mediocre or poor results.[104] Although Mazzone had the benefit of a relatively clear statutory framework to implement, his role still required considerable legal and political skills. Not surprisingly, given Mazzone's natural modesty, he was quick to downplay his role. "I didn't take bold new steps. I didn't make law. Just the Clean Water Act, that's it." On another occasion, he said, "I'm kind of proud of [the BHP], but take it easy on me. We're not done yet. Maybe someday there'll be something on my gravestone that says something about it."[105] Despite Mazzone's reluctance to take credit, Deland justifiably called him "the real hero [of the BHP] and the one who kept feet to the fire by a remarkable combination of judicial astuteness and political sagacity."[106]

The key to taking action is information, and Mazzone made sure he knew what was happening at all times through the use of a reporting system that he established at the outset of the remedial regime. On the 15th of every month the MWRA was required to submit a report to the court indicating the authority's compliance with the prior month's schedule deadlines and its progress in moving toward compliance with future deadlines. The MWRA's reports often brought up other issues relevant to the court schedule that it thought the court should be made aware of, such as political developments that could affect implementation. Other parties had the opportunity, which they often exercised, to submit their own reports to the court, in which they could comment on the MWRA's submission or raise other issues of concern that were relevant to the court schedule.

To help him digest the information in the MWRA's compliance reports, as well as the filings of other parties, Mazzone appointed a monitor to collect the submissions and to summarize what they contained, noting in particular those issues that required immediate court attention. Mazzone, then used the monitor's report, and the original submissions, to write his monthly compliance order, in which he documented the progress in meeting deadlines and discussed court decisions relating to the schedule. Mazzone also often used his monthly order to request that the parties report back to the court on various issues pertaining to the schedule. In addition to the monthly reports, Mazzone was kept up to date on the implementation of the court's order through the MWRA's submission of midyear and annual progress reports, which also identified potential compliance problems. Finally, occasional hearings on specific issues, at which time all the parties were represented, offered Mazzone another opportunity to keep abreast of the implementation process.

In addition to following the BHP through the written word and through formal oral arguments and discussions, Mazzone also often ventured out of the court and into the field to see how the project was progressing. It was, he said, a way of "showing the flag."[107] When the sandhogs broke through the final wall in the inter-island tunnel, Mazzone was there, lowered to the bottom of the shaft on Nut Island in a four-person metal cage. "This will really make a big difference for the people living around here," he said to the tired but happy workers. "I can remember when Wollaston beach was clean. For all kinds of reasons, it was worth it."[108] On a number of occasions Mazzone showed up early in the morning on Deer Island, unannounced, and jokingly told the surprised workers, "nice to see all you defendants this morning."[109] Mazzone even took his wife into the outfall tunnel once, he said, "just to make sure that she knew that this was going on."[110]

As Mazzone made clear time and again, the court-ordered schedule for the BHP was not "engraved in stone."[111] It was a dynamic document, and Mazzone was willing to change deadlines and the content of the order if there were compelling reasons for doing so. As Virginia Renick, one of the lawyers at the MWRA, noted, "Every few years the project looks quite different; it evolves over time."[112] Any changes, however, had to be presented and argued by the parties. Mazzone realized that he was not an expert on the issues contained in the schedule, and that the various parties, in particular the MWRA and the EPA, were. Here is where Mazzone's basic philosophy on remedial adjudication shone through. "The first thing I try to do," he said, "is defer to the parties during the remedy phase of this case; they knew it [what had to be done, technically], I didn't know it."[113] An example of Mazzone's approach can be seen in how he handled a revision to the schedule for long-term residuals management.

Residuals is a term that includes sludge as well as grit and screenings, the heavy solids that settle out of the wastewater during treatment and large objects, such as pieces of wood, that are trapped in screens placed at sewage pumping stations and headworks. The first interim schedule issued by the court in late 1985 established an August 1987 deadline for the MWRA to complete facilities plans for long-term residuals management. In June 1986, after further review of the feasibility of meeting that deadline, the MWRA and the EPA filed a joint motion for the court to change it to April 1988, and to establish December 1991 as the target date for ceasing the discharge of sludge to the harbor and commencing land-based disposal.[114] Mazzone gave the other parties ten days to comment on this motion, and receiving no objection, adopted it. This change in the deadline for the completion of the long-term residuals plan was not the last one. In late 1987 the MWRA presented a motion, supported by the other parties, to change the deadline again. On December 30, 1987, Mazzone wrote:

> I have stated before that any party is free to move for revision of a scheduled milestone if it can show good cause for changing that milestone. If the assumptions on which the various milestones are based prove to be

erroneous, any party is free to seek relief from imposition of the schedule and the sanctions, if any, that may be imposed for failing to meet any of the specific milestones. . . . This phase of the harbor cleanup was originally scheduled for completion in August, 1987. . . . It was revised and scheduled for completion in April, 1988. . . . The MWRA is seeking yet another revision, this time to October 31, 1989. As the parties are aware, an unambiguous, enforceable schedule is essential to moving this complex project forward. Accountability was a key factor in my adopting this schedule proposed by the MWRA. . . . I do not find at this time any good cause for changing this milestone. I will consider this matter further if a clear and unambiguous schedule is presented to me which will not affect the 1991 deadline for ending sludge discharge into the harbor.[115]

Within the next month the parties convinced Mazzone that a schedule revision was justified.

In my last Compliance Order . . . I denied the MWRA's motion for revisions to the long term residuals management portion of the schedule. At a hearing held on January 19, 1988, on other motions pending before the Court, the parties reiterated their collective belief that revisions to the schedule would be useful at this time, primarily because a prospectively achievable schedule permits the MWRA to enforce deadlines imposed on its various consultants. Because of the effort expended in arriving at an achievable schedule, I am reluctant to revise it. However, I am now persuaded by the parties that the ultimate goal will be best protected by the establishment of an achievable schedule. Therefore, I find that revisions to the milestones relating to the long term residuals management plan are necessary and appropriate at this time.[116]

Mazzone's deferential posture was very effective, and in almost every case it resulted in an agreement that was accepted and supported by the parties. According to Shelley, "a different judge might not have been as skillful in playing the negotiation role—pushing people to reach agreement and consensus without having to choose himself."[117] By encouraging the parties to work out their differences, Mazzone also helped them forge a close and positive working relationship that involved, as one of them noted, "many layers of communication and interaction."[118] Because the parties knew that Mazzone would first defer to them, they tried hard to resolve their disagreements on their own. This approach had the added benefit of creating, as Shelley noted, "a feeling of ownership of the process" that increased the parties' commitment to seeing the remedy successfully implemented.[119]

Mazzone's approach to the evolution of the court-ordered schedule worked quite well. Yet, despite his desire to defer to the parties on remedial decisions, he also made it clear that he would make the decisions if the parties failed to do so in a timely manner. "I deferred to them," he said, "until there was no action, no going forward, no progress, at which time I would step in."[120] One of the best examples of this is the initial negotiation over the long-term schedule. Mazzone first deferred to the parties, hoping that they could resolve their differences over long-term scheduling. He established a deadline for negotiations to which none of the parties objected. When the parties asked for more time to narrow their differences, he gave it. Only after the parties reached an impasse did Mazzone step in and choose the MWRA's schedule. As Mazzone noted at the time, since a long-term schedule was essential to moving the MWRA into compliance with the law and helping to clean up the harbor, continued delay in devising the schedule could not be tolerated. That Mazzone made a wise decision was reflected in the reactions of the parties. None of them opposed the judge's assumption of the remedial role. Even the CLF and the EPA felt that Mazzone had made a reasonable choice and, as a result, neither of them appealed the judge's decision. According to a CLF representative at the time, "the process was fair and the decision was made on substantial grounds and we can live with it."[121] Fowley stated that "Mazzone made a good decision. Lawyers are trained to make these choices. . . . Although we were disappointed in terms of losing . . . that was probably the right thing for the judge to do."[122]

Mazzone's posture of deference up to a point had one particularly important impact. By making clear his intentions to make a decision if the parties could not, Mazzone altered the dynamics of the negotiations. The uncertainty over how the judge would decide the issues created incentives among the parties to reach agreement on their own. Thus, Mazzone's willingness to intervene, ironically, served to reduce the need for such interventions to take place.

In four primary ways the court influenced the implementation of the BHP. The court's backing of the schedule created incentives for the MWRA and the relevant regulatory agencies to meet the schedule's deadlines. The court's presence increased the investment community's confidence in the authority's financial stability, thereby enhancing the authority's ability to float the bonds that were necessary to fund the BHP. The court's presence also decreased the potential for legislative restrictions on the MWRA's ability to secure the funding necessary to comply with the schedule. And when obstacles were placed in the way of implementation, the court used its powers to overcome them.

Incentives for Compliance with the Schedule

The court schedule served as a focal point for action. It was a clear statement of what the MWRA was supposed to complete and when. The items on the schedule rose to the top of the authority's agenda.[123] Court involvement, however, created an even stronger incentive for the MWRA to comply. As the "gorilla in the closet," the court was ready to force the MWRA to act if necessary through the application of sanctions, such as fines. When the MWRA board of directors made decisions, it knew that the court was, in effect, looking over its shoulder. As Levy noted, "When voting on something, they would ask, 'Is this on the schedule?'" If it was, chances were that "what would take years to be decided [in the absence of the court] would be decided in months."[124]

Although the "gorilla in the closet" image has negative connotations, from the MWRA's perspective the court's presence was a welcome incentive to comply. Although the MWRA was initially opposed to court intervention, the court schedule became a security blanket of sorts for the authority, giving it increased confidence that it would be able to ultimately fulfill its organizational mission. As Charles Lyons, a past MWRA board member, said while in that position, "I love judge Mazzone. From a political vantage point, the court is positive. It's not an albatross around our necks. The court is going to require politicians to be very very committed to the harbor cleanup, and that makes my job a lot easier."[125] Added Mazzone, "It is a comfort to the MWRA to know that if they don't perform they will be held to the schedule."[126] In this way, the schedule became a valuable management tool, for nothing focuses a manger's attention more than the knowledge that missing deadlines will likely result in unpleasant consequences.

Court involvement also affected the incentives of the state and federal regulatory agencies. Those agencies placed a priority on MWRA-related projects, thereby minimizing delays arising from regulatory review.[127] Here, too, the potential for the court to apply sanctions induced prompt action, for example, the head of an agency could be held in contempt if his or her agency failed to review schedule-related projects in a timely fashion. But it was not the potentially coercive power of the court alone that created incentives for compliance. As Levy noted, "the judge is like a father figure, nobody wants to tell him that it is my fault that the schedule is not being met." This sentiment reflected a larger truth—namely, that the court, as an institution, was accorded great legitimacy in the context of this case. When it placed its imprimatur on a schedule, a powerful element of moral suasion was brought into play that was based on the strongly held ideal that the court was a just arbiter of what the law required. In large part, therefore, the MWRA and the regulatory agencies sought to comply with the schedule because the court authoritatively said that was what must be done.

Calming the Bond Market

Mazzone's willingness to uphold the integrity of the schedule helped the MWRA achieve high bond ratings. As Standard & Poor's commented, major reasons for the MWRA's high bond ratings included the authority's "strong management and efficient organizational structure and the stabilizing influence of federal court oversight."[128] If anything threatened the MWRA's ability to repay its bonds with interest, the bond market had faith that the court could and would take steps to make sure the authority could fulfill its fiduciary obligations.

On one occasion, at least, Mazzone felt it necessary to specifically reassure the bond market of his resolve. This happened in late 1989, as an initiative sponsored by the Citizens for Limited Taxation began to pick up steam. That initiative was designed to roll back all fees imposed by any state authority or agency to 1988 levels, require the secretary of administration and finance to determine how much should be charged for public services, and make any changes in fees subject to legislative approval.[129] The MWRA argued that passage of such a measure, stripping the authority of its fiscal autonomy, would diminish its ability to meet its debt service obligations and to comply with the schedule. When the MWRA notified Mazzone that the credit rating agencies were concerned about the potential impact of the initiative, he wrote:

> What the parties evidently seek is an assurance that this Court will order the MWRA to meet its debt service obligations and will use its coercive powers to ensure that such an order is obeyed. . . . [U]ntil the issue is squarely presented . . . it would be inappropriate for me to speculate about a future decision. . . . However, while I cannot provide the specific assurance the parties seek, my previous statements over the course of the past four years should suffice to reassure all concerned that the Harbor cleanup will go forward in accordance with the schedule, and that there

is a vast array of remedial and equitable powers available to the Court under the law to ensure compliance with that schedule.[130]

The initiative made it onto the 1990 ballot, but was voted down. Therefore, Mazzone was not required to exercise the court's authority to ensure the project's continued implementation.

Deflecting Legislative Restrictions

A few Massachusetts politicians responded to MWRA ratepayer concerns about rising water and sewer rates resulting from the implementation of the court-ordered schedule by introducing bills in the state legislature that would have stripped the MWRA of its rate-setting powers and brought the authority more under the control of state government.[131] The court was highly aware of these developments and sympathetic to ratepayer concerns. Indeed, on numerous occasions, Mazzone encouraged the MWRA to "explore all legal and feasible means of reducing the financial burden this project will impose on the MWRA's ratepayers."[132] But when it appeared that political developments were heading toward a situation in which compliance with the schedule might be threatened, Mazzone made it clear that, no matter how the state or local political situation changed, his responsibility was to ensure that federal law was complied with and that he would do everything in his power to make sure that happened. This approach was reflected in Mazzone's response to a piece of legislation filed by two state senators in 1991.[133]

The bill in question was designed to rein in the MWRA. It included provisions that would have subjected the authority to regulation as a public utility, with the Department of Public Utilities having the right to approve rate increases and to give the MWRA advisory board control over final budgetary approvals. Mazzone reacted to the introduction of the bill with the following observation.

> Throughout the course of this litigation, this Court has consistently refrained from taking any action that intrudes on the legislative process. It is worth recalling that the legislative process first established the MWRA as an independent agency. This pending legislation seems aimed at stripping the MWRA of its independence and its ability to make the difficult, politically charged decisions that are necessary in this effort. Of course, the legislature should not ignore what it believes are important areas for increased attention. Its oversight and efforts to improve are necessary and welcome in our political system. But, the construction project under-

way as a result of the remedial order in this case is not a project that may be abandoned just because it is no longer acceptable to the "Political Environment," or because it costs too much in a temporarily stalled economy or because it sites certain facilities in the backyards of voters who elect legislative representatives. The orders of this Court are designed to compel compliance with a federal law that the Commonwealth has flouted for years. As I have repeatedly stated, the full remedial powers available to this Court will be used to scrutinize closely any attempt that would derail the project and undermine or circumvent those orders.[134]

Nothing ever came of the bill. Part of the reason was that many legislators believed that things should be left as they were, with the MWRA having the responsibility for making the difficult, costly, and necessary decisions that the legislature had earlier decided it was not willing to make. Another part of the reason, undoubtedly, was the knowledge that were the legislature to strip the authority of its ability to comply with the schedule, the court would not sit idly by. Mazzone's veiled threat raised the very real possibility that, if the bill became law, the bill's implied purpose, to keep the authority from making politically unpopular decisions, would not be realized because the court would use its powers to ensure that the unpopular decisions necessary for compliance with the schedule were made.

Overcoming Obstacles

The court used its coercive powers to maintain the integrity of the schedule on numerous occasions. During the summer of 1990, for example, the MWRA informed the court of difficulties it was having in securing local permits from the city of Quincy that were necessary for the authority to proceed with the construction of the sludge-to-fertilizer plant there.[135] In early October of that year, the MWRA still had yet to get permits for local water and sewer hookups, and it contended that if those permits were not obtained by mid-October the construction schedule would be in jeopardy.[136] As a result, Mazzone issued an order on October 18, requiring Quincy to respond to the MWRA's claims that the city was holding up the issuance of permits. Mazzone also scheduled a hearing later that month to discuss this matter, noting his concern that "any unjustified refusal to issue these permits will disrupt the schedule resulting in delay and increased costs."[137] By bringing this issue to a head at the hearing and making clear the intention of the court to intervene more coercively if the issues could not be resolved, Mazzone spurred action. According to the lawyer who represented Quincy, the threat of sanctions, in this instance and in general, created an "enormous incentive" for the parties to comply with the schedule.[138] The permits were issued by the end of the month. Reflecting on this turn of events, Mazzone wrote, "I have always encouraged the parties to reach an agreement on this and similar matters so that the Court is not compelled to intervene in what should be a local affair."[139]

Within two years another water-related issue threatened the schedule's integrity. In order to operate the new primary plant, a water line had to be routed to Deer Island. That line had to go through Winthrop, but not before issues were resolved concerning the extent and nature of the line's construction.[140] Furthermore, the town had to issue certain easements and street-opening permits before construction could proceed.[141] Throughout late 1991 and into the summer of 1992, the MWRA and Winthrop negotiated over these issues with little success.[142] On August 5, Mazzone noted this impasse and his intention to hold a hearing on the issue if the parties could not resolve it themselves by August 22. Reports that the parties were nearing agreement caused Mazzone to cancel the hearing scheduled for August 23.[143] Although the parties had narrowed their differences, negotiations stalled in mid-September and Mazzone held a hearing. Shortly thereafter, Mazzone made clear his frustration and resolve to break the impasse.

> Despite several optimistic reports that agreement was near and the holding of a hearing at which I encouraged the parties to reach agreement so that Court intervention would not be required given that the remaining areas of disagreement were very small, the parties have failed to reach agreement. As I stated at the hearing, it is deeply disappointing that an agreement could not be reached. On a project of this magnitude, it is discouraging that a dispute over the timing of approvals of the plans for one water line should require the intervention of the federal court overseeing the case. There have been, and will be far more divisive issues ahead of us, and no satisfactory explanation has been made to me by Winthrop as to why it cannot commit, without seemingly ever-increasing conditions, to a relatively straightforward schedule. . . . In light of the very generous concessions by the MWRA and in the absence of any sound explanation for Winthrop's indecision, I reluctantly conclude that my direct intervention is required.[144]

That intervention was the issuance of an order on September 25 requiring the construction to proceed by December 2, 1992.[145] In the shadow of the order, the parties were able to resolve their differences and to hammer out an agreement. On October 23, the MWRA reported to the court that it "expects the renewed spirit of good will and cooperation between the parties to prevail as the parties continue to work together closely," and asked the court to vacate its September 25 order and to approve the agreement in its place.[146] Mazzone did so gladly, commending "the parties on their diligence and efforts to resolve this matter without further court intervention."[147] Despite the agreement, however, the issue was not completely resolved. By March 1993, the easements and permits had not been issued, and Mazzone decided to turn up the pressure again, stating that if these outstanding matters were not resolved by mid-April the court would consider holding a conference on the matter.[148] Resolution came, no conference was held, and the construction of the water line through Winthrop began. According to the lawyer representing Winthrop, the pressure that the court brought to bear "did hurry things along."[149]

On the morning of August 6, 1992, a small fire occurred at the sludge pelletizing facility in Quincy. Immediately after the fire, the MWRA notified city officials, suspended operations at the facility and began taking steps to determine the causes of the fire and the steps necessary to operate the plant safely.[150] That same day, "in the interest of public safety" the Quincy fire chief issued a directive that all operations at the plant cease until he ordered otherwise.[151] This posed a serious problem for the MWRA and the integrity of the BHP. Although the pelletizing facility was temporarily shut down, the sewage plants were not. Each day, each plant produced tons of sludge. With the pelletizing plant closed, that sludge could not be converted into fertilizer that would normally be shipped off-site for sale. While the MWRA initiated the development and implementation of a backup plan to transport the sludge to a disposal site, in lieu of turning it into fertilizer, it needed to be able to store the sludge temporarily.[152]

The chief's directive, however, not only shut down the pelletizing facility; it also forbid the use of the sludge storage tanks at the Fore River Staging Area, despite the fact that those tanks were not involved in the fire. Without the use of the tanks, the MWRA would be forced to rely on the storage capacity on-site at the two treatment plants. This posed a particularly acute problem at Nut Island, where storage capacity would be exceeded by August 10. If this happened, the MWRA would be forced to discharge the sludge into the harbor, violating the court schedule's prohibition of sludge discharges to the harbor after December 1991.

To avoid this outcome, on August 10 the MWRA asked the court to issue an order overriding the fire chief's directive as it related to the storage tanks. The MWRA argued that with the use of the tanks, storage capacity would be extended to August 16, giving it much needed time to address Quincy's concerns and to put into place disposal plans.[153] Mazzone issued the order, averting sludge discharges to the harbor. Interim disposal plans were implemented, Quincy's concerns were addressed, and ultimately the pelletizing plant came back on line.

One of the most dramatic examples of the court's efforts to the keep the BHP on track involved the siting of a residuals landfill. In January 1989, the MWRA board selected a site in Walpole, Massachusetts, as its preferred location for the landfill.[154] The selection process had begun in 1986 and involved the evaluation of nearly three hundred sites within the state. The landfill was to accept grit and screenings from the sewage treatment plants and to be used as a backup for sludge disposal. It was to be a backup because another element of the authority's residual management plan was constructing a pelletizing plant in Quincy that would turn sludge into fertilizer. The Walpole landfill would be used only if the authority were unable to market the sludge as fertilizer or, in some other way, to legally dispose of it.[155]

Before the landfill could be built a number of hurdles had to be cleared. The MWRA's residuals management plan had to undergo favorable environmental review by state and federal environmental agencies, and the MWRA had to acquire the Walpole site, which was owned by the Massachusetts Department of Corrections. Under Massachusetts's law, before the MWRA could acquire ownership, the state legislature would have to pass a bill that allowed for the transfer of land. Because construction of the landfill was a crucial part of the cleanup plan, especially in relation to the December 1991 deadline for the cessation of sludge discharges to the harbor, Mazzone closely monitored the MWRA's progress in clearing these hurdles.[156]

The MWRA simultaneously began pushing for the approval of its landfill plans and the filing of the necessary land-transfer legislation. On the approval side of the ledger, things went well. On November 20, 1989, the Executive Office of Environmental Affairs accepted the MWRA's *Final Environmental Impact Report* on long-term residuals management; the report included not only the designation of the Walpole landfill, but also the decision to build the sludge pelletizing facility in Quincy.[157] On March 30, 1990, the EPA issued its own *Final Supplemental Environmental Impact Statement* approving the MWRA's long-term residuals management plan.[158]

On the land transfer side of the ledger, repeated delays occurred.

The MWRA began efforts to have the land transfer legislation filed soon after voting in favor of the Walpole site, and Mazzone ordered the authority to keep the court updated as to the status of its efforts. In June 1989, Governor Dukakis decided to postpone filing the legislation. Later that summer, the governor again decided to postpone filing the legislation, preferring to wait until the state and federal environmental review process had run its course. Although accepting this rationale, Mazzone warned, "In the event of any slippage in the schedule for completion of the . . . environmental review process, however, I will reconsider whether further action is appropriate concerning this issue."[159]

Soon after the state and federal reviews were completed, the EPA began expressing great concerns about the problems related to getting access to the Walpole site. As a result, the agency asked Mazzone to issue an order requiring the MWRA to make plans for an alternative landfill in order to maintain the integrity of the schedule.[160] Mazzone deferred his decision on the EPA's motion and held onto the hope that action would be taken soon to resolve this problem. "I will not interfere in local and state processes so long as there is no real and imminent threat to the schedule that has been imposed to remedy decades of violation of federal law. . . . The legislature and executive have always before acted on a timely and responsive basis when faced with critical decisions relating to the Harbor clean up. I have no reason to believe they will not do so at this time."[161]

At this point the Dukakis administration, which has since submitted land transfer legislation, told the court that it was committed to getting the legislation approved. At the same time, however, the House had voted to put off consideration of the legislation until December 5, 1990. Responding to this turn of events, Mazzone wrote:

> I believe the best course is to withhold current action until December 5, 1990. . . . As I have repeatedly stated throughout this litigation, this court should not become involved in the substantive decision-making process required to site, design, and build the facilities necessary to achieve full and timely compliance. . . . My role is to see that decades of violations of federal law were identified, and, once identified, terminated as quickly as reasonably possible. . . . At the same time, I am mindful of the huge risk that attends my decision to forego action until December 5, 1990. At stake is the credibility of the Court's schedule and the public's faith in the integrity of the entire project. . . . In the event that necessary legislation has not been approved by that date and that slippage in the schedule

results from the paralysis surrounding the siting issue, I will entertain and intend to grant a motion for sanctions designed to ensure immediate resolution of this matter.[162]

A large part of the paralysis Mazzone refers to was the result of the political power of the "not in my backyard" (NIMBY) syndrome.[163] The selection of the Walpole site evoked a swift and strong reaction from local residents.[164] Despite the MWRA's extensive search and site analyses and the approvals of various environmental agencies, the people of Walpole did not believe that the siting decision was either fair or environmentally sound. Neither did Norfolk, Walpole's neighbor closest to the proposed site. This opposition was not solely a reflexive case of NIMBY. Although it is true that neither wanted the facility, Walpole already housed a state maximum security prison and Norfolk a minimum security prison; both towns argued that they had done their fair share for the state with respect to unpopular local land uses.

Walpole and Norfolk filed suits in state and federal court, challenging the review processes that led to the selection of the Walpole site.[165] Beyond that, the citizens of Walpole and surrounding communities successfully pressured the local, state, and federal politicians representing them to oppose the siting decision.[166] And during the 1990 gubernatorial campaign, the ultimate victor, William Weld, ran in opposition to placing the landfill in Walpole. All of these pressures combined to stall the transfer legislation.

On October 31, 1990, the court schedule was amended with a timeline for the construction of the long-term residuals management facilities.[167] With respect to the landfill, the schedule now required facility design to be completed by November 1991, construction to commence in or before September 1992, and for the landfill to begin operation by March 1994. With these dates fast approaching, the need to quickly resolve the land transfer impasse grew. In late November 1990, Mazzone warned that if legislation were not approved by December 5, he would hold a hearing on the matter. Despite the clear intention of the court to step in if the legislature failed to pass the bill, the House voted on December 10, not for the transfer, but against it.[168] Mazzone's patience had worn out. On December 26, he wrote, "The United States suggested some months ago that awaiting legislative resolution of this issue would prove unavailing. . . . Unfortunately, the United States has proven correct. . . . My confidence was misplaced. As the Conservation Law Foundation has put it succinctly, the legislature has defaulted to the court."[169]

The EPA now asked the court to either order the commonwealth to transfer the Walpole site to the MWRA or place a moratorium on sewer hookups in the MWRA service area until the authority was able to acquire a suitable landfill site.[170] After a hearing on this motion in early January 1991, Mazzone issued a moratorium on February 25, 1991.[171] In doing so, Mazzone noted that such an action was explicitly contemplated by the Clean Water Act as an appropriate sanction in the face of continued violations of permit conditions. Although he clearly preferred not to intervene in this manner, he made it clear that it was a necessary step. "I have consistently stated my reluctance to take a substantive decision-making role in the process," Mazzone said, "and I have been sensitive to the conflict between state and federal authority that court action would implicate. However, I have also made it clear that I would consider taking action at such time that this court's scheduling order is jeopardized. That time has come."[172]

Mazzone's move placed newly elected Governor Weld in a difficult spot. He had run against the Walpole siting decision and wanted to make good on his campaign promise.[173] At the same time, the moratorium jeopardized the state's economy, which he desperately wanted to jump-start. In the hope of getting the judge to lift the moratorium, Weld announced, on April 1, the appointment of a special commission to find an alternative landfill site, within the state, to take Walpole's place. The commission's focus on in-state, as opposed to out-of-state, alternatives reflected the EPA's insistence that the MWRA construct an in-state, backup landfill, in part because of EPA concerns about the reliability of out-of-state options.

With the commission scheduled to report within 120 days, the commonwealth asked Mazzone to suspend the moratorium, pending the completion of the commission's work. When Mazzone denied this motion, the commonwealth appealed the denial as well as the moratorium to the United States Court of Appeals, First Circuit, arguing that Mazzone's actions were unreasonable.[174] The circuit court sided with Mazzone and upheld the moratorium on April 22, 1991.

Hours after the circuit court decision, Weld vowed to soon introduce the land transfer legislation, stating that "the economy of Massachusetts will grind to a halt" if the moratorium was not lifted, and, further, that his administration "really doesn't have any option but to take action to satisfy the federal judge."[175] The transfer legislation passed the legislature on May 21, 1991, and was signed the same day by Weld. Mazzone then lifted the moratorium, stating that "hopefully, this puts the [land-fill] matter behind us."[176]

Mazzone's optimism, however, was premature. On November 20, 1991, the MWRA board voted to direct the authority to develop and to issue a request for proposals to consider alternatives for residuals management backup other than the current plan of using Walpole. The vote was actually two-pronged. Given the court schedule, which contained deadlines for the construction of the Walpole landfill, the board knew that Mazzone would not allow the search for an alternative to proceed at the expense of continued progress toward complying with the schedule. Thus, part of the board's vote was a commitment to ensure that work on the Walpole landfill continue in accord with the schedule, while the search for alternatives was under way. The actual search did not begin until April 1992, when the authority appropriated $100,000 for that purpose.[177]

The MWRA's decision to reopen the search was based on politics and the belief that an acceptable alternative might still be found. Furthermore, the political pressure to find an alternative to Walpole did not disappear with the land transfer, it intensified. Although the governor's commission reported, in August 1991, that it had failed to find an acceptable, in-state alternative to Walpole, the administration did not give up the fight. Instead, the commission took the offensive, arguing that "the EPA is requiring an excessive level of certainty in requiring an in-state landfill," and that the agency should reconsider its opposition to out-of-state options.[178]

Congressman Barney Frank, who represented Walpole and strongly opposed the landfill decision, also wanted the EPA to reconsider its stance. In October 1992, a measure authored by Frank was included in an EPA appropriations bill.[179] Although giving the MWRA up to a year to find a legally acceptable alternative backup landfill, the measure also still allowed the EPA to require sufficient in-state backup landfill capacity if no acceptable alternatives were found. Although neither the commission's stance nor the Frank amendment affected the EPA's position, both certainly created substantial political pressure in favor of continuing the search for an alternative to Walpole. That pressure was not lost on the MWRA board, which included three members appointed by the governor, including the chairperson, as well as other members who were sympathetic to Walpole's and Norfolk's concerns. There was also sentiment among a majority of the board members that with one more

if the need arose. In its motion to the court, the MWRA made clear the
benefits of the new plan.

> Unlike the Walpole landfill which provides backup capacity for only two
> to three years . . . the alternative plan provides backup capacity for . . .
> the next 30 years. . . . [B]y substituting multiple backup landfills available
> through commercial means in place of sole reliance on a landfill to be
> owned by the MWRA, the alternative provides a better way to achieve
> the Court's objective of ensuring long-term compliance with the Clean
> Water Act. . . . Finally, the alternative plan can be in place within the
> original March 1994 Court-scheduled milestone for operation of the
> Walpole landfill.[191]

At the October 1, 1993, hearing on the MWRA's motion, each party
rose to support the new plan.[192] The EPA accepted the plan, but was
unwilling to call it better than the one it replaced, although the agency
agreed it was good enough and would fulfill legal requirements. Mazzone, clearly excited by this turn of events, commended the parties and
stated that the alternative was "better than" the original plan, and,
therefore, altering the schedule to reflect the alternative was a "merito-
rious modification in accordance with federal law."[193]

Reflecting on the Federal Court's Role

In a special edition commemorating its thirtieth anniversary (September 2002) the *Massachusetts Lawyers Weekly* prepared a list of the thirty
most memorable cases of the past thirty years.[194] The Boston Harbor
case, which combined the state and federal proceedings, was number
five on the list, a very respectable showing given the many high-profile
cases in Massachusetts. For example, number one on the list was the
Boston busing/desegregation case that ripped the city apart in the mid-
1970s, and number seven was the case that involved high cancer rates
in Woburn, Massachusetts, and later became the basis for a book, *A
Civil Action*, and a movie by the same name starring John Travolta.
When the *Weekly*'s reporter asked Mazzone what made the case memorable, he focused on the political and not the legal issues that it raised.
Mazzone added, "If I was a constitutional law professor, I'd point to
this case and say to the students 'the doctrine of separation of powers—
forget it!' But in the end, all three branches did what they had to do and
the case worked." As for the unique role of the courts, Mazzone said,
"Courts have no constituency. You bring a case, and we'll act independently to enforce the law."

The success of the federal court's oversight of the BHP is clearly evidenced in the comments of those who participated in the process as well as those who observed it. According to Nancy Kurtz, MWRA's general counsel, the authority

was indeed fortunate to be a defendant in the U.S. District Court of Judge Mazzone. While he made it clear from the beginning that his job was to enforce the Clean Water Act, his courtroom became a constructive forum where parties who started as adversaries were able to work together to resolve difficult legal, economic, and political issues and bring the BHP to completion under an aggressive schedule and within its original budget.[195]

To Fowley, the assistant regional counsel for the EPA's Region 1 and the lead EPA attorney on the Boston Harbor case from 1985 to 1995, the court was key to the success of the BHP for three main reasons. First, Fowley noted,

Mazzone was wise in choosing the MWRA's schedule at the outset of the case. Second, he set up a monthly reporting process that kept him informed, and he stayed on the top of the case by issuing his own monthly tracking orders, which highlighted progress and urged, and sometimes forced action to overcome obstacles to achieving the schedule's milestones. In this way, Mazzone was quite different than many other judges who leave the case once initial orders have been issued. Third, he had to confront some difficult situations of noncompliance that he dealt with very astutely. Instead of succumbing to a range of pressures, he headed off pressures that, in the absence of his involvement, would have caused the project to be scaled back.[196]

Steven Lipman, special projects coordinator at the Massachusetts Department of Environmental Protection, offered the following perspective.

Without question, the overall control and direct oversight by the Federal District Court, and Judge David Mazzone in particular, was critical to ensuring that the cleanup proceeded forward in compliance with the Court Order. The schedule . . . was reasonable and achievable while keeping everyone's "feet-to-the-fire." Judge Mazzone has been able to traverse the slippery slope of performing active and direct oversight of project decision-making, without becoming an impediment to day-to-day actions. . . . The fact that this massive public works project was implemented under budget and for the most part on-schedule is a tribute to Judge Mazzone's abilities.[197]

Vivien Li, executive director of the Boston Harbor Association, said that Mazzone "was under a lot of pressure, including from the Governor's office, but his attitude was, 'no, we're committed to this project.' If it wasn't for him . . . [there] would have been backsliding so many times."[198] Similarly, Richard Delaney, director of the Urban Harbors Institute at the University of Massachusetts Boston, added, "Judge Mazzone's detailed management of this case over many years provided for all the responsible parties a constant focus on the Boston Harbor problem as well as an occasional authoritative push when needed."[199]

This, the largest tunnel boring machine ever to operate in New England, was used to excavate the outfall tunnel.

A field of two-ton precast liner segments near the outfall tunnel shaft. Along the 9.5-mile tunnel length thousands of these segments were hoisted in place by the tailing gear of the tunnel boring machine. Later the seams were grouted to provide a watertight seal.

Muck cars in the tunnel transporting workers.

One of the diffuser heads sitting on dry land. The multiple ports on the diffuser heads help dilute the effluent discharged into Massachusetts Bay.

A telephoto lens pulls the Boston skyline closer to the jack barge, which is installing the diffuser caps.

Nine-and-a-half miles of tunnel mined and lined, the finishing shift of "sandhogs" take a bow.

Inter-island tunnel starter shaft. Photo by Massachusetts Water Resources Authority.

This dramatic shot was taken during the 1994 inter-island tunnel fire. It shows the intensity of the fire at the tunnel shaft on Deer Island. The fire started in the conveyer belt system.

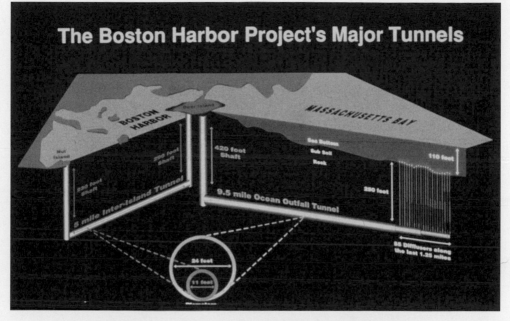

Cutaway schematic showing the tunnels of the Boston Harbor Project.

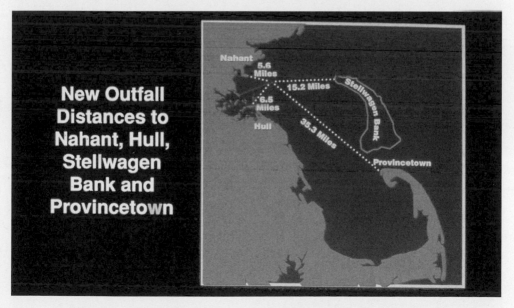

Map showing the distances between the outfall pipe and Stellwagen Bank and Provincetown, on Cape Cod.

Closeup of two of the egg-shaped sludge digesters.

Aerial shot of the pelletizing facility in Quincy.

A combined sewer overflow discharges into the Fort Point Channel, in Boston, in the early 1990s. Photo by Karen-Jayne Dodge/MWRA.

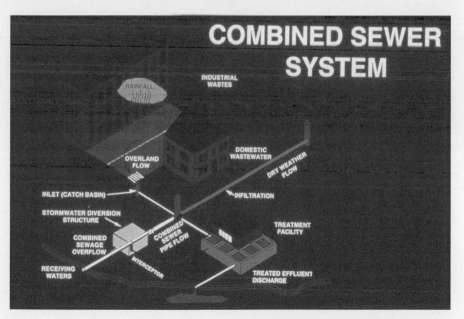

Schematic showing the basic operations of the combined sewer system.

Paul F. Levy served as MWRA executive director from 1988 to 1992.

Douglas B. MacDonald, executive director of the MWRA from 1992 to 2000, presides over the demolition ceremonies for the old Deer Island treatment plant.

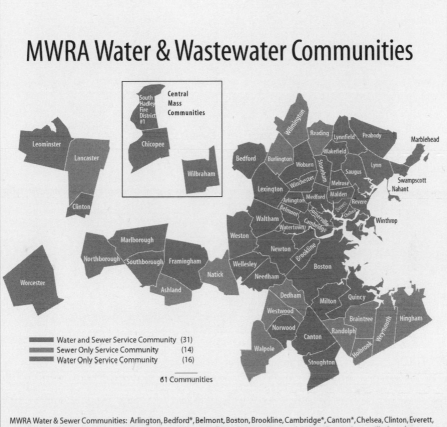

MWRA Water & Wastewater Communities

Central Mass Communities

South Hadley Fire District #1

Chicopee

Leominster

Lancaster

Wilbraham

Clinton

Marlborough

Northborough Southborough Framingham

Worcester

Ashland

Natick

Wilmington

Reading Lynnfield Peabody

Marblehead

Bedford Burlington

Wakefield

Woburn

Stoneham

Saugus

Lynn

Lexington Winchester

Melrose

Swampscott

Nahant

Arlington Medford Malden

Revere

Belmont Somerville Everett Chelsea

Waltham Watertown Cambridge

Winthrop

Weston

Newton Brookline

Wellesley

Boston

Needham

Dedham Milton Quincy

Westwood

Braintree Hingham

Norwood Randolph Weymouth

Canton Holbrook

Walpole

Stoughton

- ▬ Water and Sewer Service Community (31)
- ▬ Sewer Only Service Community (14)
- ▬ Water Only Service Community (16)

____

61 Communities

MWRA Water & Sewer Communities: Arlington, Bedford*, Belmont, Boston, Brookline, Cambridge*, Canton*, Chelsea, Clinton, Everett, Framingham, Lexington, Malden, Medford, Melrose, Milton, Needham*, Newton, Norwood, Quincy, Revere, Somerville, Stoneham, Stoughton, Wakefield, Waltham, Watertown, Wellesley, Winchester, Winthrop & Woburn.

MWRA Sewer-only Communities: Ashland, Braintree, Burlington, Dedham, Hingham, Holbrook, Lancaster, Natick, Randolph, Reading, Walpole, Westwood, Weymouth & Wilmington

MWRA Water-only Communities: Chicopee, Leominster*, Lynn*(GE only), Lynnfield(Water District), Marblehead, Marborough*, Nahant, Northborough*, Peabody*, Saugus, South Hadley(FD#1), Southborough, Swampscott, Weston, Wilbraham & Worcester*.

* Partial MWRA Water Service supplements local sources.

October 6, 2003

MWRA Sewer Service Areas.

Judge David A. Mazzone enjoying himself at the opening of the
Deer Island Public Access area.

The pathway that is part of the Deer Island Public Access area.

Swimmers at the starting line for a one-mile swim in Boston Harbor on September 5, 1992. The race was sponsored by Jantzen, Inc., for Save the Harbor/Save the Bay. Similar swims have been held in subsequent years. Photo by Karen-Jayne Dodge/MWRA.

Old Nut Island primary sewage treatment facility.

Nut Island today, with the public park in the foreground and the new head-works, or sewage screening facility, at the far end of the island. The headworks provides preliminary treatment for Deer Island–bound wastewater from twenty-one southern sewer system communities. At the headworks sewage passes through screens and grit chambers that remove large objects, sand, and gravel before conveying the flow to Deer Island for primary and then secondary treatment.

The old Deer Island primary sewage treatment plant.

Aerial view of the new Deer Island treatment facilities.

Conclusion

"How Clean is Clean Enough?"

The story of the Boston area's intimate relationship with sewage is not over, and, in fact, never will be. Since the completion of the BHP, the MWRA has entered a new and no less challenging phase of sewage operations that involves both construction and maintenance. On the construction side of the ledger, there are many years, many hundreds of millions of dollars, and many decisions to go before the CSO problem is solved, or more accurately, managed. The good news is that by reconfiguring the CSO plan in response to changing circumstances, the MWRA was able to cut roughly $600 million off the original price tag of $1.26 billion.[1] And already more than half of the CSO projects contained in the court-ordered schedule have been completed, others are under construction, and CSO volumes have been dramatically reduced while the percentage of the remaining flow that receives treatment has increased. The MWRA also has to grapple with the ongoing problems of infiltration and inflow. Every joint between pipes offers a potential entryway for freshwater into the sewers, and when it rains or snows melt, the influx of freshwater increases. Of course, the new Deer Island plant has a much greater peak capacity than did the two old plants combined, but infiltration and inflow is still serious problem. Amazingly, more than half of the volume of water that flows through the Deer Island treatment plant is groundwater or stormwater. The authority is working with local communities to address this problem and has already given them nearly $150 million in interest-free loans and grants to fund infiltration and inflow reduction projects and sewer rehabilitation. But this is a proverbial as well as a literal drop in the bucket. One estimate is that to reduce infiltration and inflow by as little as ten percent could cost from $1 to $1.5 billion.

On the maintenance side of the ledger, the job is just beginning. The minute the new sewage treatment plant went on line, its parts began wearing out. To keep the plant working properly, workers must keep it maintained. That is neither a simple nor an inexpensive task. Inertia is one obstacle. While the BHP was still under construction, there was a palpable excitement in the air. The people at the MWRA and the laborers out in the field were all pulling in the same direction to achieve a common goal, and that energy helped the project succeed. As inevitably happens when any major goal is reached, a bit of a letdown occured. Newspaper headlines announcing that a new milestone has been met are now a thing of the past, as are the photo opportunities. For even the best-run organizations, maintenance is a Herculean task. In the MWRA's case maintenance is made more difficult by virtue of the size and complexity of the sewage system and its cost. Seeing their rates go ever higher was painful enough for MWRA customers when the BHP was in full gear and they could see what they were getting for their money. But maintenance is a silent actor, rarely seen or appreciated by those who benefit from it. In the coming years, when MWRA has to justify rising assessments, it will face a growing chorus of ratepayers who balk at the costs, in effect, asking, What have you done for me lately? The rates issue, of course, is much larger than just maintenance. As rates rise to cover the various costs incurred by the MWRA, ratepayer discontent will as well.[2] Whether that compromises the authority's ability to continue its mission, only time will tell. But, given all that has been spent and all that has been achieved, it is hard to imagine a future in which such hard-won gains are sacrificed.

Unfortunately it is not impossible to imagine such a future. The Commonwealth of Massachusetts, along with the rest of the country, is going through difficult economic times. The Commonwealth's January 2003 budget-cutting decision to eliminate rate relief for the MWRA resulted in a dramatic rise in the Authority's rates. If larger rate increases become the norm, the threats to the integrity of the MWRA's mission will grow in the face of the increased political pressure that will surely be brought to bear by ratepayers who feel themselves getting squeezed. And it is not only external pressure that can throw the MWRA off course. In an effort to become "leaner and meaner," the Authority recently laid off numerous employees. As a result of the way in which the layoffs were handled as well as the relatively large numbers involved, the morale at the Authority is arguably at is lowest level ever. If such a depressed atmosphere exists too long, the performance of the staff as well as the physical plant for which they are responsible will certainly suffer.

Another reality of the cleanup of Boston Harbor is that it is not all up to the MWRA. Take the issue of stormwater management, for example. As a recent MWRA report states, "while there may be well-matched pros and cons of an expanded role for MWRA as a stormwater management agency, stormwater management is not currently part of MWRA's mission."[3] Indeed, much of the responsibility for devising and implementing stormwater management plans rests with the cities and towns in the MWRA service area, many of whom have stormwater control permits with the EPA that require the implementation of best management practices to keep stormwater from contaminating local waterways. Nevertheless, the debate over MWRA's role in this issue is not over. As this book went to press, the Science Advisory Committee of Save the Harbor/Save the Bay issued a report that highlighted the connection between stormwater discharges, sewage from illegal hook-ups and broken pipes, and CSOs, and the periodic closure of beaches in South Boston and North Dorchester because of high levels of bacteria in the water. Negotiations about what should be done to further reduce the incidence of such beach closures are ongoing among the MWRA, state and federal regulators, local politicians and environmental groups, and other interested parties. Central issues to be resolved include the nature of additional CSO and stormwater management facilities as well as the extent to which the MWRA is responsible for constructing them. Ultimately, the federal court will play a key role in resolving these issues. And while it appears that, in this instance because of some special circumstances, the MWRA will go forward with a plan that addresses CSO *as well as* stormwater concerns, the authority still believes that unless its mission is formally changed to include broader stormwater management responsibilities, it should not take on this extra task in other situations.

There are many other issues that affect the environmental quality of the harbor, in addition to stormwater, for which the MWRA has no special responsibility or power. These include coastal zoning, non-point source pollution, dredging, and boating. The limited nature of the authority's ability to address such issues is not surprising. The MWRA was established to upgrade the area's antiquated sewage treatment system and bring it into compliance with federal and state environmental law, and as a result to contribute mightily to the cleanup of Boston Harbor. The authority was not, however, established to remedy every environmental insult heaped upon the harbor.

Everyone who has a stake in the state of Boston Harbor has to ask themselves, sooner or later, how clean is clean enough? This question has been at the core of every important controversy about the environment and pollution, and it is phenomenally difficult to answer. Just look at Boston Harbor. To some, the harbor is much cleaner than it has to be, especially given the huge cost involved. What, they wonder, has roughly $4 billion gotten us, and what possible reason could we have for wanting to spend more? To others, the harbor is clean enough and anything more would be of marginal benefit. Still others are happy that the harbor has come this far, but believe that more has to be done, particularly with respect to CSOs, stormwater, and, perhaps, even urban non-point source pollution, pollution from boats, and deposition of contaminants from the air. Still others view the question purely in legal terms; if the relevant laws are complied with, then the harbor is as clean as it should be. And, of course, there are no doubt a few for whom the answer never comes. There is always more we can and should do.

The question of how clean is clean enough has swirled around the harbor for centuries, and the public, political, and legal efforts to provide an answer continue to shape the harbor's history. In fact, this fundamental question will remain an active topic of debate for centuries. Whatever the outcome of that debate, the people of Boston already have a harbor of which they can be proud. And it is up to them to make sure that their children will feel the same way.

Notes

Chapter One

1. Thomas H. O'Connor, *The Hub* (Boston, 2001), 3, 6, 8–9.
2. Ibid., 9–10.
3. Ibid., 8.
4. William Wood, *New England's Prospect* (London, 1634), 2–3.
5. Martin V. Melosi, *The Sanitary City* (Baltimore, 2000), 41.
6. Joel A. Tarr, James McCurry, and Terry F. Yosie, *The Development and Impact of Urban Wastewater Technology*, in *Pollution and Reform in American Cities, 1870–1930*, ed. Martin V. Melosi (Austin, 1980), 60.
7. John B. Blake, *Public Health in the Town of Boston* (Boston, 1959), 13.
8. George Chandler Whipple, *State Sanitation*, 2 vols. (Cambridge, Mass., 1917), 1:5.
9. Blake, *Public Health*, 15.
10. Ibid., 14–15.
11. Eliot C. Clarke, *Main Drainage Works of the City of Boston* (Boston, 1885), 7.
12. American Public Works Association (APWA) "Sewers and Wastewater Treatment," in *History of Public Works in the United States, 1776–1976* (Chicago, 1976), 400.
13. General Court of the Commonwealth, *The Acts and Resolves, Public and Private, of the Province of the Massachusetts Bay*, vol. 1 (Boston, 1869), 643.
14. Ibid.
15. "APWA, Sewers and Wastewater Treatment," 400.
16. Boston Record Commissioners, *A Report of the Record Commissioners of the City of Boston, Containing the Records of Boston Selectmen, 1736 to 1742* (Boston, 1886), 4.
17. Boston Record Commissioners, *A Report of the Record Commissioners of the City of Boston, Containing the Records of Boston Selectmen, 1716 to 1736* (Boston, 1885), 30–31.
18. General Court of the Commonwealth, *The Acts and Resolves, Public and Private, of the Province of the Massachusetts Bay*, vol. 3 (Boston, 1878), 739.

19. General Court of the Commonwealth, *The Acts and Resolves, Public and Private, of the Province of the Massachusetts Bay*, vol. 4 (Boston, 1881), 621.

20. Blake, *Public Health*, 102.

21. General Court of the Commonwealth, *Acts and Laws of the Commonwealth of Massachusetts* (Boston, 1896), 82.

22. Harold Farnsworth Gray, "Sewerage in Ancient and Mediaeval Times," *Sewage Works Journal* 12, no. 5 (September 1940): 939–946; and James L. Foil, Joel A. Cerwick, and James E. White, "Collection Systems Past and Present," *Operations Forum* (December 1993): 13–19.

23. Gray, "Sewerage in Ancient and Mediaeval Times," 942.

24. J. J. Cosgrove, *History of Sanitation* (Pittsburgh, 1909), 31–34.

25. Leonard Metcalf and Harrison P. Eddy, "The Lessons Taught by Early Sewerage Works," reprinted in *Sewering the Cities*, ed. Barbara Gutmann Rosenkrantz (New York, 1977), 1–2.

26. Justin Winsor, ed., *The Memorial History of Boston Including Suffolk County, Massachusetts, 1630–1880*, Vol. 2 (Boston, 1881), 441.

27. Blake, *Public Health*, 103.

28. Ibid., 102.

29. Ibid., 104.

30. Ibid., 210.

31. Ibid., 104.

32. Ibid., 11.

33. Ibid., 162.

34. Ibid., 163.

35. Whipple, *State Sanitation* 1:7.

36. Blake, *Public Health*, 168.

37. Whipple, *State Sanitation* 1:9.

38. Blake, *Public Health*, 169.

39. Ibid., 169, 174.

40. Ibid., 211.

41. Josiah Quincy, *A Municipal History of the Town and City of Boston during Two Centuries from September 17, 1630, to September 17, 1830* (Boston, 1852), 120.

42. Blake, *Public Health*, 227–228.

43. Boston City Archives.

44. City of Boston, *A Volume of Records Relating to the Early History of Boston Containing Minutes of the Selectmen's Meetings, 1811 to 1817, and Part of 1818* (Boston, 1908), 92–95.

45. Quincy, *Municipal History*, 65.

46. Ibid., 73.

47. City of Boston, *The Charter of the City of Boston, and Ordinance Made and Established by the Mayor, Aldermen, and Common Council, with Such Acts of the Legislature of Massachusetts, as Relate to the Government of Said City* (Boston, 1827), 103–105.

48. Ibid., 174.

49. City of Boston, *The Charter and Ordinances of the City of Boston, Together with the Acts of the Legislature Relating to the City* (Boston, 1834), 176–177.

50. Ibid., 248.

51. City of Boston, City Doc. no. 10 (1837), 2.

52. City of Boston, *Common Sewers*, City Doc. no. 12 (March 29, 1838), 3.

53. City of Boston, *Address of the Mayor to the City Council of Boston, January 4, 1847*, City Doc. no. 1 (1847), 13–15.

54. City of Boston, *Inaugural Address to the Aldermen and Common Council by John Prescott Bigelow, January 7, 1850*, City Doc. no. 1 (1850), 9–10.

55. Barbara Gutmann Rosenkrantz, *Public Health and the State* (Cambridge, 1972), 4.

56. City of Boston, Internal Health Department, *Report on the Cholera in Boston in 1849*, City Doc. no. 66 (1850), 12–13.

57. Ibid., 172–173.

58. Sarah S. Elkind, *Bay Cities and Water Politics* (Lawrence, Kan., 1998), 16.

59. Ibid., 26.

60. Stephen Halliday, *The Great Stink of London* (Phoenix Mill, U.K., 1999), 125–128; and Charles E. Rosenberg, *The Cholera Years* (Chicago, 1987), 199–200.

61. City of Boston, *Report on the Cholera*, 165.

62. Ibid., 175.

63. Rosenberg, *Cholera Years*, 120.

64. Commonwealth of Massachusetts, *Report of a General Plan for the Promotion of Public Health, Devised, Prepared, and Recommended by the Commissioners Appointed under a Resolve of the Legislature of Massachusetts, Relating to a Sanitary Survey of the States* (Boston, 1850), 425.

65. City of Boston, *Report on the Cholera*, 176.

66. Commonwealth of Massachusetts, *Report of a General Plan for the Promotion of Public Health*, 428.

Chapter Two

1. Melosi, *Sanitary City*, 46.

2. Halliday, *Great Stink of London*, 39.

3. Ibid., 40. In 1847, a witness appearing before London's Metropolitan Sewers Commission offered this graphic assessment of what he had seen: "I have visited very many places where filth was lying scattered about the rooms, vaults, cellars, areas, and yards, so thick, and so deep, that it was hardly possible to move for it. . . . The effects of the stench, effluvia, and poisonous gases constantly evolving from these foul accumulations were apparent in the haggard, wan, and swarthy countenances, and enfeebled limbs, of the poor creatures whom I found residing over and amongst these dens of pollution and wretchedness." Cited in Henry J. Jephson, *The Sanitary Evolution of London* (New York, 1972), 19.

4. Melosi, *Sanitary City*, 48.

5. Lemuel Shattuck, Nathaniel P. Banks Jr., and Jehiel Abbott, *Report of the Sanitary Commission of Massachusetts, 1850* (Cambridge, Mass., facsimile of the original, 1948), 9.

6. Ibid., 28–29.

7. Whipple, *State Sanitation* 1:185–188; and Rosenkrantz, *Public Health and the State*, 14–32.

8. Shattuck et al., *Report of the Sanitary Commission*, 10.

9. According to Duffy, "Most well-to-do Americans in Shattuck's day still believed that poverty and immorality went hand in hand and that cleanliness was next to godliness. The laws of nature and God were the same, and those who deviated from them paid the price in poverty, disease, and death." John Duffy, *The Sanitarians* (Urbana, Ill., 1992), 99.

10. Ibid., 153.

11. Ibid., 160.

12. Ibid., 162.

13. Ibid., 212.

14. Whipple, *State Sanitation* 1:30.

15. Melosi, *Sanitary City*, 65.

16. Rosenkrantz, *Public Health and the States*, 35.

17. City of Boston, *The Sewerage of Boston*, City Doc. no. 3 (1876), 14.

18. Clarke, *Main Drainage Works*, 13–14.

19. See, for example, City of Boston, *Report of Committee on Drainage in Dover Street*, City Doc. no. 47 (May 25, 1857); City of Boston, "*Report on the Drainage near Northampton Street*," City Doc. no. 63 (1858), and City of Boston, "*Report of the Committee on Dover Street Drainage*," City Doc. no. 64 (1858).

20. Fern L. Nesson, *Great Waters* (Hanover, N.H., 1983), 1.

21. Ibid., 7.

22. Whipple, *State Sanitation* 1:20.

23. John Koren, *Boston, 1822 to 1922, The Story of Its Government and Principal Activities during One Hundred Years* (Boston, 1923), 96; and Nesson, *Great Waters*, 10.

24. Joel A. Tarr and Francis Clay McMichael, "Historic Turning Points in Municipal Water Supply and Wastewater Disposal, 1850–1932," *Civil Engineering ASCE* (October 1977): 83.

25. City of Boston, *Sewerage of Boston*, appendix A; and Leonard Metcalf and Harrison P. Eddy, *American Sewerage Practice*, 3 vols. (New York, 1914–15), 1:14, reprinted in *Sewering the Cities*, ed. Barbara Gutmann Rosenkrantz (New York, 1977).

26. Halliday, *Great Stink of London*, 30.

27. Ibid., ix–xi.

28. Ibid., 71–72.

29. Ibid., 72.

30. Letter from the Consulting Physicians of the City of Boston to the Mayor and Aldermen, Health Commissioners of the City of Boston, April 14, 1870, City of Boston Archives no. 1870-0091-D.

31. Letter of resignation from three members of the Consulting Physicians of the City of Boston December 3, 1870, City of Boston Archives no. 1870-0343-C.

32. City of Boston, *First Annual report of the Board of Health of the City of Boston*, City Doc. no. 84 (1873), 22–23.

33. City of Boston, *Second annual report of the Board of Health of the City of Boston*, City Doc. no. 63, cited in Eliot C. Clarke, *Main Drainage Works of the City of Boston*, 3rd ed. (Boston, 1888), 147.

34. City of Boston, "Communication from the Board of Health upon the Necessity of Improved Sewerage in the Roxbury Canal, Stony Brook, and Muddy Brook," City Doc. no. 112 (December 28, 1874), 5.

35. Ibid., 6.

36. City of Boston, *Third annual report of the Board of Health of the City of Boston*, City Doc. no. 85 (1875), 10.

37. Whipple, *State Sanitation*, 2:379.

38. Ibid.

39. Commonwealth of Massachusetts, *Fourth Annual Report of the State Board of Health of Massachusetts*, Commonwealth Doc. no. 31 (January 1873), cited in George W. Rafter and M. N. Baker, *Sewage Disposal in the United States* (New York, 1894), 35.

40. Ibid.

41. Ibid., 20–21.

42. Ibid., 73–74.

43. Ibid., 36–37.

44. Ibid., 26.

45. Ibid., 39.

46. Ibid., 32.

47. City of Boston, *Sewerage of Boston*, 3.

Chapter Three

1. City of Boston, *Report on the Present System of Sewerage in the City of Boston*, City Doc. no. 94 (September 1, 1873), 4.

2. Clarke, *Main Drainage Works*, 3rd ed., 150.

3. City of Boston, *Sewerage of Boston*, 5.

4. Ibid., 1–2.

5. Ibid., 4.

6. Ibid., 4, 9, 11–12.

7. Ibid., 15.

8. Ibid., 17.

9. Most of the combined sewers in the Boston area were built between 1860 and

1900. Metropolitan District Commission, *Combined Sewer Overflow Project Summary Report on Facilities Planning*, (April 1982), 1.

10. Commonwealth of Massachusetts, *Eighth Annual Report of the State Board of Health*, Senate Doc. no. 75 (January 1877), 159.

11. City of Boston, *Sewerage of Boston*, 33–34.

12. City of Boston, *Improved Sewerage*, City Doc. no. 59 (May 1876), 7–8.

13. Ibid., 6–7.

14. Ibid., 8–9.

15. Clarke, *Main Drainage Works*, 3rd ed., 152.

16. Elkind, *Bay Cities and Water Politics*, 56.

17. City of Boston, *The Inaugural Address of Frederick O. Prince, Mayor of Boston, to the City Council, January 1, 1877* (Boston, 1877), 14–16.

18. Clarke, *Main Drainage Works*, 66.

19. City of Boston, *Report on Improved System of Sewerage*, City Doc. no. 70 (July 12, 1877), 2–3.

20. Elkind, *Bay Cities and Water Politics*, 56–57.

21. Clarke, *Main Drainage Works*, 87.

22. Ibid.

23. Ibid., 88.

24. Ibid., 90.

25. Ibid., 66.

26. Ibid., 69.

27. Ibid., 70.

28. Clarke, *Main Drainage Works*, 3rd ed., 170.

29. "Main Drainage-Works at Boston," *Harper's Weekly*, August 21, 1880, 534.

30. *Manufacturer and Builder* 12, no. 12 (December 1880): 268.

31. M. F. Sweeter, *King's Handbook of Boston Harbor* (Cambridge, Mass., 1883), 106

32. Clarke, *Main Drainage Works*, 3rd ed., 183.

33. Koren, *Boston, 1822 to 1922*, 162.

34. Metropolitan Sewerage Commissioners, *Main Drainage Works of Boston and Its Metropolitan Sewerage District* (Boston, 1899), 11–13.; and Ralph W. Loud, "The Metropolitan Sewerage Works," *Journal of the Boston Society of Civil Engineers* 10, no. 8 (October 1923): 333–334.

35. Elkind, *Bay Cities and Water Politics*, 88.

36. Ibid., 5.

37. Ibid., 92–93.

38. Commonwealth of Massachusetts, *Report of the Metropolitan Sewerage Commissioners upon a High-Level Gravity Sewer for the Relief of the Charles and Neponset River Valleys* (Boston, 1899), 6–7.

39. Commonwealth of Massachusetts, *Report of the State Board of Health upon the Discharge of Sewage into Boston Harbor* (Boston, 1900), 19–20.

40. Ibid., 8–9.

Chapter Four

1. X. H. Goodnough, "Examination of Sewer Outlets in Boston Harbor and of Tidal Waters and Flats from Which Shellfish Are Taken for Food," reprinted in Whipple, *State Sanitation*, 2:322–332.

2. Commonwealth of Massachusetts, *Report of the Joint Board on Conditions of South Bay*, House Report no. 1635 (1915), 4.

3. Ibid., 14.

4. Commonwealth of Massachusetts, *Report of the Joint Board Acting under the Provisions of Chapter 56 of the Resolves of 1917 Providing for an Investigation of the Discharge of Sewage into Boston Harbor*, House Report no. 1215 (January 9, 1918), 5–7, cited in Eric Jay Dolin, *Dirty Water/Clean Water* (Cambridge, Mass., 1990), 19.

5. Commonwealth of Massachusetts, *Report of the Joint Board Acting under the Provisions of Chapter 56*, cited in Charles A. Maguire and Associates, *Engineering Report on a Proposed Plan of Sewerage and Sewage Disposal for the Boston Metropolitan Area* (February 1951), 27.

6. Commonwealth of Massachusetts, *Report of the Special Commission Relative to the Discharge of Sewage into Boston Harbor*, Senate Report no. 56 (Boston, 1930), 5–7.

7. Commonwealth of Massachusetts, *Report of the Special Commission on the Investigation of the Discharge of Sewage into Boston Harbor and Its Tributaries*, House Report no. 1600 (December 2, 1936), 26.

8. Ibid.

9. Commonwealth of Massachusetts, *Report of the Special Commission Investigating Systems of Sewerage and Sewage Disposal in the North and South Metropolitan Sewerage Districts and the City of Boston*, House Doc. no. 2465 (June 15, 1939), 12–13.

10. Ibid., 14–17.

11. Ibid., 25.

12. Ibid., 38.

13. Charles M. Haar and Steven G. Horowitz, *Report of the Special Master Regarding Findings of Fact and Proposed Remedies*, Norfolk County Superior Court Civil Action no. 138477 (August 9, 1983), 12.

14. U.S. Congress, Office of Technology Assessment, *Wastes in Marine Environments* (Washington, D.C., April 1987, 213; and Eric Jay Dolin, "Boston Harbor's Murky Political Waters," *Environment* 34, no. 6 (July/August 1992): 9.

15. Metcalf & Eddy, Inc., *Wastewater Engineering* (New York, 1972), 241.

16. U.S. Environmental Protection Agency, Region 3, *Chesapeake Bay Program: Findings and Recommendations* (September 1983), 24–25.

17. Madeliene Kolb, *Wastewater Management Planning for Boston Harbor, A Status Report* (Boston Harbor Interagency Coordinating Committee, August 1980), 8.; and Dolin, "Boston Harbor's Murky Political Waters," 9.

18. Fred Pillsbury, "Our Filthy Harbor," *Boston Sunday Herald*, November 22, 1964, sec. 4.

19. John C. MacClean, "Divided Responsibilities Help Keep Harbor Dirty," *Boston Herald*, September 1, 1966.

20. Joan M. Kovalic, *The Clean Water Act with Amendments* (Washington, D.C., 1982).

21. Cynthia Cates Colella, *The Federal Role in the Federal System* (Washington, D.C., March 1981).

22. N. William Hines, "Controlling Industrial Water Pollution: Color the Problem Green," *Boston College Industrial & Commercial Law Review* 9 (1968): 585–586.

23. Thomas C. Jorling, quoted in "Congressional Staffers Take a Retrospective Look at P.L. 92–500, Part 2," *Journal of the Water Pollution Control Federation* 53, no. 9 (September 1981): 1370.

24. Massachusetts, *Clean Waters, Act General Laws* (September 6, 1966), chap. 21, Department of Environmental Management, secs. 26–53, enacted by Massachusetts Acts of 1966).

25. U.S. Department of Interior, *Conference Pollution of the Navigable Waters of Boston Harbor and Its Tributaries* (May 20, 1968), 97.

26. Federal Water Pollution Control Administration, *Report on Pollution of the Navigable Waters of Boston Harbor* (May 1968), 1, included in ibid., 87–97.

27. U.S. Department of Interior, Federal Water Pollution Control Administration, *Conference Pollution of the Navigable Waters of Boston Harbor and Its Tributaries* (April 30, 1969); and U.S. Environmental Protection Agency, *Conference in the Matter of Pollution of the Navigable Waters of Boston Harbor and Its Tributaries—Massachusetts* (October 27, 1971).

28. U.S. Environmental Protection Agency, "Grants for Water Pollution Control," *Federal Register* 36, no. 134 (July 13, 1971): 13029.

29. Joe G. Moore Jr., telephone interviews by author, January 5 and 21, 1993; and Charles V. Gibbs, telephone interview by author, February 8, 1993.

30. A. M. Rawn, "Fixed and Changing Values in Ocean Disposal of Sewage and Wastes," in *Proceedings of the First International Conference on Waste Disposal in the Marine Environment* (University of California, Berkeley, July 22–25, 1959), ed. E. A. Pearson (New York, 1960), 6–7.

31. Ibid., 11.

32. Roger Revelle, "Welcoming Address," in *Proceedings of the First International Conference on Waste Disposal in the Marine Environment*, 4.

33. U.S. Environmental Protection Agency, *Conference in the Matter of Pollution*, 132–135.

34. Ibid., 136.

35. Hydrosciences Inc., *Final Report on Development of Water Quality Model of Boston Harbor* (July 1971).

36. U.S. Environmental Protection Agency, *Conference in the Matter of Pollution*, 293–299.

37. R. S. Kindleberber, "MDC Treatment Plant Still Pollutes Harbor," *Boston Globe*, July 29, 1973.

38. James Ayres, "Ecology Bill First Step in Hub Cleanup," *Boston Globe*, July 16, 1972.

39. Seth Rolbein, "Boston's Floating Crap Game," *Boston Magazine*, May 1987, 204.

40. Micheal Rezendes, "The Treatment," *Phoenix*, August 18, 1981.

41. Noel Barrata, interview by author, October 7, 1993.

42. "Despite $20 Million New Plant, Raw Sewage Floods Harbor," *Boston Globe*, November 9, 1967.

43. Barrata interview, October 7, 1993; "MDC-Patronage Picnic, Sears: Payoff to Politicians Is Wrong," *Boston Herald*, March 29, 1973.

44. Mary A. Hague, "By Order of the Court" (Diss., Boston College, May 1994), 37.

Chapter Five

1. Harvey Leiber, *Federalism and Clean Waters* (Lexington, Mass., 1975), 1.

2. J. Clarence Davies III and Barbara S. Davies, *The Politics of Pollution* (Indianapolis, 1975), 44.

3. Kovalic, *Clean Water Act with Amendments*, 1.

4. John H. Marshall, "Sewers, Clean Water, and Planned Growth: Restructuring the Federal Pollution Abatement Effort," *Yale Law Journal* 86 (1977): 733.

5. Lieber, *Federalism and Clean Waters*, 7; and U.S. Congress, *A Legislative History of the Water Pollution Control Act Amendments of 1972*, vol. 1, 93rd Cong., 1st sess., January 1973, 3–91.

6. Ibid., 3.

7. U.S. Environmental Protection Agency, "Secondary Treatment Information," *Federal Register* 38, no. 159 (August 17, 1973): 22298.

8. "WPCF Roundtable Discussion—Congressional Staffers Take a Retrospective Look at PL 92-500—Part 2," *Journal of the Water Pollution Control Federation* 53 (September 1981): 1370.

9. Robert Zener, "The Federal Law of Water Pollution Control," in *Federal Environmental Law*, ed. Erica L. Dolgin and Thomas G. P. Guilbert (St. Paul, 1974), 731.

10. Kovalic, *Clean Water Act with Amendments*, 10.

11. Peter Crane Anderson, "The CSO Sleeping Giant," *Virginia Environmental Law Journal* 10 (1991): 381.

12. Subcommittee on Air and Water Pollution, *Water Pollution Control Legislation Part 1* (March 1971), 517.

13. Ibid., 527.

14. Phil Cummings, telephone interview by author, January 11, 1993.

15. Bill Corcoran, telephone interview by author, January 22, 1993.

16. Moore interview, January 5, 1993; and ibid.

17. Dianne Dumanoski, "Raw or Treated, the Sewage Flows into Boston Harbor," *Boston Globe*, December 19, 1982.

18. Metropolitan District Commission, *Combined Sewer Overflow Project Summary Report on Facilities Planning*.

19. Jeffrey L. Pressman and Aaron Wildavsky, *Implementation* (Berkeley, 1973), 87–124.

20. According to Pressman and Wildavsky, "Our normal expectation should be that new programs will fail to get off the ground and that, at best, they will take considerable time to get started. The cards in this world are stacked against things happening, as so much effort is required to make them move. The remarkable thing is that new programs work at all." Ibid., 109.

21. James Q. Wilson, *Bureaucracy* (New York, 1989), 377.

22. Daniel A. Mazmanian and Paul A. Sabatier, *Implementation of Public Policy* (Glenview, Ill., 1983), 43.

23. Metropolitan District Commission, *Wastewater Engineering and Management Plan for Boston Harbor—Eastern Massachusetts Metropolitan Area EMMA Study, Main Report for the Metropolitan District Commission* (March 1976), xvi–xviii.

24. Kolb, *Wastewater Management Planning for Boston Harbor*, 26–33.

25. "400 Oppose MDC Bay Fill Plan," *Patriot Ledger* October 3, 1975; and Jerry Ackerman, "Quincy Opposes Sewage Phase of Boston Harbor Cleanup Plan," *Boston Globe*, February 18, 1976.

26. Kolb, *Wastewater Management Planning for Boston Harbor*, 31.

27. Rebecca Hanmer, "EPA Statement on NSF Boston Harbor Study," in *Urban Systems Research and Engineering, Institutional Aspects of Wastewater Management* (January 1, 1979), 268.

28. Kolb, *Wastewater Management Planning for Boston Harbor*, 33; and U.S. Environmental Protection Agency, Region 1, *Draft Environmental Impact Statement on the Upgrading of the Boston Metropolitan Area Sewerage System* (August 4, 1978), 3.

29. David Doneski, "Cleaning Up Boston Harbor: Fact or Fiction?" *Boston College Environmental Affairs Law Review* 12, no. 3 (1985): 598; and Jack Kendall, "EPA Hears Disposal Dispute," *Boston Herald*, November 21, 1978.

30. Metropolitan District Commission, *Wastewater Management Plan for Boston Harbor—Eastern Massachusetts Metropolitan Area, Technical Data*, vol. 14 (October 1975), 17–22.

31. U.S. Advisory Commission on Intergovernmental Relations, *Intergovernmental Decisionmaking for Environmental Protection and Public Works* (Washington, D.C., November 1992), 82.

32. Kolb, *Wastewater Management Planning for Boston Harbor*, 86.

33. Metropolitan District Commission, *Combined Sewer Overflow Project Summary Report* (April 1982), 11.

34. Havens and Emerson, Inc., *A Plan for Sludge Management* (August 30, 1973); and Kolb, *Wastewater Management Planning for Boston Harbor*, 44–45.

35. Kolb, *Wastewater Management Planning for Boston Harbor*, 47–50.

36. U.S. Congress, House Committee on Public Works, Subcommittee on Investigations and Review, . . . *Addressing Messy Practical Issues*, Interim Staff Report, 94th Cong., 1st sess., April 1975; and U.S. Congress, House Committee on Public Works, Subcommittee on Investigations and Review, *Implementation of the Federal Water Pollution Control Act*, 94th Cong., 1st sess., May 13 and 14, 1975.

37. U.S. Congress, House Committee on Public Works, Subcommittee on Investigations and Review, *Implementation of the Federal Water Pollution Control Act*, 93rd Cong., 2nd sess., February 5, 6, and 7; April 2, 3, and 4; June 25 and 26; July 15 and 16, 1974, 39.

38. Ibid., 44.

39. Dem Cowles, telephone interview by author, January 12, 1993.

40. Cowles interview; Joan Bernard, telephone interview by author, February 23, 1993; and Moore interviews.

41. Leon G. Billings, letter to the author, January 4, 1993.

42. Bernard interview.

43. U.S. Congress, Senate Committee on Environmental and Public Works, *Legislative History of the Clean Water Act of 1977*, vols. 3 and 4, 95th Cong., 2nd sess., October 1978, 1076–1077.

44. Ibid., 639.

45. Ibid., 678–679.

46. U.S. Congress, House Committee on Public Works and Transportation, *Federal Water Pollution Control Act Amendments*, 95th Cong., 1st sess., September 15, 16, 19, and 20, 1977, 156.

47. Bernard interview; and U.S. Congress, House Committee on Public Works, Subcommittee on Investigations and Oversight, *Implementation of the Clean Water Act (Concerning Waiver Provisions for Municipal Ocean Dischargers)*, 97th Cong., 1st and 2nd sess., September 8, 1981, and February 18, 1982, 482.

48. U.S. Congress, Senate Committee on Environment and Public Works, *Legislative History of the Clean Water Act of 1977*, 434.

49. Heidi Burgess, Dianne Hoffman, and Mary Lucci, "Negotiation in the Rulemaking Process (The 301(h) Case)," in *Resolving Environmental Regulatory Disputes*, ed. Lawrence Susskind, Lawrence Bacow, and Michael Wheeler (Cambridge, Mass., 1983), 236.

50. Tom Jorling, telephone interview by author, March 10, 1993.

51. U.S. Congress, Senate Committee on Environment and Public Works, *Legislative History of the Clean Water Act of 1977*, 535.

52. Donald Baumgartner, telephone interview by author, January 12, 1993.

53. Burgess et al., "Negotiation in the Rulemaking Process," 238.

54. U.S. Environmental Protection Agency, "Modification of Secondary Treat-

96. Pat Choate and Susan Walter, *America in Ruins* (Washington, D.C., 1981); and Robert Royer and Cathleen Carr, Thinking about the Infrastructure (Washington, D.C., 1986).

97. Associated Press, "To MDC, Sewers Were 'Stepchild,'" *Boston Globe*, December 9, 1984, 3

98. Snedecker interview, April 7, 1989; and Barrata interview, April 14, 1989.

99. Associated Press, "To MDC, Sewers Were 'Stepchild.'"

100. Madeliene Kolb, interview by author, October 18, 1993.

101. Peter Shelley, telephone interview by author, May 10, 1993.

102. Boston Harbor Association, *Boston Harbor—An Uncertain Future* (December 1978), 5.

103. Dumanoski, "The Cycle: Breakdowns, No Money".

104. Ibid.

105. "According to Bill Geary, MDC Commissioner from 1983 to 1989, it was always possible for him to get legislative appropriations for swimming pools or skating rinks that were not really necessary, but it was virtually impossible to get appropriations for the 'invisible' underground infrastructure that was essential to the region's health and well-being." Paul F. Levy, "Sewer Infrastructure, An Orphan of Our Times," *Oceanus* (spring 1993): 57.

106. Margot Hornblower, "Boston Harbor Sewers Back Up into Litigation," *Washington Post* (December 9, 1984).

107. Barrata interview, October 7, 1993.

108. Associated Press, "To MDC, Sewers Were 'Stepchild.'"

109. Barrata interview, October 7, 1993; and Rolbein, "Boston's Floating Crap Game," 204.

Chapter Six

1. Dudley Clendinen, "Raw Sewage Fouls Harbor 11 Years After Pollution Law," *New York Times*, July 24, 1983.

2. Anthony Wolff, "Boston's Toilet: The True Story," *Audubon*, March 1989, 28.

3. Ibid.

4. Dolin, *Dirty Water/Clean Water*, 63.

5. Hague, "By Order of the Court," 61.

6. Wolff, "Boston's Toilet," 28.

7. Judy Foreman, "Judge Asks Reagan for Harbor Cleanup Help," *Boston Globe*, August 24, 1983.

8. *Conservation Law Foundation of New England, Inc., v. Metropolitan District Commission et al.*, 83-1614-MA, Complaint (June 7, 1983), 1–2.

9. Rolbein, "Boston's Floating Crap Game," 202.

10. Peter Koff, telephone interview by author, May 12, 1993.

11. Rolbein, "Boston's Floating Crap Game," 202.

12. Koff, interview, May 12, 1993.

13. Rolbein, "Boston's Floating Crap Game," 202; Paul Garrity, interview by author, December 14, 1993; and Hornblower, "Boston Harbor Sewers."

14. Charles M. Haar and Lance Liebman, *Property and Law* (Boston, 1985), 447–450.

15. *City of Quincy v. Metropolitan District Commission and Boston Water & Sewer Commission*, Norfolk Superior Court, C.A. 138477 (hereafter cited as *Quincy v. MDC/BWSC*), Findings, Rulings, and Orders on Plaintiff City of Quincy's Application for Preliminary Injunctive Relief (June 27, 1983), 4.

16. Owen M. Fiss and Doug Rendleman, *Injunctions*, 2nd ed. (Mineola, N.Y., 1984), 331.

17. Andrew Blake, "Dukakis Names Sargent to Lead Harbor Cleanup," *Boston Globe*, May 27, 1983.

18. *Quincy v. MDC/BWSC.*, Findings, Rulings, and Orders, 9. For a later description of the committee and its charge, see Francis W. Sargent, "All Must Help Clean Up the Harbor," *Boston Globe*, September 16, 1983.

19. Ibid.

20. *Quincy v. MDC/BWSC*, Memorandum in Support of Motion for Further Consideration and Clarification (July 6, 1983), 3.

21. Ibid.

22. *Quincy v. MDC/BWSC*, Findings, Rulings, and Orders, 4.

23. Haar and Horowitz, *Report of the Special Master*, 4.

24. According to Garrity, "The Boston Harbor case was not a complex case scientifically at all. It was one of the least complex cases I've ever had where institutional litigation was involved." Garrity interview.

25. Steven T. Seward, "The Boston Harbor Dispute," in *Of Judges, Politics, and Flounders*, ed. Charles M. Haar (Cambridge, Mass., 1986), 4.

26. Wolff, "Boston's Toilet," 28.

27. Charles M. Haar, "What Only Courts Can Do," *National Law Journal* (January 4, 1982): 13–14; and Charles M. Haar, "A Helpful Judicial Tool," *National Law Journal* (January 11, 1982): 11, 16.

28. Gary McMillan, "Charles Haar—the Lawyer as 'More of a Mason than an Architect," *Boston Globe*, December 15, 1984.

29. Timothy G. Little, "Court-Appointed Special Masters in Complex Environmental Litigation," *Harvard Environmental Law Review* 8 (1984): 445.

30. Haar and Horowitz, *Report of the Special Master*, 5.

31. Ibid., 133 n. 27.

32. U.S. Environmental Protection Agency, Tentative Denial of the Administrator Pursuant to 40 CFR Part 125, Subpart G (June 30, 1983), 6–7.

33. James Hoyte, telephone interview by author, March 8, 1989.

34. Metropolitan District Commission, Application for a Waiver of Secondary Treatment for the Nut Island and Deer Island Treatment Plants (June 30, 1984).

35. Haar and Horowitz, *Report of the Special Master*, ix–x.

36. Ibid., 114.

37. Paul Hirshson, "As Legalities Fly, the Sewage Flows," *Boston Globe*, December 9, 1984.

38. Haar and Horowitz, *Report of the Special Master*, 102.

39. Ibid., 42.

40. Ibid., 47–48.

41. Ibid., 70.

42. Ibid., xi, 91–92, 95–96, 114, 116.

43. Ibid., 125.

44. Ibid., 136.

45. Ibid., 165.

46. Judy Foreman, "Harbor Pollution Remedies: Giant Step or Just Stopgap?" *Boston Globe*, August 14, 1983.

47. Noel Barrata, quoted in Scott T. McCreary, "Resolving Science-Intensive Public Policy Disputes: Lessons from the New York Bight Initiative (Ph.D. diss., Massachusetts Institute of Technology, May 1989), 145.

48. Ibid.

49. Judy Foreman, "Court Given Plans to Clean Hub Harbor," *Boston Globe*, August 11, 1983.

50. Seward, "The Boston Harbor Dispute," 6.

51. Foreman, "Court Given Plans to Clean Hub Harbor."

52. *Quincy v. MDC/BWSC*, State Defendants' Objection to the Report of the Special Master (August 22, 1983), 2.

53. Garrity interview.

54. *Quincy v. MDC/BWSC*, Procedural Order (September 12, 1983); 1–2.

55. Garrity interview.

56. McCreary, "Resolving Science-Intensive Public Policy Disputes," 149.

57. Foreman, "Harbor Pollution Remedies."

58. *Quincy v. MDC/BWSC*, Procedural Order, Exhibit A.

59. McCreary, "Resolving Science-Intensive Public Policy Disputes," 149.

60. Barrata interview, October 7, 1993.

61. Barrata, quoted in McCreary, "Resolving Science-Intensive Public Policy Disputes," 150.

62. Doug MacDonald, quoted in McCreary, "Resolving Science-Intensive Public Policy Disputes," 150.

63. Shelley interview, May 10, 1993.

64. *U.S. v. MDC et al.* (September 5, 1985), cited in Bureau of National Affairs, *Environmental Law Reporter* 16 (July 1986): 20622.

65. Charles A. Radin, "Cleanup of Boston Harbor Defies Effort at Tidy Solution," *Boston Globe*, April 22, 1984, 1, 22; and Little, "Court-Appointed Special Masters," 468 n. 264.

66. Seward, "The Boston Harbor Dispute," 7; and Judy Foreman and Andrew Blake, "MDC Harbor Receivership Eyed," *Boston Globe*, October 10, 1984.

67. Judy Foreman, "Boston Harbor Gets 10-year Plan," *Boston Globe*, September 7, 1983.

68. Charles M. Haar, interview by author, November 8, 1993.

69. For an excellent review and analysis of the public authority mechanism, see Annmarie Hauck Walsh, *The Public's Business* (Cambridge, Mass., 1978).

70. "The common wisdom for much of this century has been that public authorities . . . are simply too businesslike and efficient to fall prey to the corruption and managerial disarray that infect less businesslike, less efficient, more 'political' units of traditional government." Diana Henriques, *The Machinery of Greed* (Princeton, N.J., 1982), 1.

71. Doneski, "Cleaning Up Boston Harbor," 564.

72. Ian Menzies, "Cleaning Up the Harbor," *Boston Globe*, January 9, 1984.

73. Jerry Ackerman, "MDC Breakup to Be Urged in Dukakis Budget," *Boston Globe*, January 25, 1984.

74. Haar addressed the impact of the special master's report as follows: "A legal proceeding, with its attendant public fact-finding, proves to be a good way to put information before the public. Even if the information is openly available, the court process—especially if it includes a special master's report—provides a mechanism for consolidating a mass of information from disparate sources and molding it into a coherent story that can catch the attention of the public and the media. In this case in particular, the special master's on-site visits to sewage plants with representatives of the press and television drew widespread attention to the needs of the harbor." Charles M. Haar, "Boston Harbor: A Case Study," *Boston College Environmental Affairs Law Review* 19, no. 3 (1992): 647.

75. Garrity interview.

76. Menzies, "Cleaning Up the Harbor."

77. Barrata interview, October 7, 1993; and Boston Harbor Associates, *Boston Harbor . . . Who Cares?* (June 5, 1975).

78. According to Victor Hugo, "Greater than the tread of mighty armies is an idea whose time has come." Quoted in John W. Kingdon, *Agendas, Alternatives, and Public Policies* (Boston, 1984), 1.

79. Bank of Boston, Public Finance Group, *Protecting Water Resources: A Financial Analysis* (February 8, 1984).

80. Ibid., 15.

81. According to the Bank of Boston report, "Under the existing structure, [MDC] management is unable to plan expenditures with any certainty or to obtain adequate human and material resources to support the Agency's activities. Possible solutions include the creation of a separate dedicated fund solely under Agency control, granting of authority to independently set rates and exemption from State Civil Service Provisions. Any or all of these changes, however, represent a radical departure from existing policies and procedures related to the management of State government. In our judgment, neither the Legislature nor the Executive Branch would deem it responsible to relinquish their respective oversight responsibilities

for a single line agency. In addition, this could set a precedent for the management and governance of other line agencies which would be institutionally unacceptable." Ibid., 30.

82. Ibid., 15, 31.

83. For an extended and more critical review of the Bank of Boston report, see Greg D. Peterson, "After the Deluge: A Critical Evaluation of the Governance Structures of the Massachusetts Water Resources Authority," in Haar, *Of Judges, Politics, and Flounder*, 77–83.

84. Charles A. Radin, "Harbor Help Insufficient, Monitor Says," *Boston Globe*, April 13, 1984.

85. Norman Lockman, "Dukakis Proposes Sewer Authority as New MDC Unit," *Boston Globe*, April 20, 1984.

86. John Strahinich and J. William Semich, "Inside the Shadow Government," *Boston Magazine*, November 1989, 131. Other authorities include the Massachusetts Convention Center Authority, State College Building Authority, Massachusetts State Lottery Commission, and the Boston Water and Sewer Commission. The 506 estimate is subject to question. According to a 1990 survey, Massachusetts was not even among the fifteen states with the most public authorities, and the last state on that list, Wisconsin, had only one hundred such entities. The divergences are probably due to different assumptions as to what constitutes a state or local authority. Whatever the number actually is, there is no disputing that Massachusetts has quite a few authorities. Jerry Mitchell, "The Policy Activities of Public Authorities," *Policy Studies Journal* 18, no. 4 (summer 1990): 931.

87. See, for example, Massachusetts, Senate Ways and Means Committee, *State Authorities: The Fourth Branch of Government?* (1985); Donald Axelrod, *Shadow Government* (New York, 1992), 9.

88. "Sewers on the Legislative Agenda," *Boston Globe*, June 15, 1984.

89. Andrew Blake, "Dukakis Pushes Bill for a Sewer Authority," *Boston Globe*, June 20, 1984.

90. Andrew Blake, "Dukakis Urges New Agency on Visit to Old Sewer Plant," *Boston Globe*, June 26, 1984.

91. Andrew Blake, "Time Is with Dukakis in Push for Programs," *Boston Globe*, July 15, 1984.

92. "Sen. Bulger's Sewer Coup," *Boston Globe*, October 10, 1984.

93. Neil O'Brien, telephone interview by author, October 8, 1993.

94. Peterson, "After the Deluge," 58; and Foreman and Blake, "MDC Harbor Receivership Eyed."

95. Ian Menzies, "A Great Week for Harbor," *Boston Globe*, October 11, 1984.

96. Ibid.

97. Foreman and Blake, "MDC Harbor Receivership Eyed."

98. Ibid.

99. Jerry Ackerman, "MDC Says It's Overwhelmed by Harbor Cleanup," *Boston Globe*, October 31, 1984.

100. Steve Angelo, telephone interview by author, August 1993.

101. Robert L. Turner, "Legislature Again Passing the Buck?" *Boston Globe*, December 12, 1984.

102. Ackerman, "MDC Breakup to Be Urged in Dukakis Budget."

103. Kovalic, *Clean Water Act with Amendments*, 24–30; and Glenn E. Deegan, "Judicial Enforcement of State and Municipal Compliance with the Clean Water Act," *Boston College Environmental Affairs Law Review* 19 (1992): 772–773.

104. Jerry Ackerman, "Legislature Faces Deadline for Harbor Cleanup Vote," *Boston Globe*, November 15, 1984.

105. Judy Foreman, "Receivership Threat for Harbor Cleanup," *Boston Globe*, November 16, 1984.

106. Ibid.

107. John DeVillars, Dukakis's chief of operations, quoted in Foreman, "Receivership Threat for Harbor Cleanup."

108. Foreman, "Receivership Threat for Harbor Cleanup."

109. Ibid.

110. Laurence Collins, "The Politics behind the Stalled Bill," *Boston Globe*, November 30, 1984.

111. Ibid.

112. Judy Foreman, "Court Bans Tie-ins to MDC Sewers, Sets Receivership Trial," *Boston Globe*, November 30, 1984; and Lynda Gorov and Jan Wong, "Businessmen Call the Decision a Ploy and Say It Could Cripple Development," *Boston Globe*, December 1, 1984.

113. Hornblower, "Boston Harbor Sewers Back Up into Litigation."

114. Foreman, "Court Bans Tie-ins to MDC Sewers, Sets Receivership Trial."

115. Haar interview.

116. Hornblower, "Boston Harbor Sewers Back Up into Litigation."

117. Rolbein, "Boston's Floating Crap Game," 207.

118. Ibid.

119. Laurence Collins, "Attorney General's Office to Ask Court to Lift Ban on MDC Sewer Hookup," *Boston Globe*, December 1, 1984; and Judy Foreman, "Sewer Tie-in Ban Is Lifted," *Boston Globe*, December 6, 1984.

120. Rolbein, "Boston's Floating Crap Game," 208.

121. Foreman, "Sewer Tie-in Ban Is Lifted."

122. Ibid.

123. Comments by Michael Deland at the Boston Harbor Project Symposium, co-sponsored by University of Massachusetts Boston, the Massachusetts Water Resources Authority, and the Massachusetts Executive Office of Environmental Affairs (May 16, 2001).

124. Judy Foreman, "Garrity Vows a New Ban on Tie-ins to Sewer System," *Boston Globe*, December 8, 1984.

125. "The Subject Is Boston Harbor," picture on the front page of the *Boston Globe*, December 11, 1984.

126. Peter Mancusi, "Objection, Your Honor, Say Some," *Boston Globe*, December 13, 1984.

127. Garrity interview.

128. Robert C. Wood, ed., *Remedial Law* (Amherst, Mass., 1990, 74.

129. Hornblower, "Boston Harbor Sewers Back Up into Litigation."

130. Andrew Blake, "House Begins Debate on Sewer Authority Bill," *Boston Globe*, December 11, 1984.

131. Chris Black, "Legislature Likely to OK Only Harbor Bill," *Boston Globe*, December 12, 1984.

132. Laurence Collins, "House Approves Sewer Authority," *Boston Globe*, December 13, 1984.

133. Mancusi, "Objection, Your Honor."

134. Andrew Blake, "House-Senate Panel Agrees on State Water Authority," *Boston Globe*, December 14, 1984.

135. Ibid.

136. Andrew Blake, "Ultimatum Given on Harbor Bill," *Boston Globe*, December 15, 1984.

137. Andrew Blake, "Conferee: Harbor Bill is 'Close,'" *Boston Globe*, December 17, 1984.

138. Andrew Blake, "Panel OK's Harbor Bill; Voting Due Tomorrow," *Boston Globe*, December 18, 1984.

139. Ibid.

140. Andrew Blake, "Conferees Agree to Compromise on Harbor Bill," *Boston Globe*, December 19, 1984.

141. Hague, *By Order of the Court*, 109.

142. Andrew Blake, "Harbor Bill OK'd, Signed into Law," *Boston Globe*, December 20, 1984.

143. Hague, *By Order of the Court*, 109.

144. Ibid.

145. Jerry Ackerman, "Garrity, in Last Move as Judge, Orders 3-year Harbor Supervision," *Boston Globe*, December 22, 1984.

146. Rolbein, "Boston's Floating Crap Game," 208.

147. Peter Koff, telephone interview by author, November 1, 1994.

148. Neil O'Brien, telephone interview by author, November 11, 1994.

149. Shelley interview. May 10, 1993.

150. Jeffry Fowley, telephone interview by author, November 23, 1993.

151. Wood, *Remedial Law*, 72.

152. Mancusi, "Objection, Your Honor."

153. Blake, "Harbor Bill OK'd, Signed into Law."

154. Mancusi, "Objection, Your Honor."

155. Haar interview.

156. Garrity interview.

157. Ibid.

158. Peter Boynton, "The Boston Harbor CleanUp: Two Decades of Battles Over 'That Dirty Water,'" *Massachusetts Lawyers Weekly* (September 16, 2002), accessed online at www.masslaw.com/mlw30/mlw30.cfm.

159. O'Brien interview, October 8, 1993.

160. Ackerman, "Garrity, in Last Move as Judge."

Chapter Seven

1. *U.S. v. MDC et al.*, Complaint, 1.

2. Rolbein, "Boston's Floating Crap Game," 204.

3. Michael R. Deland, Affidavit, 12 April, 1985, *U.S. EPA v. MDC et al.*, 1.

4. Deland quoted in Rolbein, "Boston's Floating Crap Game," 206.

5. Deland, Affidavit.

6. Haar interview.

7. Jeffry Fowley, telephone interview by author, September 20, 1994.

8. Deland, Affidavit.

9. Peter Shelley, telephone interview by author, November 16, 1994.

10. Commonwealth of Massachusetts, Defendants' Memorandum of Law in Opposition to Motions for Partial Summary Judgment, *U.S. v. MDC.*

11. Andrew Blake, "MDC Now Facing Federal Harbor Suit," *Boston Globe*, December 21, 1984.

12. Dianne Dumanoski, "Boston Harbor Pollution Case Will Be in Federal Jurisdiction," *Boston Globe*, May 23, 1985.

13. Ibid.

14. A. David Mazzone, interviews by author, May 4, 1993, and December 6, 1993.

15. *U.S. v. MDC et al.*

16. Dumanoski, "Boston Harbor Pollution Case."

17. *Almanac of the Federal Judiciary*, 1st Circuit, vol. 1 (1993): 8.

18. Ibid., 9.

19. Mazzone interview, December 6, 1993.

20. Mazzone interview, May 4, 1993.

21. Mazzone interview, December 6, 1993.

22. *U.S. v. MDC et al.*, 23 ERC 1350, 1351.

23. *U.S. v. MDC et al.*, cited in *Environmental Law* Reporter 16 (July 1986): 20621.

24. *U.S. v. MDC et al.*, Memorandum and Order (September 5, 1985), 1–2.

25. *U.S. v. MDC et al.*, 23 ERC 1350, 1363.

26. Mazzone at The Boston Harbor Project Symposium, May 16, 2001.

27. *U.S. v. MDC et al.*, Memorandum to All Parties (October 1, 1985), 2.

28. Dianne Dumanoski, "Court Set to Enforce Harbor Cleanup," *Boston Globe*, September 6, 1985.

29. Dolin, *Dirty Water/Clean Water*, 75.

30. Massachusetts Water Resources Authority briefing packet given to board members in early 1986, before the siting decision. It included information on the siting options under consideration and the mitigation measures being offered, plus the transcripts from January hearings on the siting of wastewater treatment facilities for Boston Harbor, which were held in Quincy and Winthrop.

31. U.S. Environmental Protection Agency, Tentative Decision of the Regional Administrator on the Revised Application Pursuant to 40 CFR Part 125, Subpart G (March 29, 1985).

32. Massachusetts Water Resources Authority, *The Clean-up of Boston Harbor Status Update* (September 23, 1985), 13.

33. Phil Shapiro, interview with author, April 10, 1989.

34. *U.S. v. MDC et al.*, Comments of the Massachusetts Water Resources Authority on the Status Report of the United States (November 7, 1985).

35. *U.S. v. MDC et al.*, Memorandum by the United States Regarding Proposed Form of First Interim Order (December 2, 1985); and *U.S. v. MDC et al.*, Response and Comments of the Massachusetts Water Resources Authority to Proposed Orders and Schedules of CLF and the United States (December 10, 1985).

36. *U.S. v. MDC et al.*, Order (December 23, 1985), 2.

37. *U.S. v. MDC et al.*, Schedule One Compliance Order No. 1, December 1985 (February 7, 1986), 1.

38. *U.S. v. MDC et al.*, Long Term Scheduling Order (May 8, 1986), 2.

39. Ibid., 8; and *U.S. v. MDC et al.*, Report of the Conservation Law Foundation on Dates for the Completion of Treatment Plant Construction (February 18, 1986).

40. *U.S. v. MDC et al.*, Second Interim Order (MWRA Proposed Form, February 18, 1986).

41. *U.S. v. MDC et al.*, Report by the United States on Schedules for Construction of Treatment Plants and Related Facilities, and Certain Other Matters (February 18, 1986), 4.

42. *U.S. v. MDC et al.*, Memorandum by the United States in Support of Its Motion for Establishment of Long Term Target Dates (March 19, 1986), 4.

43. *U.S. v. MDC et al.*, Schedule One Compliance Order No. 3, February 1986 (April 8, 1986).

44. *U.S. v. MDC et al.*, Report of the United States on Its Proposed Form of Order on Long Term Construction Scheduling (April 28, 1986); and *U.S. v. MDC et al.*, Long Term Scheduling Order, 7.

45. *U.S. v. MDC et al.*, Report of the Massachusetts Water Resources Authority concerning Long-Term Scheduling (April 18, 1986); and *U.S. v. MDC et al.*, Long Term Scheduling Order.

46. *U.S. v. MDC et al.*, Long Term Scheduling Order, 3.

47. Ibid., 8; *U.S. v. MDC et al.*, Second Affidavit of James J. Colantonio (February 18, 1986); and *U.S. v. MDC et al.*, Opposition of Conservation Law Foundation to Massachusetts Water Resources Authority's Motion for Order Entering Its Compliance Schedule (February 28, 1986).

48. *U.S. v. MDC et al.*, Memorandum by the United States in Support of Its Motion for Establishment of Long Term Target Dates (March 19, 1986).

49. "CLF and EPA place overriding emphasis on advancing by few years the target completion date of a plant that is to last a century. They advocate this short-sighted aim, which in fact is not even superior in the short run, at the cost of large potential sacrifices of quality of technology and reliability of performance and without any regard whatsoever to the resulting great financial burden on the public. The Authority believes that such a course is irresponsible." *U.S. v. MDC et al.*, Report of the Massachusetts Water Resources Authority on Scheduling and Compliance and Memorandum in Support of Adoption of Proposed Second Interim Order (February 18, 1986), 14.

50. *U.S. v. MDC et al.*, Long Term Scheduling Order, 7.

51. *U.S. v. MDC et al.*, Affidavit of David Standley, consultant to the City of Quincy (April 28, 1986), 7; and *U.S. v. MDC et al.*, Third Affidavit of Richard D. Fox, P.E. (February 27, 1986).

52. *U.S. v. MDC et al.*, Second Affidavit of Mark S. Ferber (April 30, 1986).

53. *U.S. v. MDC et al.*, Memorandum by the United States in Support of Its Motion for Establishment of Long Term Target Dates, 18–19; and *U.S. v. MDC et al.*, Affidavit of John E. Petersen (March 14, 1986).

54. *U.S. v. MDC et al.*, Long Term Scheduling Order, 3–4.

55. Ibid., 5.

56. Ibid.

57. Ibid., 11–13.

58. Ibid., 4.

59. Mazzone interview, December 6, 1993.

Chapter Eight

1. Larry Tye, "$6.1B Cleanup of Boston Harbor Gets Underway," *Boston Globe*, August 11, 1988.

2. Larry Tye, "EPA Official Says Dukakis to Blame for 6-year Delay," *Boston Globe*, August 11, 1988.

3. Christine Chinlud, "In Boston, Bush Blames Rival for Delays in Harbor Cleanup," *Boston Globe*, September 2, 1988.

4. Bill Dietrich, "Clearing Up a Muddy Issue—Both Dukakis, GOP Linked to Problems at Boston Harbor," *Seattle Times*, October 20, 1988.

5. Beth Daley, "Pipe Dreams: Boston Completes Harbor Cleanup," *Boston Globe*, September 11, 2000.

6. *Boston Globe*, "Achieving Outfall," September 9, 2000.

7. Douglas MacDonald, *The Massachusetts Water Resources Authority: Turning the Tide on Pollution* (MWRA), 20.

8. Paul Eckler, "MWRA Tunnels into the 21st Century," *AUA News* 15, no. 3 (fall 2000).

9. Massachusetts Water Resources Authority, "Sandhogs at Work on the Boston Harbor Tunnel," *Construction Outlook* (January 1992): 31.

10. Massachusetts Water Resources Authority, "Hard Mining: All in a Day's Work for Tunnelers," in *Under Construction* (MWRA booklet, 2001), 92.

11. Erik Calonius and Gilles Peress, "60 Fathoms beneath the Sea," *Fortune*, April 15, 1996, 128.

12. Eckler, "MWRA Tunnels into the 21st Century," 2.

13. Massachusetts Water Resources Authority, "Miners Score Bull's Eye: Tunnel Dig Is Completed," in *Under Construction*, 91.

14. Massachusetts Water Resources Authority, "Did You Know That . . . ?" in *Under Construction*, 12. The first use occurred at the Mamaroneck, New York, facility.

15. Massachusetts Water Resources Authority, *Facts about BHP Construction* (winter 1998).

16. Massachusetts Water Resources Authority, website, www.mwra.state.ma.us/.

17. Massachusetts Water Resources Authority, "Boston Harbor Project, Sludge Digesters" (spring 1994).

18. Kristen Patneaude, MWRA project manager, Residuals Management, e-mail to the author, September 17, 2002.

19. Gloria Rodriguez, "Group Protests Use of Sewage Sludge," *Boston Globe*, August 8, 2002; Beth Greenburg, "Sludge: A Terrible Thing to Waste," *Boston Globe*, September 1, 2002.

20. The National Academies, "Sewage Sludge Standards Need New Scientific Basis," press release, July 2, 2002.

21. Eckler, "MWRA Tunnels into the 21st Century."

22. Massachusetts Water Resources Authority, "Diffuser Team: Finished," in *Under Construction*, 3.

23. Massachusetts Water Resources Authority, "Splash of Green Water Greets Outfall Tunnelers," in *Under Construction*, 105.

24. Daniel Vasquez and Rob Nelson, "9 Miles into Tunnel, Air Ran Out for 2, Co-workers Travel with Stricken Pair through Water, but Help Is Too Late," *Boston Globe*, July 22, 1999; Eckler, "MWRA Tunnels into the 21st Century."

25. Eckler, "MWRA Tunnels into the 21st Century."

26. Massachusetts Water Resources Authority, *5 Year Progress Report, 1995–1999* (2000): 21.

27. Scott Allen, "Closing In on a Healthy Harbor," *Boston Globe*, March 15, 2000.

28. Comments by Jekabs Vittands, Metcalf & Eddy, Inc., at the Boston Harbor Project Symposium.

29. Massachusetts Water Resources Authority, *Facts about History: Deer Island* (fall 1999).

30. F. W. Dodge, "Boston Harbor Cleanup," *F. W. Dodge Profile* (July 20, 1992): 19.

31. Massachusetts Water Resources Authority, *Facts about History: Deer Island*.

32. Dodge, "Boston Harbor Cleanup," 19.

33. Scott Allen, "Closing In on a Healthy Harbor."

34. Dodge, "Boston Harbor Cleanup," 8.

35. Massachusetts Water Resources Authority, *5 Year Progress Report, 1995–1999*, 22.

36. Comments by Joseph Nigro, Greater Boston Building Trades Council, at Boston Harbor Project Symposium.

37. Rene Becker, "More Than Just a Water Boy," *Boston Magazine*, March 1989, 143.

38. Massachusetts Water Resources Authority, *5 Year Progress Report, 1995–1999*, 22.

39. Tye, "$6.1B Cleanup of Boston Harbor Gets Underway."

40. Personal communication from Tim Watkins, MWRA Office of Public Affairs, August 2002.

41. Tye, "EPA Official Says Dukakis to Blame for 6-year Delay."

42. Massachusetts Water Resources Authority, website, www.mwra.state.ma.us, accessed on September 6, 2002.

43. Scott Allen and Judy Radowsky, "300 Burn MWRA Bills in Chelsea," *Boston Globe*, May 14, 1993.

44. N. Brockway, R. D. Colton, S. Dorn, and A. Quinn, *The Impact of Rising Water and Sewer Rates on the Poor* (Boston, 1991), and Dolin, "Boston Harbor's Murky Political Waters," 31.

45. Massachusetts Water Resources Authority, news release, "MWRA Board of Directors Approves 2.9% Increase in Community Assessments for FYO3" (June 13, 2002).

46. Dianne Dumanoski, "Sludge Reaches End of the Line," *Boston Globe*, December 25, 1991.

47. Massachusetts Water Resources Authority, *The State of Boston Harbor: Mapping the Harbor's Recovery* (2002).

48. For background on this controversy, see, for example, Robert Buchsbaum, "Fallout from the Outfall," *Sanctuary* (September/October 1992): 13–16.

49. Dolin, "Boston Harbor's Murky Political Waters," 28.

50. MWRA news release, "Scientists Help End Sewage Discharges to Boston Harbor" (September 6, 2000).

51. Beth Greenburg, "Boston's Riviera for Years, South Boston's Three Miles of Beaches Were Often Less than Inviting—but Now, the Harbor's a Lot Cleaner and the Beaches Are Looking Up, and the Crowds—Many from the Suburbs—Are Back," *Boston Globe*, July 28, 2002.

52. Gloria Rodriguez, "TV Ad to Tout Hub's Cleaner Beaches," *Boston Globe*, August 3, 2002.

53. National Park Service website for the park, www.nps.gov/boha/.

54. Massachusetts Water Resources Authority, *Facts about History: Deer Island* (fall 1999).

55. Beth Daley, "Harbor Cleanup Falls Short at Beaches," *Boston Globe*, September 10, 2001.

56. Massachusetts Water Resources Authority, *State of Boston Harbor*.

57. Mark Sappenfield, "America's 'Filthiest Harbor' Now a Model," *Christian Science Monitor*, December 20, 2000.

58. Tom Bell, "Boston Harbor Cleanup: A World-Class Environmental Feat," *Environmental & Climate News*, December 2000.

59. Comments by James Hoyte and Michael Dukakis at the Boston Harbor Project Symposium.

60. Comments by James Hoyte at the Boston Harbor Project Symposium.

61. Dianne Dumanoski, "Who Speaks for the Harbor?" *Boston Globe Magazine*, September 20, 1987, 87.

62. Becker, "More Than Just a Water Boy," 144.

63. Norman Boucher, "The Dirtiest Job," *Boston Globe Magazine*, May 8, 1988, 66–67.

64. Dumanoski, "Who Speaks for the Harbor?" 87.

65. Ibid.

66. Comments by James Hoyte at the Boston Harbor Project Symposium.

67. Dumanoski, "Who Speaks for the Harbor?" 87.

68. Ibid.; and Boucher, "The Dirtiest Job," 66.

69. Becker, "More Than Just a Water Boy," 150.

70. Paul F. Levy, "Why the Boston Harbor Project Succeeded," *Newtown Magazine* 2, no. 1 (March 2002): 6.

71. Larry Tye, "Fox to Get $125,000 a Year to Clean Up Harbor," *Boston Globe*, October 29, 1987.

72. Ibid.

73. Levy, "Why the Boston Harbor Project Succeeded."

74. Boucher, "The Dirtiest Job," 69.

75. Ibid., 72.

76. Paul Levy, "Financing the Boston Harbor Project," *Civil Engineering Practice* (spring/summer 1994): 78–79.

77. Becker, "More Than Just a Water Boy," 115; and comments by James Sheets at the Boston Harbor Project Symposium.

78. Liz Kowalczyk, "A Strong Hand Grips Hospital's Helm," *Boston Globe*, January 7, 2002.

79. Dolin, "Boston Harbor's Murky Political Waters," 27.

80. Robert L. Turner, "A Record of Accomplishment in Harbor Cleanup," *Boston Globe*, October 22, 1991.

81. David L. Chandler, "Man Who Designed It to Run MWRA," *Boston Globe*, January 30, 1992.

82. *Boston Globe*, editorial, "A Model at MWRA," April 10, 2001.

83. John Carroll, town manager of Norwood, Massachusetts, referring to MacDonald in George Foster, "MacDonald Steps in at State DOT," *Seattle Post-Intelligencer*, April 24, 2001.

84. Comments by Sheets at The Boston Harbor Project Symposium.

85. Doug MacDonald, personal communication, September 10, 2002.

86. *Boston Globe*, "A Model at MWRA."

87. Scott Allen, "Closing In on a Healthy Harbor," *Boston Globe*, March 15, 2000.

88. Massachusetts Water Resources Authority, news release, "Laskey Named MWRA Executive Director" (May 9, 2001).

89. "City Officials Rail against MWRA Water/sewer Hikes," *Boston Herald*, June 14, 2002.

90. Comments by Robert Ciolek at Boston Harbor Project Symposium.

91. MacDonald personal communication.

92. Scott Allen, "MWRA Sewage Facility Reduced Deer Island Change Aims to Save $165m," *Boston Globe*, October 19, 1995.

93. Massachusetts Water Resources Authority, "The MWRA's Six Billion Dollar Man," *Construction Outlook* (March 1, 1989): 31.

94. Levy, "Financing the Boston Harbor Project," 79–81.

95. Ibid., 80.

96. Ibid., 82.

97. Massachusetts Water Resources Authority, *5 Year Progress Report, 1995–1999*, 48.

98. Frederick A. Laskey, *Report to the House and Senate Committees on Ways and Means and the Secretary of Administration and Finance* (April 23, 2002), 4.

99. Comments by Joe Nigro at the Boston Harbor Project Symposium.

100. Massachusetts Water Resources Authority, "Boston Harbor Project Credits Unions with Job Harmony," in *Under Construction*, 35.

101. Massachusetts Water Resources Authority, "Union Veterans on the Boston Harbor Project," in *Under Construction*, 48.

102. Massachusetts Water Resources Authority, "Boston Harbor Project Credits Unions with Job Harmony."

103. Dumanoski, "Who Speaks for the Harbor?" 16.

104. See, for example, John J. DiIulio Jr., *Courts, Correction, and the Constitution* (New York, 1990); Christopher E. Smith, *Courts and Public Policy* (Chicago, 1993); Donald L. Horowitz, *The Courts and Social Policy* (Washington, D.C., 1977); and Lino A. Graglia, *Disaster by Decree* (Ithaca, N.Y., 1976).

105. Scott Allen, "Low-Key, but Hands-On: A Judge's Oversight Pays Off," *Boston Globe*, March 15, 2000.

106. Ibid.

107. Comments by Mazzone at the Boston Harbor Project Symposium.

108. Eric Niiler, "Harbor Cleanup Judge Visits Tunnel," *Patriot Ledger*, November 7, 1995, 1.

109. Allen, "Low-Key, but Hands-On."

110. Comments by Mazzone at the Boston Harbor Project Symposium.

111. Ibid.

112. Virginia Renick, interview by author, August 25, 1994.

113. Comments by Mazzone at the Boston Harbor Project Symposium.

114. *U.S. v. MDC et al.*, Schedule One Compliance Order No. 6 (June 27, 1986).

115. *U.S. v. MDC et al.*, Schedule One Compliance Order No. 24 (December 30, 1987), 6.

116. U.S. EPA v. Metropolitan District Commission et al., Schedule One Compliance Order No. 25 (January 29, 1988): 4.

117. Shelley interview, November 16, 1994.

118. Virginia Renick, telephone interview by author, May 9, 1993.

119. Peter Shelley, telephone interview by author, August 5, 1994.

120. Comments by Mazzone at the Boston Harbor Project Symposium.

121. Shelley interview, August 5, 1994.

122. Fowley interview, September 20, 1994.

123. Virginia Renick, interview by author, May 3, 1993; Paul Levy, interview by author, September 14, 1993; Shelley interview, May 10, 1993; and Fowley interview, November 23, 1993.

124. Levy interview.

125. Dumanoski, "Who Speaks for the Harbor?" 93.

126. Mazzone interview, May 4, 1993.

127. Fowley interview, November 23, 1993; Levy interview; Renick interview, May 3, 1993. According to Douglas Wilkins, the assistant attorney general who worked on this case from 1985 through 1992, "The court does raise things to the top of the agenda"; telephone interview, November 2, 1994.

128. "Boston Harbor Clean-Up Makes Progress," Standard & Poor's *CreditWeek*, May 6, 1991, 38.

129. *U.S. v. MDC et al.*, MWRA Monthly Compliance Report for August 1989 and Progress Report as of September 15, 1989, 6.

130. *U.S. v. MDC et al.*, Schedule Three Compliance Order No. 47 (November 30, 1989), 2.

131. *U.S. v. MDC et al.*, Schedule Four Compliance Order No. 68 (August 28, 1991).

132. *U.S. v. MDC et al.*, Schedule Three Compliance Order No. 64 (April 25, 1991), 2.

133. Scott Lehigh, "Judge Says Bill Could Declaw MWRA," *Boston Globe*, September 25, 1991.

134. *U.S. v. MDC et al.*, Schedule Four Compliance Order No. 68 (August 1991), 2–3.

135. *U.S. v. MDC et al.*, Schedule Three Compliance Order No. 56 (August 22, 1990), 3

136. *U.S. v. MDC et al.*, Schedule Three Compliance Order No. 57 (October 2, 1990), 2–3.

137. *U.S. v. MDC et al.*, Order (October 18, 1990).

138. Koff interview, November 1, 1994.

139. *U.S. v. MDC et al.*, Schedule Three Compliance Order No. 58 (October 31, 1990), 3–4.

140. *U.S. v. MDC et al.*, Schedule Three Compliance Order No. 79 (August 5, 1992).

141. *U.S. v. MDC et al.*, Special Report of the Massachusetts Water Resources Authority concerning Winthrop Water Line (October 23, 1992); and *U.S. v. MDC et al.*, Order (September 25, 1992).

142. *U.S. v. MDC et al.*, Schedule Four Compliance Order No. 71 (November 26, 1991); and *U.S. v. MDC et al.*, Schedule Five Compliance Order No. 79 (August 5, 1992).

143. *U.S. v. MDC et al.*, Schedule Five Compliance Order No. 80 (August 26, 1992).

144. *U.S. v. MDC et al.*, Schedule Five Compliance Order No. 81 (September 25, 1992), 4–5.

145. *U.S. v. MDC et al.*, Order (September 25, 1992).

146. *U.S. v. MDC et al.*, Special Report of the Massachusetts Water Resources Authority concerning Winthrop Water Line.

147. *U.S. v. MDC et al.*, Schedule Five Compliance Order No. 82 (October 26, 1992), 6.

148. *U.S. v. MDC et al.*, Schedule Five Compliance Order No. 87 (March 31, 1993).

149. Harlan Doliner, telephone interview by author, November 2, 1994.

150. *U.S. v. MDC et al.*, Memorandum of the Massachusetts Water Resources Authority in Support of Motion concerning Sludge Storage at Fore River Staging Area (August 10, 1992).

151. Ibid.; Thomas F. Gorman, chief, Quincy Fire Department, Official Directive (August 6, 1992).

152. *U.S. v. MDC et al.*, Special Report of the Massachusetts Water Resources Authority concerning Sludge Pelletizing Facility (August 7, 1992); *U.S. v. MDC et al.*, Memorandum of the Massachusetts Water Resources Authority in Support of Motion concerning Sludge Storage at Fore River Staging Area.

153. *U.S. v. MDC et al.*, Memorandum of the Massachusetts Water Resources Authority in Support of Motion concerning Sludge Storage at Fore River Staging Area.

154. Dolin, *Dirty Water/Clean Water*, 93.

155. *U.S. v. Metropolitan District Commission*, 757 F. Supp. 121 (D. Mass. 1991), 123.

156. Ibid., 124.

157. Massachusetts Water Resources Authority, *Residuals Management Facilities Plan/Final Environmental Impact Report* (August 1989).

158. U.S. Environmental Protection Agency, Region 1, Public Record of Decision on the Final Supplemental Environmental Impact Statement, Long-Term Residuals Management for Metropolitan Boston (March 30, 1990).

159. *U.S. v. MDC et al.*, Schedule Three Compliance Order No. 44 (August 24, 1989), 3.

160. *U.S. v. Metropolitan District Commission*, 757 F. Supp. 121, 125.

161. *U.S. v. MDC et al.*, Schedule Three Compliance Order No. 53 (May 30, 1990), 9.

162. *U.S. v. Metropolitan District Commission*, 757 F. Supp. 121, 125.

163. For an analysis of NIMBY, see Daniel Mazmanian and David Morell, "The 'NIMBY' Syndrome: Facility Siting and the Failure of Democratic Discourse," in *Environmental Policy in the 1990s*, ed. Norman J. Vig and Michael E. Kraft (Washington, D.C., 1990), 125–144.

164. David Arnold, "Walpole Residents Say They've Done Their Share for the State," *Boston Globe*, December 22, 1988; Renee Graham, "Day of Decision on Walpole Landfill Norfolk Residents to Join Protest," *Boston Globe*, January 4, 1989; and Alexander Reid, "400 Protest Sludge Landfill for Walpole," *Boston Globe*, March 18, 1990.

165. *U.S. v. Metropolitan District Commission*, 757 F. Supp. 121, 124.

166. James L. Franklin, "Congressional Delegation Agrees to Help in Walpole Fight," *Boston Globe*, March 8, 1991.

167. *U.S. v. MDC et al.*, Long-Term Residuals Management Scheduling Order (October 31, 1990).

168. James Franklin, "House Kills Measure to Transfer Walpole Site for Use as Landfill," *Boston Globe*, December 11, 1990.

169. *U.S. v. MDC et al.*, Schedule Three Compliance Order No. 60 (December 26, 1990), 2.

170. Franklin, "EPA Asks Court for Landfill in Walpole," *Boston Globe*, December 7, 1990.

171. It was not a blanket moratorium. Exceptions were allowed for facilities necessary to protect public health and safety, sources discharging less than 2,000 gallons of wastewater per day, and facilities needed to carry out the schedule. *U.S. v. Metropolitan District Commission*, 757 F. Supp. 121, 129–130. On April 1, the moratorium was expanded to include hookups for less than 2,000 gallons.

172. *U.S. v. Metropolitan District Commission*, 757 F. Supp. 121, 126.

173. Ross Gelbspan, "Panel Finds No Option to Walpole Landfill," *Boston Globe*, August 9, 1991.

174. *U.S. v. Metropolitan District Commission*, 757 F. Supp. 121, 134.

175. Ross Gelbspan and Frank Phillips, "Weld Will File Bill for Landfill on Walpole Site Plan," *Boston Globe*, April 23, 1991.

176. Sean P. Murphy and Jerry Ackerman, "Judge Lifts Sewer Hookup Ban with Landfill site in MWRA Hands," *Boston Globe*, (May 22, 1991).

177. Ross Gelbspan, "Agency's New Landfill Search Revives Old Dispute," *Boston Globe*, April 1, 1992.

178. Gelbspan, "Panel Finds No Option to Walpole Landfill."

179. Ross Gelbspan, "Frank Amendment May Provide Another Year to Find Sludge Site," *Boston Globe*, September 28, 1991.

180. Gelbspan, "Agency's New Landfill Search Revives Old Dispute."

181. *U.S. v. MDC et al.*, Response of the United States to certain recent filings (November 21, 1991), 2.

182. Julie Belaga, administrator, U.S. EPA, Region 1, quoted in Gelbspan, "Agency's New Landfill Search Revives Old Dispute."

183. Gelbspan, "Agency's New Landfill Search Revives Old Dispute."

184. Mazzone interview, December 6, 1993.

185. *U.S. v. MDC et al.*, Schedule Four Compliance Order No. 71 (November 26, 1991), 7–9.

186. *U.S. v. MDC et al.*, Schedule Five Compliance Order No. 85 (February 1, 1993).

187. *U.S. v. MDC et al.*, Schedule Five Compliance Order No. 91 (July 30, 1993), 6.

188. Ibid.

189. Stephen Power, "Court Gives MWRA Sewage Ultimatum," *Boston Globe*, August 3, 1993.

190. *U.S. v. MDC et al.*, Memorandum of the Massachusetts Water Resources Authority in Support of Motion to Modify Long-Term Residuals Management Scheduling Order (September 9, 1993).

191. Ibid., 3–4.

192. The MWRA, the CLF, Quincy, and a representative of Walpole who was allowed to speak all lauded the new plan as being better than the old. In an interview the week before the hearing, the acting regional administrator said the EPA's decision to support the MWRA proposal "was not based on politics, but on the merits of the plan." Quoted in Scott Allen, "EPA Ends Push for Walpole Landfill, Approves Sending Sludge to Utah," *Boston Globe*, September 24, 1993. Also see, Michael Grunwald, "Judge Buries Walpole Dump Plan, Group Triumphs: MWRA Moves Sludge Site," *Boston Globe*, October 10, 1993.

193. Author's notes at the October 1, 1993, hearing.

194. Boynton, "Boston Harbor CleanUp."

195. Nancy Kurtz, e-mail to the author, September 27, 2002.

196. Jeffry Fowley, e-mail to the author, March 21, 2003.

197. Steven Lipman, e-mail to the author, September 23, 2002.

198. Scott Allen, "Low-Key, but Hands-On."

199. Richard Delaney, e-mail to the author, September 25, 2002.

Conclusion

1. Massachusetts Water Resources Authority, *5 Year Progress Report, 1995–1999*, 23.

2. Boston Herald, "City Officials Rail against MWRA Water/Sewer Hikes."

3. Massachusetts Water Resources Authority, *5 Year Progress Report, 1995–1999*, 27.

Interviews

Steve Angelo, state representative, (D) Saugus, Massachusetts, telephone (8/93)

Noel Barrata, former chief engineer, MDC, telephone (4/14/89 and 10/7/93)

Donald Baumgartner, former sanitary engineer and physical oceanographer with EPA laboratory in Corvallis, Oregon, telephone (1/12/93)

Joan Bernard, former staff, U.S. Congress, House Public Works Committee, telephone (2/23/93)

Bill Corcoran, former staff, U.S. Congress, House Public Works Committee, telephone (1/22/93)

Dem Cowles, former staff, U.S. Senator Mike R. Gravel, telephone (1/12/93)

Phil Cummings, former staff, U.S. Congress, Senate Committee on Public Works, telephone (1/11/93)

Ron DeCeasare, former manager, 301(h) Task Force (1/14/93)

Harlan Doliner, lawyer representing Winthrop, Massachusetts, telephone (11/2/94)

Jeffry Fowley, chief of Water Office, Office of Regional Counsel, U.S. EPA, Region 1, telephone (11/23/93 and 9/20/94)

Dick Fox, former head of construction, MWRA (fall 1992)

Paul Garrity, former superior court judge, Massachusetts (12/14/93)

Charles V. Gibbs, former head of Seattle Metro Sewage District and past president of Association of Metropolitan Sewerage Agencies, telephone (2/8/93)

Charles M. Haar, Louis D. Brandeis Professor of Law, emeritus, Harvard Law School (11/8/93)

Eric Hall, Water Quality Standards coordinator, U.S. EPA, Region 1 (11/8/94)

Donald R. F. Harleman, former Ford Professor of Civil Engineering, Massachusetts Institute of Technology (fall 1993)

James S. Hoyte, former secretary, Massachusetts Executive Office of Environmental Affairs, telephone (3/8/89)

Tom Jorling, former assistant administrator, Water and Hazardous Materials, U.S. EPA, telephone (3/10/93)

William Kane, former CSO program manager, MWRA, telephone (3/3/89)

Peter Koff, lawyer representing Quincy, Massachusetts, telephone (5/12/93 and 11/1/94)

Madeleine Kolb, former analyst at Massachusetts Department of Environmental Quality Engineering, telephone (10/18/93)

Paul F. Levy, former executive director, MWRA (9/14/93)

Steven Lipman, Boston Harbor coordinator, Massachusetts Department of Environmental Protection (11/15/94)

John Lishman, former member of 301(h) Task Force, telephone (1/14/93)

A. D. Mazzone, district court judge, District of Massachusetts (5/4/93 and 12/6/93)

Joe G. Moore Jr., former head of Federal Water Pollution Control Administration, telephone, (1/5/93 and 1/21/93)

Kenneth Moraff, assistant regional counsel, Water Office, U.S. EPA, Region 1, telephone (fall 1993)

Neil O'Brien, director of research, House Committee on Natural Resources, Massachusetts House of Representatives, telephone (10/8/93 and 11/11/94)

Brian Pitt, environmental engineer, Management Division, U.S. EPA, Region 1 (4/12/89)

Virginia Renick, former associate general counsel, MWRA (5/3/93, 5/9/93, 8/25/94, and 11/8/94)

Phil Shapiro, former director of finance and development, MWRA, telephone (4/10/89)

Peter Shelley, senior attorney, Conservation Law Foundation of New England, telephone (5/10/93, 8/5/94, and 11/16/94)

Michael Sloman, former assistant attorney general, Massachusetts, telephone (1/16/94)

John Snedeker, former commissioner, MDC, telephone (4/7/89 and 10/20/93)

Jekabs Vittands, with consulting firm of Metcalf & Eddy and former project manager for MDC's waiver application, telephone (4/12/89)

Douglas Wilkins, former assistant attorney general, Massachusetts, telephone (11/2/94)

A Note on Sources

All the sources used in writing this book are documented in the endnotes. If you are interested in learning more about a specific event detailed in the text, the best approach is to track down the references cited for that section. But tracking down references begs the question of where those references can be found. The following is intended to help facilitate your search.

Most of the early historical documents pertaining to sewage and the situation in Boston Harbor can be obtained through the State Library of Massachusetts or Boston's Archives and Records Center. The State Library, located in the Massachusetts State House, is a good source for state statutes and reports, as well as general books on the history of Massachusetts. The Archives and Records Center, located in Hyde Park, Massachusetts, contains a wealth of documents covering the history of Boston and was especially useful for documents from the 1700s and 1800s.

Readers interested in learning more about the federal court case should contact the Archives and Special Collections at the library of the University of Massachusetts, Boston Campus, the institution to which Judge A. David Mazzone donated his papers. The documents for both the federal and the state court cases are also available through the respective courts. The MWRA has created thousands of documents relating to the cleanup of Boston Harbor, and has collected thousands more from a great variety of sources. To learn about the MWRA's holdings, visit the authority's website, www.mwra.state.ma.us/, or its library, which is located in the MWRA complex at the Charlestown Navy Yard.

Because so much of the real-time history of the cleanup of Boston Harbor was first written by the scores of newspaper reporters who diligently covered this enormous story, I strongly encourage readers to look at the chapter notes to see which newspaper articles might be worth tracking down. I would also like to offer a special thank you to those reporters, for the information they provided was invaluable in piecing together the story. Of all the papers consulted, the *Boston Globe* deserves special mention. Its reporting on the Boston Harbor court cases, in particular, was thorough and engaging.

The best way to find all the other sources cited in the text, such as federal reports, magazine articles, and books, is to go to your local library. If your library doesn't have what you need, you can probably get it through inter-library loan. While working on this book I had the great fortune to have access to two of the greatest "local" libraries in the world—the U.S. Library of Congress and the Boston Public Library. But even those two behemoths didn't have everything I wanted. Thus, wherever your search takes you, keep digging. If what you seek is available, you'll find it eventually.

Index

ERIC JAY DOLIN, Ph.D., has published more than sixty articles and six books, including the *Smithsonian Book of National Wildlife Refuges*; *Snakehead: A Fish Out of Water*; and *The Duck Stamp Story: Art—Conservation—History*. Born in Queens, New York, he was educated at Brown University, the Yale School of Forestry and Environmental Studies, and the Massachusetts Institute of Technology. His work experience includes being a program manager at the U.S. Environmental Protection Agency, a Knauss Sea Grant Fellow at the U.S. National Oceanic and Atmospheric Administration (NOAA), an environmental consultant, a Pew Research Fellow at Harvard Law School, an American Association for the Advancement of Science writing fellow at *Business Week*, and a fisheries policy analyst at NOAA's National Marine Fisheries Service. He lives in Marblehead, Massachusetts, with his wife, Jennifer, and children, Lily and Harrison.